Women in Motion

Women in Motion

Globalization, State Policies, and Labor Migration in Asia

NANA OISHI

Stanford University Press
Stanford, California
2005

Stanford University Press
Stanford, California

Printed in the United States of America on acid-free, archival-quality paper

Library of Congress Cataloging-in-Publication Data

Oishi, Nana.
    Women in motion : globalization, state policies, and labor migration in Asia /
Nana Oishi.
        p.   cm.
    Includes bibliographical references and index.
        ISBN 0-8047-4637-0 (cloth : alk. paper)—ISBN 0-8047-4638-9 (pbk. : alk. paper)
        1. Women alien labor—Asia.   2. Women's rights—Asia.   3. Women in
development—Asia.   4. Migration, Internal—Asia.   5. Asia—Emigration and
immigration—Government policy.   I. Title.
HD6181.85.I37 2005
331.4'086'912095—dc22   2005014912

Original Printing 2005

Last figure below indicates year of this printing:
14   13   12   11   10   09   08   07   06   05

Typeset by G&S Typesetters, Inc. in 10.5/12.5 Bembo

To Soya, Shinya, and my parents

Contents

List of Tables and Figures

TABLES

FIGURES

WRITING A BOOK is often compared to having a child. Both entail similar processes: inception, development, and delivery. Each is a long and difficult effort requiring much perseverance. That is why many authors affectionately call their output a "baby." I like this analogy very much, especially since giving birth to my real baby, Shinya, two years ago. At the same time, delivering this book was much harder in at least one way: I was "pregnant" with it for almost ten years!

International female migration—the theme of this book—has been my research interest since 1993, which was the year I joined the United Nations agency International Labour Organization, headquartered in Geneva. Once the number of migrant women began to surge in the 1980s, so did the number of cases of their mistreatment and abuse. The concerns of the international community were just beginning to grow at that time. In 1996, when I coauthored a report on the policy dimensions of women's migration in Asia, I found myself stunned by the extent and severity of the abuse and exploitation that migrant women were experiencing; soon, I also grew frustrated with the limitations of international legal mechanisms. Many research questions and puzzles emerged as I began looking into the complexities of international female migration. All of these things became the seed for this book.

I took study leave from the ILO to tackle these issues. I was tempted to conduct ethnographic research that focused entirely on individual women, but in the end I established a broader framework, having decided that not nearly enough policy-oriented research had been done. Also, after being emotionally engulfed by so many stories of suffering migrant women during my work with the ILO, I wanted to step back and see the broader picture.

After completing the theoretical groundwork, I visited ten countries in Asia to conduct fieldwork. I knew that traveling alone through so many countries was going to be arduous, yet I felt compelled to interview migrant women, policy makers, and NGOs in person; this had not been possible for me until I entered academia. I traveled to major destinations of migrants such as Japan, Hong Kong, and the United Arab Emirates, as well as to countries of origin such as the Philippines and Sri Lanka. I also visited some developing countries from which far fewer women emigrated—Bangladesh, Thailand, India, Pakistan, and Vietnam.

It was an adventurous trip. On one occasion, I stayed at a returned migrant's house in the Philippines and had my first experience of living without electricity and running water. On another, I hiked through the Sri Lankan tropical forests to visit the homes of returned migrants. Sometimes there was no road and my interpreter refused to walk with me because of the leeches. Although I was a little scared of walking through the forests, it was fascinating to interview women who shared with me great (and sometimes sad) stories. In Hong Kong, I interviewed migrant women in the streets and parks, in shelters, and at union meetings. Wherever I went, their stories broke my heart and forced me to question my hypotheses, which had been derived from academic theories and UN perspectives. This humbling experience reminded me of the importance of fieldwork. This firsthand experience and information was vital to me, for out of them I would build up the picture of international female migration that I present in this book.

I have written this book mainly for scholars but also for policy makers, international organizations, and NGOs. Having spent some time in an international organization, in academia, and "out there" in developing countries, I recognized the necessity of producing a book, which could speak to people in various social positions. I also wanted to take an "integrative approach," one that does not side with either the receiving or the sending countries—an approach that includes even those countries which send few migrant women. I saw an indispensable need to adopt three levels of analysis-macro, meso, and micro-in order to truly understand the mechanisms of women's migration. Because of this rather ambitious approach, this book can only sketch the situation in each country. Some readers may find the writing style too simple, others too academic. My hope is that most will understand my goals for this book, and that they will still find some added value no matter how small it may be.

My own journey as a migrant woman for fourteen years ended a year and a half ago. Like all migrant women, I am still going through a reintegration process. It has not always been easy, but my long experience of migration has empowered me to face any challenges. Migration does indeed help one grow as an individual. Yet at the same time, reintegration also has many positive aspects. Being reunited with family is certainly one of them. I do not know if I will ever be a migrant again, but for now I will let myself indulge in the comforts of "home."

Acknowledgments

THIS BOOK became a reality because of the support I received from many individuals. First I must thank all of those migrant women who generously shared their life stories with me. Their inner strength and faith were always energizing.

This project has benefited greatly from the comments and suggestions made by many individuals during various phases. First I must thank my mentors at Harvard University for their advice and comments on my manuscript while it was still in the form of Ph.D. dissertation. Ezra F. Vogel spent copious time reading and discussing my work despite his extremely busy schedule. His amazing energy for new intellectual endeavors has been a great inspiration to me. Barbara Reskin provided me with many insights and constructive comments. She consistently helped me clarify my ideas and think a step further. I was also very fortunate to have a prominent migration scholar, Mary C. Waters, on my committee. I could always count on her to discuss my empirical findings and theoretical interpretations. Her support and encouragement have been greatly appreciated.

I also thank my former mentors at the ILO, Roger Bohning and Manolo Abella, for their guidance and help throughout this project. Their strong commitment to the cause of migrants influenced my work and way of thinking in many ways.

Many friends and colleagues shared their thoughts on all or part of this manuscript: Marla Asis, Rieko Kage, Pei-Chia Lan, Kristin Maher, Phil Martin, Chiho Ogaya, and Kyoko Shinozaki, to name a few. I am also grateful to Wayne Cornelius and Gaku Tsuda at the Center for Comparative Immigration Studies at the University of California, San Diego, for offering me a visiting research fellowship. This opportunity enabled me to exchange ideas with many other migration scholars who offered constructive comments on the earlier version of this manuscript.

My fieldwork went smoothly thanks to the help of many friends. Some were former colleagues at the ILO: Anees Ahmad, Anis Hassanein, Shengjie

Li, Naoko Otobe, Pongsri Phantumvanit, and Shizue Tomoda. Others were government officials whom I got to know through my work: Sharful Alam, Carmelita Arriola, Tran Thanh Binh, and Kanti Yapa. I am also thankful to many NGOs, including the Asian Migrant Centre, the Asian Pacific Mission for Migrant Filipinos, Bethune House, St. Andrew's Church, the Mission for Filipino Migrant Workers Society, and the Association of Sri Lankans (Hong Kong); Kaibigan and Scalabrini Migration Center (Philippines); the Migrant Services Centre and the American Center for International Labor Solidarity (Sri Lanka); and the Welfare Association of Repatriated Bangladeshi Employees, Ain O Salish Kendra, the Refugee and Migratory Movements Research Unit, and the Christian Commission for Development in Bangladesh (Bangladesh).

Many other friends extended warm and generous help during my fieldwork. Robert Wihtol at the Asian Development Bank in Manila not only lent me a helping hand with logistics but also offered me advice and insights with regard to many facets of this project. I must also thank Hiroshi Mihara, a former diplomat, for helping my fieldwork in the United Arab Emirates. Given my limited knowledge of Arabic culture, my fieldwork there would have been enormously difficult without his help. Hideki Matsunaga and Anura Krariksh were also kind enough to provide logistic assistance in Sri Lanka and Thailand respectively.

I gratefully acknowledge the financial support extended to me by the following institutions which enabled me to complete the various stages of this project: the Harvard University Graduate School of Arts and Sciences, the Harvard Center for Population and Development Studies, the Fulbright Commission, the International Federation of University Women, the Toyota Foundation, the Matsushita International Foundation, and the Gregory C. Carr Foundation.

It was a wonderful experience to work with the superb editorial staff at Stanford University Press. Patricia Katayama, a former editor, helped me with the initial revisions. Kate Wahl provided me with detailed professional comments, helpful suggestions, and much encouragement, which got me through the revision process. I also thank Mariana Raykov for all her efforts in the final stages of book production. The research assistance of Fancy Zhu, Kumiko Nagasawa, Mio Ietomi, and Toshinori Asano was valuable during the final revisions.

I extend my deepest gratitude to my family. My parents Takeshi and Eiko Oishi are unusual Japanese parents; they were strongly supportive of their tomboy daughter while she passed many years "migrating" around the world. Their constant encouragement and long-distance love have meant so much to a sojourner daughter. I also thank my extraordinary parents-in-law,

Toru and Yurie Hirase, who have been helping me in so many ways since I became part of the family. My deepest thanks go to both my parents for providing generous child-care assistance during the last few months of writing this book.

My final words of thanks go to my husband, Soya Hirase, for his love, understanding, and perseverance. I give him the Best Husband Award for doing more than his best to let me focus on my work, for providing comfort whenever I need it, and for making our home a fun place. Shinya, thank you for being such a joyful child. Although we are still heavily sleep-deprived, dad and I love you so much and will be forever grateful to God for bringing you into our life.

Nana Oishi
Tokyo, Japan

ADB	Asian Development Bank
AMC	Asian Migrant Centre
ANGOC	Asian NGO Coalition for Agrarian Reform and Rural Development
ASEAN	Association of South East Asian Nations
ASK	Ain O Salish Kendra
BEPZA	Bangladesh Export Processing Zones Authority
BMET	Bangladesh Bureau of Manpower and Employment Training
CFO	Commission on Filipino Overseas
DOLE	Department of Labor and Employment (Philippines)
EPZ	export processing zone
ESCAP	Economic and Social Council for Asia and Pacific
ESCWA	United Nations Economic and Social Commission for Western Asia
FDI	foreign direct investment
GCC	Gulf Cooperation Council
ILO	International Labour Organization
IMF	International Monetary Fund
INSTRAW	International Research and Training Institute for the Advancement of Women
IOM	International Organization for Migration
JISEA	Japan Institute for Social and Economic Affairs
MFA	Migrant Forum in Asia
MNC	multinational corporation
MSC	Migrant Services Centre
NCRFW	National Commission on the Role of Filipino Women
NGO	non-governmental organization
ODA	official development assistance

PEFDA	People's Forum for Development Alternatives
POEA	Philippine Overseas Employment Administration
SLBFE	Sri Lanka Bureau of Foreign Employment
UAE	United Arab Emirates
UN	United Nations
UNDP	United Nations Development Programme
WCSDG	World Commission on the Social Dimensions of Globalization

Women in Motion

CHAPTER 1

Introduction: Women in Global Migration

IT WAS IN THE QUIET evening after a tropical rain shower. We were relaxing in Rena's modest house in a small village when she glanced affectionately at her son and said softly, "I will never leave him again." She had just come back to the Philippines after working in Hong Kong for twelve years. Although she had some college education, she had chosen to work as a domestic worker[1] for a Hong Kong family because of the higher and more stable wages. "I thought my family would need more money for our son's future," she told me. However, Rena's life had gone into upheaval as soon as she left home. Her husband Jose, who had been against her migrating, passed away only eight months later. "He had an accident earlier, but his health got worse after I left. He was lonely and missed me badly. I missed him, too." Rena also lost her parents while away. "I regret that I went to Hong Kong, but what can I do now?" Left with her only son Paolo, she seemed determined to stay in the Philippines and put her life back together. Yet only a few years later, I found her back in Hong Kong as a domestic worker again. She had not been able to find a stable job in the Philippines, and had to leave her home again to support her son and herself.

Rena is one of the world's 175 million migrants—a number that has been increasing rapidly.[2] Migration has emerged as a critical global issue, one that now touches almost every corner of the world. Most countries are no longer categorized as destinations, origins, or points of transit, but rather as some combination of those three. Migration's socioeconomic, political, and cultural impact on societies has become enormous; so have the implications for states, for civil society, and for the individuals involved. Heeding the complexity and growing challenges that migration entails, UN Secretary-General Kofi Annan has declared migration a priority issue for the international community.[3]

Rena's case reflects one of the distinctive characteristics of global migration today—the feminization of migratory populations around the world. The forces of globalization are increasing the demand for cheap and docile migrant female labor in all regions. Between 1960 and 2000, the number of migrant women around the world increased more than twofold, from 35 million to 85 million; by 2000, women constituted 48.6 percent of the world's migrants.[4] Contrary to the traditional image, migration is no longer a solely male phenomenon. More and more women are migrating not as dependents of a father or husband but as autonomous workers. Men have always worked overseas to support their families back home; now women are choosing to do the same. More women are becoming breadwinners, migrating abroad on their own in order to support a family from far away.

Global restructuring of economy is playing a significant role in this change in a number of ways. First, it is pushing more middle-class women in wealthier countries to enter the labor market and thereby increasing the demand for female migrant caregivers. Around the world over the past few decades, the number of double-income households has been growing. Traditionally secure "male" jobs are becoming more precarious as a consequence of deregulation, corporate restructuring, and contracting out. Some women have been forced into the labor market by their partner's economic insecurity and by their shared desire to maintain a middle-class lifestyle.

Second, the pressures of work have been increasing in recent years so that many professionals are now working more overtime. Some have to take night shifts or early morning shifts as their workplace extends its operation hours due to growing business competition. Many families have become "time-starved," carrying great burdens and having difficulties balancing both family and work.[5] Because of the shortage of public child-care facilities and of time to do household chores, dual-income families are now relying on migrant nannies and housekeepers to take care of the children and to keep the home in order.

Third, the global economy is generating a class of "new rich" not only in the industrialized world, but also in semi-industrialized and developing countries. These people have benefited from international business expansion and can afford to pursue more affluent and comfortable lives. They seek migrant domestic workers and nannies who can provide better care for their homes and children. Live-in migrant caregivers also work on call 24 hours a day whenever a need arises. Their care is preferred to institutional care because of its personal attentiveness, long hours, and affordability.

Fourth, populations in many industrialized countries are aging, and this has increased the need for nurses and other caregivers for the elderly. Some nurses and caregivers are men, but especially in Asia, most in this occupational category are women.[6] The United States and the United Kingdom, for instance, are accepting many female nurses from the Philippines. Canada now allows many Asian migrant women to enter the country through its Live-in Caregiver Program; these women provide care for a child or a disabled or elderly person and also do some household work.[7]

All of this points to a care gap between state welfare services and the actual needs of working families.[8] Welfare states have been eroding worldwide; the care provisions of these countries are no longer able to keep pace with their aging populations and with the growing need for quality child care. In many countries, female migrant labor has become the answer to this shortfall. As many scholars have already pointed out, using terms such as "nanny chain," "global care chain,"[9] and "international division of reproductive labor,"[10] global economic restructuring has increased the worldwide demand for migrant domestic workers who often serve as both caregivers and housekeepers. At one time, this trend was visible only in industrialized countries; today, globalization is reaching beyond the industrialized world to affect middle- and low-income countries.

Migrant women are also in high demand in the global manufacturing sector. Globalization has started a "race to the bottom"; that is, countries around the world are now competing to provide corporations with the cheapest and most docile labor. This global competition has created a large niche for female migrant labor. Many corporations—especially those which cannot afford to relocate or outsource overseas—have found migrant women to be the most "qualified" workers in this regard. More and more migrant women are being incorporated into the production system—into "global commodity chains"[11] or, more recently, "global value chains," which include entire value-added activities leading to goods and services.[12] In the newly industrialized economies (NIEs)[13] and even in some developing countries, export-led industries are recruiting a large number of migrant women from neighboring countries. For instance, many Filipino women are now working in factories in Taiwan, and Indonesian women are doing the same in Malaysia. Most importantly, an increasing number of migrant women are working in other developing countries that are at a similar economic level. For instance, some Sri Lankan women are working in factories in countries such as the Maldives because they cannot find work nearer home.

All of these facts together suggest that the international division of labor by gender is becoming increasingly complex. In the past, the international gender division of labor simply incorporated Third World women into export manufacturing in their own countries; these women produced goods for consumers in the industrialized world.[14] Today, the international gender division of labor is integrating migrant women into various segments of value chains; through their labor, these women are now serving "the global new rich" in industrialized, semi-industrialized, and even some developing countries. In this sense, the international migration of women now involves a tremendously complex system of inequalities, not only between the North and the South, but also within the South itself. This poses a new challenge when it comes to understanding and responding to the international gender division of labor.

Finally, the global "sex industry" that has been developed by international criminal networks is creating a demand for migrant women. In Japan, where the sex industry accounts for about 1 percent of the GNP, more than 150,000 migrant women work in the sector.[15] Many of them come from the Philippines and Thailand, but an increasing number of women from Eastern Europe, Latin America, and other parts of Asia have been arriving in recent years.[16] Some enter Japan legally as "entertainers," but many others enter through illegal channels. This situation is not limited to industrialized countries. Many developing countries in Asia employ migrant women in the sex sector: 20,000–30,000 Burmese in Thailand; 100,000 Nepalese in India; and 200,000 Bangladeshis in Pakistan.[17] Many of these women are the victims of human trafficking and irregular migration.

Women and Migration in Asia: The Puzzles

This book will examine women's migration in Asia[18] by focusing on temporary flows of a legal nature. Temporary migration, which up to this point has received less attention than permanent migration, now forms a large component of international migration both in Asia and elsewhere in the world. The popular perception is that permanent migration[19] from Asia to industrialized countries is quite significant; in fact, temporary migration within Asia is much larger in terms of sheer numbers. Since the 1970s, as a consequence of rapid economic growth, many Asian countries have been adopting temporary migration schemes, accepting a larger number of migrants from other parts of the region. The industrialized countries, especially in North America, have been accepting a large number of Asian immigrants, but in terms of annual intake, far more Asian migrants are ending up in other Asian countries. In part, this reflects industrialized countries' restrictive policies toward low-skilled and unskilled workers.[20] For instance, ten times as many Filipino migrants go to other Asian countries as go to North America: 582,584 Filipinos migrated to Asian countries as temporary migrants in 2001, whereas only 51,308 migrated to the United States and Canada as permanent migrants.[21]

Another reason why I have focused my research on Asia is that the fem-

TABLE 1.1
Temporary Migration from Selected Asian Countries, Circa 2002

Country	GDP per capita (US$)	UNEMPLOY-MENT (%) Male	UNEMPLOY-MENT (%) Female	ANNUAL OUTFLOWS OF MIGRANTS (THOUSANDS) Men	ANNUAL OUTFLOWS OF MIGRANTS (THOUSANDS) Women	ANNUAL OUTFLOWS OF MIGRANTS (THOUSANDS) Total	Women's Share in Migration Outflows (%)	Total Stock of Migrants (millions)
Sending Countries								
Philippines	4,170	9.4[a]	10.3[a]	189.8	453.5	682.3	69.2	7.6
Sri Lanka	3,570	8.7	12.8	70.7	133.0	203.7[1]	65.3	1.0
Indonesia	3,230	n.a.	n.a.	116.8	363.6	480.4	75.7	1.4
Non-Sending Countries								
Bangladesh	1,700	3.2[b]	3.3[b]	266.9[d]	0.8[d]	267.7[d]	0.3[d]	2.5
India	2,670	4.3[b]	4.3[b]	333.5	34.2	367.7	9.3	3.1[b]
Pakistan	1,940	6.7	16.5	104.2[d]	0.2[d]	104.4[d]	0.2[d]	n.a.

NOTES: n.a. = not available. a = 2001; b = 2000; c = 1999; d = 1998. 1 = provisional; 2 = In Gulf States only.

SOURCES: AMC and MFA (2003); ILO (2004); SLBFE (2004); UNDP (2004); Zachariah et al. (2002). Gender-differentiated data on annual outflows from India are the high-end estimates arrived at by using the gender composition of emigrants from Kerala.

inization of migration has been especially salient in this region. The number of migrant Asian women has increased significantly since the late 1970s; Asia is now both a major destination for female migrant labor *and* a source of that labor to the world. Between 1978 and 2002, the proportion of women among emigrants rose from 17 to 65 percent in Sri Lanka, from 15 to 69 percent in the Philippines, and from 41 to 76 percent in Indonesia. It is estimated that more than 4 million Asian migrant women were working in the region in 2002.[22] These figures refer only to legal migrants and would be much higher if irregular migrants[23] were included.

When I was at the International Labour Organization and coauthoring a report on the migration of Asian women,[24] I noticed a strange pattern to female migration vis-à-vis male migration. Men emigrated from almost all developing countries across the region, yet most migrant women tended to originate in only a few countries: the Philippines, Sri Lanka, and Indonesia. There were some migrant women from Thailand, Nepal, India, and Bangladesh, but their numbers were relatively small even though all countries shared major "push factors" such as high unemployment, low wages, and poverty, which tend to induce emigration. According to neoclassical economic theory, individuals move in search of higher wages from regions where labor is relatively abundant and capital is scarce to regions with labor shortages and capital surpluses.[25] This seemed to hold for male migration, but not for female migration. As Table 1.1 indicates, *more men emigrate from low-income countries (Bangladesh, India, and Pakistan), but more women emigrate from better-off countries (the Philippines, Sri Lanka, and Indonesia).*

Poverty has indeed driven many women to emigrate—numerous studies have illustrated this.[26] Yet few women have emigrated from Bangladesh, which is one of the poorest countries in the world. If economic hardship is the main driver of migration, why do so few women migrate from low-income countries? Poverty may well be the principal cause of international female migration at the individual level, but it does not explain cross-national differences in migration patterns within the region.

Furthermore, the data do not support the conventional economic assumption that high unemployment rates lead to migration. In Pakistan, as seen in Table 1.1, the unemployment rate among women is more than twice the rate among men. However, very few Pakistani women migrate overseas: they comprise only 0.2 percent of emigration flows from Pakistan. In Sri Lanka, Indonesia, and the Philippines, the unemployment rates are also higher among women than among men; yet in those countries, the gender difference in unemployment rates is much narrower than in emigration rates. In sum, then, unemployment does not always result in female migration. The international labor market always has a demand for female workers; even so, many poor women in low-income countries in Asia are not responding to that demand.

The emerging patterns of female migration in Asia also pose a challenge to structuralist theories that explain patterns of international migration in terms of a country's role in the international division of labor. Dual labor market theory, for instance, views international migration as a form of exploitation of the "periphery" nations by the "core" nations in the international system. Piore asserted that international migration is caused not only by "push" factors (such as low wages and high unemployment) in peripheral countries, but rather mainly by "pull" factors (such as a chronic need for foreign workers to perform menial jobs) in core countries.[27] However, neither this approach nor the world systems theory can explain why most women in middle- and low-income developing Asia are pulled into the middle-income countries within the region rather than into the high-income countries of the West. Some argue that most poor people cannot afford the high fees they must pay in order to migrate to the West. In recent years, however, more and more poor have been migrating abroad through "salary deduction schemes" that do not require the payment of high migration fees prior to departure. An increasing number of poor women in the Philippines and Sri Lanka are now emigrating by means of such schemes. However, many women in other developing countries are not willing to take that same option.

Even though there is a strong demand for migrant women in the international labor market, the vast majority of low-income women in Bangladesh, Pakistan, and India are still not responding to that demand. Some might suggest that religion is the reason; that is, Muslim and Hindu women do not work overseas because they are discouraged from wage employment even in their own countries. However, this is largely a myth. Some Muslim countries (Pakistan, Bangladesh, Afghanistan) send few migrant women overseas, but others (Indonesia and the Philippine island of Mindanao where Muslims dominate) are major sources of migrant women. India is 80 percent Hindu, yet Indian women have been participating in the labor force at roughly the same rate as Filipino women.[28] Despite that fact, very few Indian women emigrate on their own to work abroad. Religion seems to constrain female employment in some countries but does not explain women's migration pattern in all countries.

The puzzle of cross-national patterns leads us to seek a fundamental cause for international female migration. As Table 1.1 suggests clearly, poverty and unemployment are not the only determinants. What, then, are the true determinants of large-scale female migration? Before we answer this question, it would perhaps be useful to review how scholars have approached the topic of international female migration.

Gender and Migration: Overview

Many scholars have been examining the causes of international migration for a long time. However, the gender dimension rarely received much attention before the 1980s. Most research reflected the long-held assumption that migration is a male phenomenon. Furthermore, most countries have not collected gender-related statistics on migration.[29] In the 1960s, after family reunification became a key principle of immigration policies in many industrialized countries, scholars began to include women in their analyses as part of family migration. Yet women were still treated as dependents of male immigrants and not as significant contributors to the economy. Some studies added gender-differentiating variables yet continued to focus on associational migration by including "women's marriage probabilities" in their migration models.[30]

Some scholars started paying attention to women's rural–urban migration in the 1980s, and these studies were gradually expanded to include international female migration.[31] Nevertheless, gender had still not been integrated into mainstream migration theories. Traditional approaches such as neoclassical economic theory and structurist theory (both mentioned earlier) focus sharply on macrolevel push–pull factors such as wage differentials and labor demand and supply. Such approaches are mostly gender-blind; they assume either that migration is a male phenomenon or that the causes of migration are the same for women as they are for men.

More recent approaches have also been rather slow in mainstreaming gender into migration theories. Network theorists focus on the concrete interpersonal ties of migrants, seeing these as important triggers for migration.[32] This theory has been supported by many empirical studies;[33] however, it has treated networks as gender-neutral until recently. More scholars have begun to address the resource implications of gendered networks *within* destination countries.[34] Yet the gendered impact of networks on migration flows has still been understudied. The work of Curran and Rivero-Fuentes is a wonderful starting point in this regard: they found that in Mexico, social ties induced *international* migration of men and women equally but had no impact on the *internal* migration of men.[35] The gender implications of social networks will require further analysis.

With network theory, it is rather difficult to explain the differences in migration patterns—for example, why and how such networks were developed between certain countries but not between others. In this regard, the theory of migration systems is useful in explaining how such networks developed through historical, geographical, and political ties between countries that had existed long before large-scale migration started.[36] However, such close ties did not always exist between major countries of origin and destination in Asia, as seen in the example of the Philippines and Saudi Arabia before the 1970s. In general, the network approach can tell us much about how migration flows expanded, but not about how they originally started.

The new economics theory provides different insights: it incorporates a microlevel context by examining "household strategies."[37] According to this theory, a household assesses its members' reproductive and productive abilities and then strategically organizes its labor to maximize its collective income.[38] Many scholars have recognized that it is useful to consider both households and individuals, but many also question the theory's basic assumption that households are neutral and autonomous actors.

Some household strategists have shifted their analytical focus to power dynamics and patriarchal ideology within households—both of these affect the mechanisms of migration decision-making.[39] By doing so, they have elucidated the ways in which women and men are molded by the intrahousehold power hierarchy and by wider sociocultural expectations concerning gender roles. Other scholars have been more critical of the household strategy approach, arguing that a household does not necessarily act collectively, nor does it always maximize the interests of its members.[40] In their view, household members often pursue their own individual interests, such as earning money for their own education or gaining independence from family control. In her study of Mexican migrants, Hondagneu-Sotelo found that the independent migration of young women is accepted as a rite of passage for their independence, not as a sacrifice for the family.[41]

A clear definition of household roles is difficult to establish, since a household can represent not only a space for collective well-being but also a locus of struggle in which the members' interests clash within the web of power relations.[42] Moreover, perspectives on marital status and the life stages of women are missing from the household strategy approach. My research and other case studies indicate that young single women tend to migrate for their own individual self-fulfillment and independence, whereas older and married women migrate to support the family and to finance the children's education.[43] The degrees of patriarchy and sexual division of labor within households are not necessarily static; they are capable of changing over time along with women's life stages.

It is still difficult to theorize international female migration, yet it is an exciting development that more scholars have begun to study migrant women since the mid-1990s. In particular, we have seen the burgeoning of research on the international migration of Asian women. Constable provided rich ethnographic accounts of Filipina domestic workers in Hong Kong, examining their problems as well as their own interpretations of the migration experience.[44] She offered new insights for migration research by shedding light on women's agency and subjectivity. Parreñas linked agency-level research on Filipina migrant women in Los Angeles and Rome to a broader context—the international division of reproductive labor.[45] Gamburd focused on a migrants' home country, Sri Lanka, by examining the communities and families left behind and by interviewing former migrant women who had come back after working in the Middle East.[46] Her rich ethnography illustrated how migration has transformed migrant women, their families, and their communities. Chin conducted rigorous analyses on Asian domestic workers in Malaysia from a political economy perspective.[47] By focusing on the role of the state, she presented fascinating analyses on how Third World women were being incorporated into the international labor market through state modernization strategies.

All of these studies have significantly advanced our understanding of international female migration, especially the experiences of migrant women and the nature of the international political economy that pulls Third World women into domestic service around the world. Yet my questions about *cross-national migration patterns* and *the causal mechanisms of international female migration* remain unanswered. The few studies available on multiple countries[48] have been compilations of excellent case studies by different authors, but these studies did not use the same variables to systematically compare and contrast the cases to extract the common factors that induced female migration. The work of Parreñas[49] was perhaps the first major comparative research on female migration, but her research focused on the receiving side, and it can be complemented by analyses of the sending side. Moreover, as I mentioned earlier, the vast majority of Filipina and other Asian women (and men) migrate *within* Asia, not to North America and Europe. Thus it is important to expand research beyond the Western hemisphere and to incorporate "South–South migration" into the picture, especially since its flow is now much more significant than North–South migration. Furthermore, on the basis of my preliminary work at the ILO,[50] I recognize the importance of the state and the international community, as well as the differential impact of the global economy on migration. The suprastate and macropolitical factors, in particular, need to be taken into account in analyses of international female migration.

Integrative Approach to Female Migration

The aim of this book is to explain the causal mechanism of cross-national patterns of international female migration through an integrative approach. As Goss and Lindquist suggest, there have been many attempts to achieve a comprehensive understanding of migration.[51] These attempts do not comprise a unified theory; rather, they are reflected in a variety of theories that identify the connecting elements between the macro and micro levels, such as households, networks, and institutions. Although they focus on the different entities, these approaches share a common aim, which is to link "different levels of social organization, analyze simultaneously the origin and destinations, and consider both historical and contemporary processes."[52] My goal is to build my research on these approaches, while developing their framework further by integrating the gender dimension of migration.

My integrative approach examines various factors not only in migrant-sending and migrant-receiving countries,[53] but also those in the countries from which relatively few migrant women emigrate, which I label "non-sending countries" for analytical purposes. As macrocausal analysts have argued, to fully understand the causal mechanisms of social phenomena, one must adopt (1) the "method of agreement," which examines a set of cases with a similar outcome and attempts to identify common causal factors (assuming that similar outcomes have a similar cause); and (2) the "method of difference," which compares two sets of cases with similar conditions and a dissimilar outcomes and then identifies at least one dissimilar condition to account for the difference.[54] I will adopt both of these methods for three comparisons. First, for *within-group comparisons* of major migrant-sending countries (such as the Philippines, Sri Lanka, and Indonesia), the method of agreement will be used to ascertain which factors have led to the feminization of migration in these countries. The same method will be applied to compare "non-sending countries" (Bangladesh, Pakistan, and India), the point being to seek common threads that discourage female migration. By contrast, for *between-group analyses* on "sending countries" and "non-sending countries," the method of difference will be adopted to highlight the elements that set them apart.

Essentially, my integrative approach will compare country cases. However, given the complexity of the phenomenon, it will adopt a multilevel analysis. Specifically, it will examine the following four levels: suprastate (global), macro-state, meso-society, and micro-individual. At the suprastate level, I will examine the impact of globalization on women's employment, changes in the international labor market, international relations, and the lack of an international migration regime. Although some migration scholars have already pointed out that global restructuring has incorporated Third World women into the low-paying service sectors in industrialized countries,[55] more careful analyses will be required if we are to understand why many more Asian migrant women go to the middle-income countries in the same region than to the United States and Europe. Furthermore, it is important to note that globalization is not a monolithic force that affects all Third World women in the same manner. The impact of globalization varies in different countries because its processes involve different economic, political, and social interventions. In fact, globalization has been criticized for excluding many countries and people in the developing world.[56] Therefore, it is necessary to examine the differential impact of globalization on female migration—in particular, why globalization is pushing many women in some countries, but not in others, to migrate.

Another suprastate factor that affects policies for female migration is the lack of an effective international legal framework—an "international migration regime"—to protect migrant workers abroad. The existing international protection mechanism is working poorly because many receiving countries are unwilling to commitment themselves to it. In light of this, in order to protect their own citizens, many developing countries have adjusted their own emigration policies. These policies have taken various forms; some are extremely protective and restrict female migration, whereas others are relatively open. Chapters 3 and 4 will review how various countries have developed their emigration policies, and discuss the factors that account for these differences.

MACRO LEVEL: THE ROLE OF THE STATE

At the macro level, I will analyze the role of the state[57] in international female migration. International migration matters greatly to the state on both receiving and sending ends because it involves crucial economic and political interests that the state is compelled to act upon. Through their immigration policies, destination states determine the skill levels and socio-economic characteristics of incoming workers. Many scholars have already acknowledged the importance of immigration policies,[58] and some of them have explained the differences in these policies as a function of a nation's self-definition or self-understanding as established over a long time.[59]

Nevertheless, there have been few in-depth studies dealing with states on *the sending side*. This is partly because scholars generally assume that countries of origin have virtually no leverage. Migration is viewed as a demand-driven phenomenon, and it is assumed that the only role developing states can play is to promote and facilitate labor export. Some scholars have pointed to the negative consequences of state economic policies on rural populations in the Third World as a determinant of migration;[60] yet as the data above suggest, levels of poverty and unemployment do not by themselves lead automatically to large outflows of female labor. Only in the past decade have studies on emigration policies begun to emerge.[61] These studies have focused mainly on the contents of policies; cross-national differences in emigration policies have rarely received much attention.[62] The mainstream migration theories have largely ignored the gender dimensions of emigration policies.

This book takes an integrative approach in an effort to elucidate how migrant-sending countries—both as states and as societies—affect gender-differentiated migration outcomes. In particular, I intend to explain the variations in state responses toward the international migration of women. Although it is true that migration is a demand-driven phenomenon, workers in developing countries do not respond to this demand in the same manner, and this is especially the case with female migration. As far as traditional male migration is concerned, no state discourages or prohibits it; in fact, many states promote male migration or adopt a laissez-faire approach to it. However, the policies of states vary, sometimes strongly, with regard to female migration. As will be discussed later, the state tends to exert control over women through emigration restrictions or bans. I call these "value-driven emigration policies," since such restrictions for women signify an underlying social value: namely, that women need to be protected by the state—more so than men. I hypothesize that these value-driven emigration policies, which crystallize various sociocultural, political, and institutional factors, influence the flows of female migration in Asia.

MICRO LEVEL: INDIVIDUAL AUTONOMY

At the micro level, I will examine women's autonomy and decision-making power. The role of individuals is important because the formulation of policies does not necessarily guarantee blind compliance by the citizenry. For instance, state efforts to ban female migration in the Philippines failed because some women kept migrating abroad through unofficial channels. Conversely, attempts to promote female migration in other countries did not succeed because women were not interested in migrating. Therefore, in addition to macro policy factors, microlevel analyses of individuals and households are also necessary to uncover the true determinants of female migration. In particular, this study tries to emphasize the importance of women's autonomy and decision-making power within households. Female migration is not a simple outcome of pull–push factors or global restructuring; rather, it is a complex process in which women themselves actively participate and on which they carefully reflect. Examining the role of women's autonomy and decision-making power will constitute an important component of the integrative approach I am taking.

Here, I should briefly discuss households. In my samples for Sri Lanka and Bangladesh, most migrant women belonged to a household that consisted of a nuclear family, and their financial obligations and responsibilities were largely contained within it. By contrast, Filipina migrant women often sent money and gifts from overseas not only to their parents and children but also to grandparents, siblings, nephews, nieces, and in-laws. These people did not necessarily belong to the same "household," understood here as a shared residential unit. In analyzing women's migration behavior, therefore, we must look beyond households and recognize the role played by the extended family and sometimes even the community. This study will incorporate the impact of gender roles within households on women's decision-making and the influence of family members, friends, and neighbors in the microlevel analyses.

MACRO–MICRO LINK: SOCIAL LEGITIMACY

This study will present a concept of "social legitimacy" as a heuristic tool for linking globalization forces with state policies and individual autonomy. I define social legitimacy as a particular set of social norms—norms that accept women's wage employment and geographical mobility and that establish an environment conducive to international female migration. The historical legacy of women's wage employment (for example, the incorporation of female labor into colonial agricultural estates) has tended to prepare society to accept women's economic activities outside the home; in this way, it has helped extend social legitimacy to female labor migration.

A country's integration into the global economy through export-oriented industrialization policies and the resulting increase in foreign direct investment also contribute strongly to the emergence of social legitimacy for international female migration. This is because these things increase women's rural–urban mobility by creating jobs in urban manufacturing sectors. However, my idea veers from the existing literature which maintains that women's internal mobility directly increases the number of migrant women by creating a potential migrant labor reserve in free trade zones.[63] I argue instead that *women's increasing rural–urban mobility transforms the gender norms within communities*; furthermore, *this transformation itself lends social legitimacy to international female migration*. I will examine how women's rural–urban mobility has changed community norms and helped establish a more acceptable environment for women to migrate to foreign countries. In doing so, I will illustrate the impact that globalization has had on the experience of Third World women with internal and international migration.

In summary, the patterns and causal mechanisms of female migration can be explained by the "integrative approach" which examines (1) the impact of globalization, (2) the absence of an international migration regime, (3) gendered policies for immigration and emigration, (4) women's autonomy within households, and (5) the social legitimacy of international female migration. I reiterate here that I will limit this study to the legal migration of women. Irregular migration and human trafficking have been increasing, and both now pose a difficult challenge to the international community. I have decided, however, to exclude these particular types of migration from my research. The lack of reliable data is one reason; a more important reason is that both phenomena involve factors such as criminal networks, border controls, and law enforcement, which might require a different type of research from the sort that I have conducted. My research findings can be applied to a particular form of irregular migration but are not generalizable to the entire phenomenon.

Data

Most of the data in this book were collected during my fieldwork in nine Asian countries (Japan, Philippines, Thailand, Vietnam, Bangladesh, Sri Lanka, India, Pakistan, and the United Arab Emirates) and one Special Administrative Region (Hong Kong) in 1999 and 2000. I have supplemented these data with additional data on other countries that I gathered while working at the ILO between 1993 and 1996 and in 2002–03. I will be using both qualitative and quantitative data. The qualitative data are based on my interviews with 249 individuals, including 116 migrant women, 22 "non-migrants," and 111 key informants in state offices, recruitment agencies, NGOs, international organizations, and research institutions. Where useful or necessary, I will also be using quantitative data on macroeconomic indicators (such as GDP per capita, unemployment rates, women's labor participation rate, and levels of FDI) as well as demographic profiles of migrant women.

Regarding the immigration policies of receiving countries in Asia, I will mainly be comparing the data on Japan, two newly industrialized economies (Hong Kong and Singapore), and the Gulf States (mainly Kuwait and United Arab Emirates).[64] I have divided the main destination countries in the region into these three groups because each reflects distinctive immigration patterns and economic development processes. The gender dimensions of immigration outcomes will be highlighted in the analyses.

Regarding the emigration policies of "senders" and "non-senders," I will be focusing on the Philippines and Sri Lanka (senders) as well as Bangladesh (non-sender), because each of these countries represents a certain pattern of state response to female migration: Sri Lanka is the most lenient, the Philippines moderate, and Bangladesh the most restrictive. Most states have adopted similar emigration policies for men; the same countries vary in their responses to female migration. To highlight the differences between the two groups, this part of the study will be supplemented by additional data from one "sender" (Indonesia) and two "non-senders" (India and Pakistan).

For this policy analysis, I have obtained and will use various sources, including interview data, policy documents, and other secondary information. The policy documents include Executive Orders, ministerial ordinances, memorandums exchanged within state agencies, government reports, and so on. The institutional analyses will be based on interviews with politicians, NGOs, recruitment agencies, international organizations, other interest groups, and officials in various ministries (foreign affairs, labor, justice, and so on).

The microlevel analyses in this study are based on my interviews with 116 migrant women. Since most of the respondents from Sri Lanka and Bangladesh could not speak English well, I conducted interviews with them through interpreters. Some were working abroad during my fieldwork; others had already returned to their home countries. This study incorporates data from an additional 22 women who were either "attempted migrants" (those who tried unsuccessfully to emigrate) or "non-migrants" (those who had not taken any actions toward migration). The interviews with the latter were especially important for identifying the factors influencing individual decisions.

In general, it is extremely difficult to conduct a systematic survey of migrant workers based on random sampling, because in no country is there a list that comprehensively covers the entire migrant population, be it male or female. Given this situation, and given the general paucity of data on female migration in developing countries in particular, all the respondents were identified through the "snowball sampling" method. I followed this practice in conjunction with participant observation.

I conducted 55 interviews with Filipino women: 15 with "returnees" in the Philippines and 40 with migrants still working abroad at the time of interview (14 in Hong Kong and 26 in the United Arab Emirates). I also conducted 50 interviews with Sri Lankan women: 21 with returnees and 29 with migrants working in Hong Kong. Most of these migrant women were domestic workers, but some were entertainers, caregivers, factory workers, or office clerks. I interviewed a few male migrants as well, although I did not include them in my sample because there were so few of them.

My approach to Bangladeshi women had to be adjusted to reflect the ban on migration of unskilled women that was in place at the time of my field-work, as well as the fact that there are far fewer Bangladeshi migrant women compared with Filipina and Sri Lankan women. I interviewed 33 women in total: 11 returned migrants and 22 non-migrants. The latter included two women who were about to leave the country, seven who had paid fees to migrate but had been defrauded by a recruitment agent, four who were in-terested in migration but had not taken actions yet, and nine who had no interest in migration, at least at the time of interview.

Interviews varied in length. Most of them lasted between sixty and ninety minutes. Sometimes I interviewed the same person two or three times in order to gather more in-depth information. To protect the privacy of the migrant women, I use fictitious names for all respondents who appear in this book.

FIELD INTERVIEWS: IDENTIFYING RESPONDENTS

During my fieldwork, I was fortunate to have access to ILO offices as my contact points. Although I was on study leave, my colleagues in each country office were kind enough to help me make appointments with state officials, NGO staff, and academics. State officials in various countries whom I met through my work with the ILO also helped me in my research. This enabled me to identify key informants for interviews. However, identifying migrant women was quite difficult and time-consuming. As noted earlier, none of the countries in this study kept a comprehensive list of migrants. Some state agencies kept lists of registered migrants, but most such lists were kept confidential. And I was told that even with such a list, it would be difficult to identify respondents because those on the list might be still overseas or have changed their residence without reporting to the agency. Furthermore, the addresses on those lists were scattered throughout the country, so it would have been almost impossible for me to draw a random sample from it and visit interviewees.

Faced with these constraints, in the Philippines, I first interviewed a few former migrant women who were working as domestic workers at my friends' houses in Manila. After this, I asked migration NGOs[65] for help identifying former migrant women. Some migration NGOs hold pre-departure orientation courses for future migrant workers every week. I monitored one of these and interviewed a group of women who already had some migration experience. Through one NGO, I met Rena, a former migrant domestic worker in Hong Kong. We became friends after going through a long interview session, and she was kind enough to take me to her home village, three hours north of Manila. Many of her friends there were like her—they had emigrated and returned. I visited that village twice, staying at her house and interviewing returned migrants in her neighborhood.

A Sri Lankan NGO, the Migrant Services Centre (MSC), helped me greatly in identifying migrant women. The MSC also holds regular pre-departure orientation sessions for prospective migrant women. I attended one of these, where I conducted participant observation; later on, I also interviewed some of the participants. The MSC also showed me one of their projects in Kegalle, four or five hours northwest of Colombo, where many former migrant women were learning to run their own small businesses so that they would not need to migrate abroad again. I met a group of about twenty "returnee" women at their monthly meeting there; after that, I visited the homes of those who were willing to be interviewed again.

In Hong Kong—one of the most popular destinations for Asian migrant women—I interviewed migrants working "on site." Finding respondents here was relatively easy because most migrant women are given every Sunday off and gather in public spaces. Each ethnic group has its own favorite place to hang out—Filipinas in Statue Square in the heart of downtown, Sri Lankans in Kowloon Park, and Indonesians in Victoria Park. On Sundays I went to these spots and interviewed migrant women. As I had heard and read about it many times, these were indeed massive gatherings. In Statue Square, well over a thousand Filipino women were filling the entire space and its neighboring areas. Like many of the migrant women, I spread a newspaper on the ground; from my new "office," I interviewed those who were sitting around me or passing near. Besides attending these Sunday outings, I visited church-based shelters and legal aid offices for migrant women. In these places, I interviewed mostly Filipina and Sri Lankan domestic workers who were in trouble or who had run away from their employers after experiencing violence, sexual abuse, or other problems. During my stay in Hong Kong, I also interviewed some employers and recruitment agencies.

In the United Arab Emirates—another popular destination for migrants—it was extremely difficult to identify and interview migrant women from Asia. In most countries in the Middle East, unskilled migrant women are given no days off and are not allowed to go outside alone. This means there is no place where migrant women gather on the weekends the way they do in Hong Kong. Faced with this constraint, I visited the embassies and consulates instead. From my earlier research, I knew that the diplomatic missions of major migrant-sending countries had shelters for migrant women inside their compounds. With the help of my friends in the Philippine government, I was able to interview migrant women in two shelters—one in the Philippine embassy in Abu Dhabi, the other in the Philippine consulate in Dubai. I also visited the embassies of Bangladesh, Sri Lanka, and Indonesia, but interviewing migrant women was not possible in any of them.

Conclusion

This book examines cross-national patterns and causal mechanisms of international female migration that have received relatively little attention in the literature on migration. Its "integrative approach" compares migrant-receiving and migrant-sending countries and also looks at non-sending countries, the goal being to identify the factors that encourage and discourage female migration. This approach involves analysis at four different levels: suprastate, state, societal, and individual. The suprastate factor—more specifically, the globalization of production and services—has dramatically changed the lives of Third World women. The lack of an international legal framework for protecting migrant workers is another important element to be considered in analyses of emigration policies. The role of the state is crucial; even when there is a high demand in the international labor market, states often try to prevent women from working overseas. However, the enforcement power of states is hardly absolute; they cannot entirely dictate individual behavior. This means that we must also analyze women's decision-making processes and social environment that affects them. An integrative approach based on these multiple levels of analysis will help us understand the causal mechanisms of female migration and answer this question: Why does the feminization of migration occur in some countries but not others?

In the next chapter I focus on the role of migrant-receiving countries in Asia and explain how the demand for migrant women emerged and how immigration policies have evolved to accommodate that demand. In particular, I will elucidate the ways in which different types of economic development have resulted in the different types of labor demand and variations in immigration policies for migrant women. After this, Chapter 3 addresses the role of migrant-sending countries and examines "value-driven" emigration policies. It reveals how policies for women's migration differ from those for men, and why. Chapter 4 examines the factors affecting emigration policies for women and how they yield cross-national differences in migration outcomes. The importance of the colonial legacy, civil society, and state identity, and the symbolic politics of gender, will be highlighted. Chapter 5 focuses on individual migrant women. Based on the interview data, it presents the "face" of migrant women: who they are, why they do or do not migrate, and how some of them fall into traps that keep them away from home. Chapter 6 examines the social environment that surrounds women in developing countries. In particular, it suggests that "social legitimacy" is a crucial element for fostering female migration on a large scale. It discusses how social legitimacy for women's migration is developed, enhanced, and sometimes undermined. The final chapter then sums up the findings and addresses some of the critical political implications, including the challenges facing states and the international community.

Economic Development and Immigration Policies: The Role of the State and Society in Destination Countries

A WALK AROUND STATUE Square in Hong Kong or Lucky Plaza in Singapore on Sunday is probably the best possible introduction to female migration in Asia. Thousands of migrant women gather in both places to hang out with one another and chat with their friends. This is their break from a long and stressful week. On Sundays and public holidays, local residents suddenly become the "minority" in both places. Viewing such huge crowds of migrant women, one cannot help wondering: Why are there so many foreign women?

This chapter examines the processes through which international female migration has grown in Asia by focusing on the role of the receiving countries. Women's autonomous migration is not necessarily new in the region. In the nineteenth century, a large number of Chinese women migrated to Singapore and Malaysia (then called "British Malaya") as domestic workers. After World War II, the demand for migrant women—especially for nannies, housekeepers, and caregivers—continued to expand in many parts of Asia. At the same time, less developed Asian countries became major "suppliers" of migrant women for the region and across the world. As discussed in the previous chapter, the feminization of migration has been accelerating in Asia, particularly in recent decades.

It is worth noting that the demand for "women's work" (such as domestic work) is barely affected by economic downturns, unlike "men's work" (such as construction). For many middle-class working couples in Southeast Asia, a domestic worker is a status symbol as well as a necessity. In addition, among upper-class families in the Arab countries of West Asia, the number of domestic workers one has is an important indicator of wealth. A former Philippine state official put it this way:

> Filipina domestic workers are like Mercedes [Benz]. They are a status symbol for employers. That's why they don't want to fire their domestic workers easily even when they face salary cuts or financial difficulties.

Indeed, the Asian financial crisis had little impact on the demand for migrant women in these sectors. The demand for female migrant labor cannot be understood simply in economic terms.

This chapter starts with a brief history of female migration in the colonial era. Then it examines various factors that fueled the growing demand for migrant women in the postwar period. Almost all middle- and high-income countries in Asia have migrant women on their soil; however, these countries vary greatly with regard to their acceptance processes and the types of migrant women they allow in. For instance, Hong Kong and Singapore accept a large number of migrant domestic workers, whereas Japan accepts very few of these but a significant number of migrant entertainers. How do differences like these arise? This chapter compares and contrasts migrant-receiving countries in Asia.

To explain the diversity among destination countries, it is important to examine the development processes, demographic challenges, and sociocultural factors that affect immigration policies for women. I will analyze receiving countries in terms of three subcategories: (1) Southeast Asia (Hong Kong and Singapore); (2) Japan; and (3) West Asia (the oil-rich Gulf States). My goal is to illustrate the differences and similarities in the state response to female migration through which international gender division of labor has been structured.

Finally, this chapter will analyze how migrant women are chosen by destination countries, and why. That is, why do some countries accept mainly Filipina migrant women whereas others accept mainly Indonesians? What kinds of factors determine decisions like this? I will approach this as a question of "political selectivity" in terms of macrolevel immigration policies, and then as a "social selectivity" question in terms of the choices made by the society—particularly by individual employers and recruitment agencies. Based on my interviews with these employers and agencies, I will highlight the sociocultural stereotypes that shape the demand structure for migrant women of certain nationalities at the individual level.

Economic Development and Women's Migration: The Newly Industrialized Economies

The autonomous migration of women into Hong Kong, Singapore, and Malaysia is not a new phenomenon. Large-scale female migration to these places dates back to the colonial era. In the mid-nineteenth century, women from southern China—especially from Guangdong province—migrated to these places to work in private homes. Emigration from China was officially prohibited at the time, yet a sizable female migration from Guangdong began in 1851 when the Manchus lost control over the Chinese borders—a consequence of the Taiping Rebellion and the deteriorating economic situation.[1] The number of migrant women increased rapidly once the ban on emigration was lifted in 1860. Most of these migrant women were single, since traditionally, married women were expected to stay home to look after children and parents-in-law. Guangdong became the main source of migrant women because foot-binding and the killing of newborn girls were not as prevalent as in other parts of China. Geographical isolation (it is ringed by mountains) enabled Guangdong province to develop a distinct culture—one that was much more accommodating to women. Because their feet had never been bound, Cantonese women found it much easier to go overseas than women from other areas.[2]

These migrant domestic workers from Guangdong were generally called *amah*. Chinese families in the British colonies also depended on girl slaves, *mui tsai*, for household help. The *mui tsai* were purchased or leased at a young age and worked for the master and his family until they were married off.[3] According to a 1918 report by the Hong Kong governor, almost every Chinese household that could afford one had a *mui tsai*.[4] A campaign to abolish this form of slavery took root in the early 1920s; in 1923 the British authority prohibited the sale and purchase of *mui tsai*. Although the practice continued until World War II under the new term "adopted daughters," the demand for household help shifted from *mui tsai* to *amahs*.[5]

In the 1930s, a large number of women migrated from Guangdong to Hong Kong and Malaya (the present Malaysia and Singapore) to serve as domestic workers. This was partly owing to the Great Depression, during which male migrants in the British colonies were repatriated back to China. In Malaya in 1930, as a response to high unemployment, an immigration quota system was introduced; as a consequence, between 1931 and 1933 half a million more Chinese men returned to China than arrived in Malaya.[6] After the immigration restriction was incorporated into the Straits Settlements Aliens Ordinance of 1933, male migration from China declined sharply.[7] The policy of sending migrant men back home increased the burden on rural Chinese families which already had difficulty making ends meet. This led to a sharp increase in the number of Chinese women to Malaya between 1934 and 1938 because women were exempt from the quota restrictions. A large number of Chinese women began to arrive in Malaya in place of their husbands in order to support their families.[8] In addition, the growth of the synthetic fiber industry after 1924 led to more than 100,000 poor women losing their jobs in Guangdong's silk industry.[9] The economic conditions in Guangdong were made even worse by natural disasters (mainly floods) and by political turmoil—specifically, the Japanese invasion and Chinese Civil War. More than 190,000 Chinese women left Guangdong between 1933 and 1938 in response to the demand for domestic workers in Malaya and Hong Kong.[10] This large-scale female migration from Mainland China to Malaya continued until 1938 when high unemployment led the colonial authorities to impose immigration restrictions on women as well.[11] At the same time, the population flows into Hong Kong became even greater. It is possible that the closed door to Malaya redirected the migrants; it is certain that the prolonged Sino-Japanese war drove people out of southern China. Between 1938 and 1940, more than half a million Chinese fled to Hong Kong.[12]

In the postwar era, these migrants' destinations went through socioeconomic upheaval. They all experienced strong export-oriented industrialization, rapid growth in local women's labor force participation, and the nuclearization of families. These things led to a strong demand for domestic workers and the opening of the immigration gates for women from other Asian countries. However, these destinations are dissimilar in many ways with regard to both processes and policies. The factors at play are both social and geographical. The next sections compare and contrast the cases of Hong Kong and Singapore.

HONG KONG

Decades before World War II and into the 1950s, Hong Kong prospered as the center of entrepôt trade with China and the rest of the world. Hong Kong's major industrialization began in 1949, the year the Communists took control of Mainland China. The colony absorbed an influx of refugees from the mainland, many of whom were gifted capitalists and managers. These middle-class refugees reestablished themselves in the light manufacturing sector in Hong Kong.[13] At the same time, the unskilled refugees contributed to the economy as a pool of cheap labor. With an abundance of local capital and labor, the manufacturing industry started growing in Hong Kong in the 1950s. In 1947, only 10 percent of Hong Kong's exports were manufactured goods; by 1959, the figure was 70 percent.[14] Multinational corporations increased their capital investments, until by the end of the 1960s, Hong Kong had developed a vibrant industrial economy.

Women played a crucial role in Hong Kong's economic development. The manufacturing industry preferred young unmarried women because of their supposed docility, obedience, and manual dexterity. The number of female workers in Hong Kong factories rapidly increased. The labor force participation rate of men dropped by 11.2 percent between 1961 and 1991, while that of women grew by 10.8 percent. By 1981, 49 percent of Hong Kong's workers were women.[15] Most of them worked in light industry, reflecting the colony's initial stages of industrialization; in the early 1970s, 85 percent of them worked in garment, textile, plastics, electronics, and wig-making factories.[16] At that point, however, Hong Kong underwent a profound structural change and began to shift toward a services-oriented economy. During this transition, a large number of middle-class women joined the labor force.

As more women began working outside the home, or aspiring to do so, finding domestic help became a serious challenge. Labor migration from China had declined since the Communist takeover in 1949, which is the year the border with China was officially closed. The supply of *amahs* decreased as a consequence. Middle-class families managed for some time with the help of extended family or undocumented migrants from China. However, by the 1970s, the traditional large, extended family had become less common owing to rapid urbanization, a growing population, and the resulting housing shortage. The large-scale state housing projects were being designed to accommodate nuclear families, and this also accelerated the change in family structure. At the same time, young couples began to prefer living away from their parents. Between 1971 and 1990, the average household size in Hong Kong dropped from 4.5 persons to 3.5.[17] As small nuclear families slowly replaced traditional large, extended families, it became more and more difficult for women to seek household help from family members. Furthermore, the rise in household incomes made people feel it was more appropriate to hire a domestic worker than to ask an aging mother or mother-in-law to assume onerous household duties.[18]

Yet by then, getting outside help had become difficult in Hong Kong. The supply of *amahs* had already declined after the closing of the Chinese border. In addition, more and more women were leaving domestic work (especially live-in domestic work) because it often entailed punishing conditions—not only low wages and long working hours but also difficult employee–employer relationships which sometimes included abuse. As more factories opened up, *amahs* shifted to factory jobs which paid better, had regular hours, and offered higher social status and an independent lifestyle.

The rise in overall income levels of Hong Kong households was another reason why fewer Chinese women were taking household jobs. The shortage of domestic workers was accompanied by a decline in the reputation and quality of *amahs*. In the 1970s and 1980s, *amahs* were developing a reputation for being difficult and demanding. According to Constable, Hong Kong residents were beginning to lament that *amahs* were in such high demand that they could refuse to do what they were asked and even quit whenever they liked.[19]

Despite the increasing need for household help among many working families, effective social policies were not being developed to address this problem. Reflecting the laissez-faire economic principles, Hong Kong's social policies offered "minimal support" with few resources allocated to the working-class families. Even large public housing projects were not equipped with day-care facilities.[20] The state viewed child care as a family responsibility and contended that state welfare services could threaten the traditional value that family members should be cared for at home. It did not provide adequate public day-care facilities except to families on the lowest income rung. The Hong Kong government's first policy statement on social welfare reflected its position clearly:

> It is of the greatest possible importance that social welfare services should not be organized in such a way as to . . . accelerate the breakdown of the natural or traditional sense of responsibility—for example by encouraging the natural family unit to shed on to social welfare agencies, public or private, its moral responsibility to care for the aged or infirm. . . . It is clearly desirable, on social as well as economic grounds to do everything possible in Hong Kong to support and strengthen the sense of "family responsibility."[21]

With the population aging, eldercare has become a serious concern for nuclear families in Hong Kong. Yet levels of public assistance continue to be minimal, and the responsibility for eldercare falls on families. Most often, that means wives or unmarried daughters.

Given the lack of public welfare assistance, working couples in Hong Kong had to rely on the meager supply of *amahs*. However, more and more *amahs* were abandoning live-in domestic work and only working part-time, as "commuting domestic workers." This made the lives of dual-career families difficult, especially when there was a newborn baby in the home, or elderly parents requiring constant care.

IMMIGRATION POLICIES

In 1974 the Hong Kong government opened a legal immigration channel for domestic workers from other Asian countries. Until this point, the government had been allowing unskilled workers to enter only if they were from China;[22] this is because the local population was growing quickly and the inflow of Chinese refugees was quite large. For many years, the government had been allowing Mainland Chinese to stay in Hong Kong whether they entered legally or illegally. In 1974 it adopted a stricter "touch base" policy that denied illegal migrants the right to enter if they were caught crossing the borders. Yet even this policy was lenient, since it granted residency to migrants who had already arrived illegally in the urban zones of Kowloon and Hong Kong Island.[23]

According to one Labour Department official, the change in policy toward foreign domestic workers had been prompted by pressure from the growing number of Western expatriates in the colony. Most of these people were from Europe (mainly Britain) and North America and were employed by the Hong Kong offices of multinational corporations (MNCs). They earned high salaries and lived affluent lives in spacious homes, and most of them wanted English-speaking domestic workers. However, now that the Chinese border was closed, Hong Kong did not have enough domestic workers even for the local population, let alone the expatriates. The government realized that it would have to accommodate the Westerners' needs if it hoped to attract foreign investment. Even today, the Hong Kong government is using the availability of foreign domestic workers in its sales pitches to foreign investors. One of the government websites targeting foreign investors and MNC executives advertises the "wonderful life experience" offered by Hong Kong—an experience that includes easily available domestic help:

> The executive lifestyle in Hong Kong includes affordable, live-in domestic help. Specialist recruitment agencies can source domestic workers with particular strengths to suit individual needs, including professionally trained child carers, nurses or cooks. Most executive-style flats and houses include domestic helper quarters. For families with children, the difference that one (or two) live-in workers can make is tremendous. Parents are freed from daily chores to spend quality time with their children and enjoy what Hong Kong has to offer. In fact, for many executive mothers in particular, it can be difficult to readjust to life back home without the depth of household support provided by domestic workers in Hong Kong. . . . Most domestic workers are from the Philippines or elsewhere in Southeast Asia. Workers work . . . at a minimum wage equivalent to US$471 per month.[24]

It was not just foreign executives who required domestic help. The demand for domestic workers was also growing among the local population, especially with regard to working couples who could not find child care. The government responded to such needs and began allowing Hong Kong residents—be they expatriates or locals—to bring in foreign domestic workers through two-year renewable contracts from any country except China.[25] By 1976,

TABLE 2.1

Nationalities of Foreign Domestic Workers in Hong Kong (stock data)

Country	1990	1993	1995	1997	1999	2001
Philippines	63,643	105,410	131,176	138,085	140,066	155,370
Indonesia	1,023	6,148	16,357	24,706	36,769	66,130
Thailand	4,274	6,999	6,708	5,142	5,433	6,900
India	838	1,027	1,228	1,157	1,179	n.a.
Sri Lanka	344	632	831	1,089	1,177	n.a.
Nepal	32	104	318	528	606	n.a.
Others	181	284	408	264	219	3,890
Total	70,335	120,604	157,026	178,971	185,449	232,290

SOURCES: Hong Kong Immigration Department (1999); Asian Migrant Centre and Migrant Forum in Asia (2003).

an administrative framework had been established: a new Foreign Domestic Workers Service Section within the Department of Labour assumed the role of controlling and administering matters relating to foreign domestic workers.[26] As a result of all this, the number of foreign domestic workers in Hong Kong increased from a few thousand in the late 1970s to 232,000 in 2001. The great majority of these were Filipino women (see Table 2.1).

Hong Kong's acceptance of foreign domestic workers was driven by four factors: (1) a laissez-faire industrial policy that led to rapid economic growth in the 1980s and 1990s; (2) a concurrent increase in foreign investment and in business expatriates who required English-speaking domestic workers; (3) an increase in local women's entry into the labor force; and (4) the closing of the Chinese border, which choked off the supply of *amahs*. The need to attract Western executives was an especially important trigger.

The situation was rather different in other countries in Southeast Asia. The following section on Singapore presents a more typical example of state-led economic development that fostered female migration.

SINGAPORE

After achieving full independence in 1965, the city-state of Singapore adopted an aggressive, export-oriented industrial strategy. Hong Kong has long been guided by a laissez-faire economic policy; by contrast, Singapore is a typical "developmental state," to use Johnson's term.[27] That is, it has taken a strongly state-interventionist approach to economic and social development. In particular, the Singapore government has made every effort to attract MNCs. At the time it started taking this approach, the local business community consisted almost entirely of small merchants and financiers—people who lacked technical and management skills.[28]

The demand for labor generated by increases in foreign investment and export-led manufacturing was initially met through cheap and abundant local labor.[29] Quickly, however, because of its small population—only 1.9 million at the time of independence—Singapore had to open its doors to foreign labor. In 1965 its government passed the Regulation of Employment Act; this introduced a one-year permit scheme for unskilled labor. In the first year, only 2,109 work permits were issued to foreign migrant workers, who comprised only 0.4 percent of the total labor force.[30] However, as export-led manufacturing started growing, their number increased from 5,449 in 1969 to around 100,000 in 1973.[31]

Singapore crafted its immigration policy with painstaking caution in order to ensure that it was not overwhelmed by foreign workers. Its government perceived too much foreign labor as a threat to the national identity. This was especially important from the perspective of ethnic balance. Singapore's leaders were Chinese, and to remain in control, they would have to ensure that the Chinese retained a numerical majority. Already accommodating Malays and Indians as a significant portion of the population, the government placed restrictions on the number of Malays who could enter Singapore to work. The point of this was to prevent an influx of Malays from Singapore's heavily populated neighbor, Malaysia.

Given these constraints, the Singaporean authorities pursued a deliberate policy of mobilizing the entire local labor force. If there were labor shortages, it would bridge the gap with Singaporeans if it possibly could; it would not open the immigration gates any more than it absolutely had to. As a result of this policy and the growth of foreign direct investment, the labor force participation rate of Singaporean women more than doubled between 1957 and 1980, from 21.6 to 44.3 percent; not only that, but their share in the total labor force increased from 17.5 percent in 1957 to 34.5 percent in 1980.[32] By 1980, manufacturing industries—especially textiles and electronics—had absorbed more than 130,000 women, that is, 34.9 percent of all female workers.[33] Then in 1979 the government launched a major economic restructuring, the goal of which was to move Singapore from a labor-intensive to a capital-intensive economy. By the early 1980s, services and technology had replaced manufacturing as the linchpin of Singapore's economy.

The labor force participation rate among married women had barely grown between 1957 and 1970, from 14.0 to 14.7 percent. Even after industrialization took off, the proportion of married women in the labor force remained at 22.1 percent in 1975.[34] This became a concern for the government which had been counting on further growth in the labor force to enhance Singapore's economic growth. Prime Minister Lee Kuan Yew commented on this:

Women are equal to men in intellectual capacity. With more jobs open to them and separate income tax for married women, the status of women in our society has been changed. . . . With economic independence, the dependent position of wives must also change. . . . It has been government policy to encourage the education of women to their fullest ability and their employment commensurate with their abilities. . . . However, what has not taken place in traditional male-dominant Asian societies is . . . change in social attitude [which] cannot come by legislation. Such adjustments should be allowed to develop naturally.[35]

However, many women still faced difficulties: the "social attitude" among men was difficult to change, especially with regard to sharing household work equitably. Furthermore, by the late 1970s the supply of local domestic workers in rural areas had been depleted. The Singaporean authorities had been permitting the recruitment of domestic workers from Malaysia since the late 1960s, but Malaysia itself was beginning to face labor shortages as a consequence of strong economic growth in the late 1970s. As part of an effort to encourage more married women to enter the labor force, a "foreign domestic workers scheme" was introduced in 1978. Foreign domestic workers would now be accepted from "non-traditional sources" such as the Philippines, Sri Lanka, and India.[36] The point of this was to provide a viable option for local housewives who wished to work outside the home.

This scheme turned out to be effective in releasing local housewives from home: the labor force participation rate among married women in Singapore increased from 29.3 percent in 1980 to 40.3 percent in 1989.[37] By 1992, married women actually outnumbered single women in the labor force—a trend that has strengthened since. In 1998, married women constituted 55.7 percent of the total female labor force.[38]

To prevent a massive influx of unskilled foreign labor, state policies also required employers to bear an additional financial burden for each foreign domestic worker. At first, employers were required to pay 30 percent of each worker's monthly salary to the Central Provident Fund—Singapore's version of social security.[39] In 1982 this policy was replaced by a levy system that required employers to pay the government a fee for each migrant worker hired. This system counters any cost advantage that employers might gain by employing migrant workers, and in doing so slows down the increase in the migrant population. The monthly levy varies among occupations, and has been increasing for all occupations. The levy for a foreign domestic worker is especially high—the highest of all. The levy for a manufacturing worker is only S$50 (US$30); for a domestic worker it is S$250 (US$154). Clearly, the government's intention is to discourage Singaporean households from relying too heavily on foreign domestic workers.

At the same time, the government has been exerting strict control over foreign domestic workers to prevent their settlement in Singapore. For instance, it limits them to two-year contracts, which are renewable only for those who are under fifty and physically fit and who have not broken any of the work permit conditions. Foreign domestic workers are also prohibited from marrying Singaporeans or becoming pregnant. They have been required to take not only a general medical exam but also medical screenings for pregnancy, HIV/AIDS, and venereal diseases every six months.[40]

Besides allowing the recruitment of foreign domestic workers, the government has been attempting to lighten the child-rearing burdens of Singaporean women. After the population policy was shifted toward pronatalism in 1983, the government set up public child-care centers and began encouraging non-governmental organizations and the private sector to establish similar facilities. The number (and capacity) of child-care centers increased from 33 (for 2,023 children) in 1982 to 319 (for 23,235) by the mid-1990s.[41]

However, the child-care centers have not been a perfect solution for working couples. Most centers do not take children under two. Furthermore, their hours of operation are highly restricted, and the care they provide is not as intensive as that provided by a live-in domestic worker, who is often available to the children twenty-four hours a day in the home. In addition, the child-care centers do not have medical facilities and thus cannot accept sick children; this means that parents have to take their sick child to a doctor and then stay home with them.[42] Perhaps the biggest problem, however, is the cost of this care. In the early 1990s in Singapore, the average cost for a space in a child-care facility was S$350−400 (US$200−230) per month per child. This was not too high by Singaporean standards. More exclusive (presumably "better") facilities cost up to S$800 (US$460).[43] By contrast, the monthly salary of foreign domestic workers is around S$300 (US$170); S$330−350 for Filipina and S$230−250 for Indonesian domestic workers.[44] Although the employer must pay the levy in addition to that, the total cost would be less than that of upscale child-care facilities. Clearly, for couples with two or more children, it is a more economical choice to hire a foreign domestic worker who can take care of the children and do the household chores besides.

Another concern for Singaporean families is eldercare. Singapore is one of the fastest-aging societies in Asia. In 2002, 7.6 percent of Singaporeans were over sixty; this figure is expected to reach 13.1 percent by 2015. Low birth rates (especially among the Chinese ethnic majority) and prolonged life expectancy are combining to increase the burden of eldercare for many working families in Singapore. Although the government provides some welfare services such as public nursing homes, the strong tradition of filial piety has led almost 90 percent of Chinese and Malays to care for their elderly parents at home.[45] The same study indicates that most elderly couples live with their son; of course, it is often the daughter-in-law who bears the actual responsibility for providing care. In a society where almost 50 percent of women work outside the home, arrangements like these are becoming increasingly unmanageable, especially when no outside help is available. Therefore, despite the cumbersome employment procedures and high levies, many families have been opting to hire foreign domestic workers and caregivers. This makes more financial sense to most working couples, especially if they have more than one child and/or elderly parents at home. A foreign domestic worker is a practical help; she also confers status on middle-class Singaporean families.

Singaporeans' dependence on foreign domestic workers has been increasing rapidly. Between 1990 and 2002, the percentage of households employing foreign domestic workers more than doubled, from 6.7 to 14.3 percent.[46] This figure is among the highest in the world.[47] In 2000 there were more than 140,000 foreign domestic workers in Singapore; of these, 80,000 were from the Philippines. The rest were from Indonesia, Sri Lanka, Myanmar, and Thailand.[48]

The number of foreign domestic workers will continue to increase now that Singapore has accepted them as a component of its population policies. The Singaporean government sees foreign domestic workers as key to reducing child-care costs. It has recently decided to reduce the levy on domestic workers from S$345 to S$250 for families with small children or elderly parents.[49] By facilitating the employment of foreign domestic workers, it hopes to increase the fertility rate among Singaporeans and maximize female labor force participation. Expanding welfare programs—for example, by creating and improving child-care and eldercare facilities—is not considered a viable option, perhaps because of the cost. More and more migrant women in domestic and care work in Singapore are now bearing the burden of the state's withdrawal from the welfare sector.

THE NIE MODEL FOR INTERNATIONAL FEMALE MIGRATION

Notwithstanding some slight differences, the above cases—Hong Kong and Singapore—represent a particular immigration model broadly shared by newly industrialized economies (NIEs). Both cases embraced strong industrialization policies and experienced rapid growth in the export-manufacturing sector, along with an increase in the demand from female labor. In factories all over Asia and around the world, women are preferred as workers; supposedly, relative to men they are docile, obedient, and good with their hands. Because of the higher wages and better working conditions, many local women choose factory work rather than domestic work.

The most distinct characteristic of the NIE model is that the state responded promptly to labor market needs and opened the immigration gates to foreign domestic workers as a means to push local women into the labor force. In other words, bringing in migrant women was clearly seen as a part of the state industrialization policy. In the case of Hong Kong, the acceptance of foreign domestic workers was also part of a strategy to attract more MNCs (and their executives). The priority was apparently to enhance economic productivity and increase foreign direct investment. Another common factor was that the state used the foreign domestic worker program as an alternative to investing in social services. In order to push local women into the labor market, the government opened the doors to cheap labor instead of providing more child care and eldercare services. There was no campaign to encourage husbands to contribute more to household work. Existing gender roles and ideologies remained intact. Chin, who found similar situations in Malaysia, pointed out that many Malaysian men refused to assume their share of responsibility for domestic labor, while the state elite were "unprepared to encourage the middle classes to use child-care centers."[50]

In recent years other newly industrialized economies have been shifting to this model. These include Korea and Taiwan, both of which long ago adopted restrictive immigration policies. Both of these countries have been bringing in more foreign domestic workers in order to push more women into the labor force. Taiwan officially opened its immigration gates to foreign domestic workers in 1992. The number of foreign domestic workers in that country has been increasing rapidly since then; in 2001 in Taiwan, there were 114,519 caregivers and domestic workers from overseas.[51] Korea was an important labor-exporting country until the 1980s, but has been evolving into a major destination for Asian migrant workers since 1991.[52] Because the government officially prohibited the entry of unskilled foreign labor, for a long time most of these workers were undocumented or were disguised as "trainees." However, Korean immigration policies have been more open in recent years. In November 2002 the government started admitting foreign domestic workers, albeit only if they were Chinese citizens of Korean decent.[53] Another important policy change came in August 2004, when Korea finally began openly accepting unskilled foreign labor. Now all NIEs in Asia officially allow foreign domestic workers to enter temporarily.

JAPAN: IN ISOLATION OR TRANSITION?

Japan is the only high-income country in Asia that does not accept foreign domestic workers. (As an exception to the rule, foreign diplomats in Japan are allowed to bring in domestic workers from abroad.) Its highly restrictive immigration policies are an important reason why. Japan is unique in another way: most of the female migrant workers there are in the entertainment industry. Why is Japan different from other countries? And will it always remain so? This section focuses on Japanese immigration policies, especially as they relate to migrant women.

As many scholars have pointed out, Japan is not an entirely homogeneous nation; it contains a number of small ethnic minorities.[54] These include (1) the Chinese and Koreans who were forced to migrate to Japan during the colonial era; (2) the Ainu on the northern island of Hokkaido, who have been forced to assimilate over the years; and (3) the Okinawans on their Pacific islands, who were once citizens of the Ryukyu Kingdom that Japan conquered in the nineteenth century.[55]

Japan was an emigration country in the early twentieth century. When it opened itself to the world in 1868 after two hundred years of self-imposed isolation, many Japanese emigrated abroad. Most of them went to Hawaii, California, and British Columbia until the United States and Canada closed the door to Asian immigration in the mid-1930s. After that, Brazil and Peru became the destination countries. By 1940 there were about half a million Japanese migrants (and their descendants) in the Americas. Japanese also migrated to their colonial territories, including Manchuria, Korea, and Formosa. In Manchuria alone there were 1.8 million Japanese immigrants by 1937. Most of these returned to Japan after the war.[56]

The first significant immigration flows *into* Japan started during the colonial period. After Japan invaded Korea in 1911, the Japanese government brought in roughly 400,000 Korean workers (mostly men) to serve as forced labor in mines and on construction sites. This practice continued until the end of World War II. Around the same time, a significant number of Korean women were forced to work as "comfort women," providing sex services for Japanese soldiers. After the war, 1.2 million Koreans and Chinese returned to their home countries. Some of them stayed, however, and established ethnic communities. In 2003 these people and their descendants comprised 24.9 percent of all foreign residents in Japan.[57] These communities of "special permanent residents" have been declining in size; however, the total number of Chinese and Koreans in Japan has been increasing because of the more recent immigration of students, technical trainees, and workers from these countries.

The postwar economic recovery created a large demand for foreign labor—a demand that has become especially strong since the 1970s. However, Japan has maintained its "closed-door" immigration policy for unskilled workers, although in 1990 it revised its Immigration and Refugee Recognition Act to open "back doors" for *Nikkeijin* (the descendants of Japanese immigrants) and for technical trainees who serve, in effect, as unskilled labor.

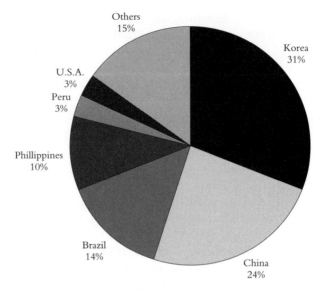

FIGURE 2.1. The Nationalities of Migrants in Japan, 2003
SOURCE: Ministry of Justice (2004).

The number of *Nikkeijin* from Latin America has soared drastically since then. In 1985 there were only 2,000 Brazilians in Japan; since the new immigration law came into force, that number has increased to 268,332.[58] In 2003, Brazilians and Peruvians together comprised 17.1 percent of the total number of registered foreigners in Japan.

Overall, though, the number of temporary and permanent foreign residents is still very small. In 2003 they represented only 1.5 percent of Japan's population. As indicated in Figure 2.1, most of these migrants came from Asia.

The feminization of migration has also been observed in Japan in recent years. Migration inflows had long been male-dominated; but since 1996, the majority of registered foreigners in Japan have been women. In 2003, women comprised 53.8 percent of registered foreign residents.[59] However, the patterns of female migration to Japan are fairly unique relative to those of other countries. Most migrant women working in West and Southeast Asia are domestic workers, nurses, and factory workers; by contrast, in Japan most of them are entertainers. This is largely attributed to the nature of Japan's immigration policy which officially bars all unskilled migrants and even some types of skilled migrants. Japanese immigration law stipulates only fourteen occupational categories for foreign workers; these categories do *not* include domestic workers, factory workers, and nurses—the categories in which most Asian migrant women are concentrated elsewhere. In Japan, "entertainment" is the only major immigration category easily accessible to Asian women.

Entertainers comprise the largest segment of foreign migrant workers in Japan. In 2003, 133,103 entertainers arrived in Japan, out of whom 60 percent (80,048) were Filipinas.[60] The overwhelming majority of them were young single women from the Philippines. Many of them work for less than US$1,500 per month, which is the official minimum monthly salary stipulated by the Philippine government for entertainment workers. Some of them, however, work for as little as US$350 per month.[61] Some of the women arriving in this category do actually work as performers, but most of them have been recruited to serve as bar hostesses or even as prostitutes. A Ministry of Justice survey found that 81.6 percent of the Asian women arriving in Japan on entertainment visas were actually working as waitresses or hostesses in bars and pubs.[62]

Foreign women who work in the Japanese entertainment industry are called *"Japayuki-san"*—a derogatory term rooted in *"Karayuki-san,"* which refers to those destitute Japanese women who went to China before World War II to engage in sex work. The demand for *Japayuki-san* in the entertainment and sex industries developed in the late 1970s, after general prosperity and better education came to Japan. At that point, fewer Japanese women were driven into these sectors. Besides this, the rapidly growing economy increased the demand for entertainment and sex workers until it exceeded the domestic supply. Initially, this resulted in sex tourism; Japanese men began flying to Southeast Asian countries to find inexpensive leisure and entertainment. In 1981, the government responded to mounting public criticism of these junkets by taking measures to stop sex tourism. At that point the crime syndicates—the *yakuza*—changed their strategy; they began bringing Asian women into Japan instead of flying Japanese men overseas.[63]

The immigration category of "entertainment" was introduced in 1981 in response to the strong demand for overseas entertainment workers. From the beginning, this category was seen as breaching the state policy of not accepting unskilled foreign labor. Work visas in Japan were supposed to be for "skilled" workers. (Strictly speaking, the Japanese government issues "certificates of residential status," not "visas." I use the term "visas" for simplicity's sake.) However, it was difficult to prove the qualifications of entertainers because of the nature of the occupation.[64] This is precisely how the crime syndicates were able to take advantage of entertainment visas, using them as means to import women for the sex industry. Tourist visas have also been used to bring in foreign women to work in the entertainment and sex industries. In 1979 only 9,100 Filipinos entered Japan as "tourists"; by 1981 this number had more than doubled to 20,512; by 1986 it had reached an all-time high of 77,275. The majority of these "tourists"—63 percent—were young women.[65] As of January 2004, 106,352 migrant women were "over-staying" in Japan; most of them were "tourists" or "entertainers."[66]

Marriage migration is another major category of female migration to Japan. These women are not counted as foreign workers. More and more Asian women have been entering Japan for marriage. Foreign wives are especially sought after in rural areas because of low birth rates in the country-side and high out-migration of young Japanese to cities. Farmers in remote villages find it extremely difficult to locate young Japanese brides. In terms of income and property ownership, Japanese farmers are generally perceived as middle class; however, they work long, hard hours, and so must their adult family members. The burden is especially heavy for young wives, who are typically responsible for the housework and caregiving (for children and par-ents-in-law) in addition to much of the agricultural work. Traditional fam-ily values persist in rural Japan and are often accompanied by lower status for women and a lack of freedom and material comforts. All of this dis-courages many young Japanese women from marrying farmers. As a con-sequence, many single men in the agricultural sector cannot find wives on their own. To solve this problem and to arrest the fall in rural populations, local authorities have been helping unmarried middle-aged farmers find for-eign wives.

Most foreign wives are Asians because of the cultural affinity—an affinity that is often presumed and sought by Japanese intermediary agencies and their clients. Many of these wives come from China, the Philippines, Korea, Thailand, and Sri Lanka. According to Philippine government data, Japan accepted 4,237 Filipina wives in 1998—the highest number of all Filipino nationals who officially left the country through the channel of marriage mi-gration.[67] According to the director of the Commission on Filipino Over-seas (CFO), this type of marriage arrangement—"the mail-order bride"—has been popular for many years and is fairly endemic even though it has been prohibited in the Philippines. Many overseas operators and illegal in-termediary agencies have penetrated the system, nowadays mainly through the Internet. Arrangements like these are more popular among North Americans and Europeans, but more and more Asians are resorting to them. In Japan, some municipal governments actively assist their residents in find-ing marriage partners and provide the follow-up. For instance, Yamagata prefecture in northern Japan has dispatched a volunteer teacher to Manila to give Japanese-language lessons to prospective wives of Yamagata residents. Such channels, however, are official. The Philippine authorities are concerned that international marriage is sometimes being used as a disguise for human trafficking. Because a spouse visa is the easiest kind to obtain, some underground brokers are arranging "paper" marriages as a cover for bringing in women to work as bar hostesses and sex workers.

The Japanese government had long been reluctant to take any effective actions on the aspect of human rights violations in the migration of entertainers, tourists, and spouses. Japan became a signatory of the United Nations Protocol to Prevent, Suppress and Punish Trafficking in Persons in December 2002, but critics have said it has done little to stop the trade.[68] However, its attitude began to change in 2004 with the release of the U.S. government report on trafficking. The report placed Japan in the "Tier 2 Watch List" together with Azerbaijan, Zambia, and other developing countries as "not meeting the minimum standards" for anti-trafficking efforts.[69] It was a serious political humiliation for the Japanese government.

With such *gaiatsu* or external pressure, the Japanese government finally admitted that the problem of trafficking existed and began to take action for tackling the problem. It presented the Action Plan for Anti-Human Trafficking in December 2004, and is in the process of preparing legislation that would lead to the revisions of immigration law and criminal law. These legal changes would penalize traffickers more severely and provide the victims of trafficking with more care and protection. One of the major actions also included a severe immigration restriction of entertainers from the Philippines; this has already resulted in some debates and protests inside and outside the country.

JAPANESE IMMIGRATION POLICIES
AND GENDER IDEOLOGY

Overall, Japan presents a stark contrast to other industrialized Asian countries that have opened their doors to foreign domestic workers. Those other countries began to welcome them much earlier in their economic development. The reasons stem partly from demography. Singapore and Hong Kong, for instance, were confronted with small populations and had to "free" women in order to maximize their workforces. By contrast, Japan had a fairly large population in the 1960s—110 million compared to 2 million in Singapore and 5 million in Hong Kong in the 1960s—as well as an ample labor supply in rural areas. The Japanese government did not face an acute need to import unskilled foreign workers because throughout the economic boom, it was able to absorb its rural workforce into the industrial sector. Japan faced serious labor shortages in the early 1970s and opened a serious debate on accepting unskilled foreign labor; however, the oil shock of 1973 and the subsequent economic downturn eased the tight labor market situation. In the 1970s and 1980s, the part-time workforce—which mainly consisted of women—expanded to meet the increased labor demand in the manufacturing and service sectors.

During the "bubble economy" of the late 1980s and early 1990s, the labor shortage became so acute that the labor pool in the countryside could no longer meet the country's needs. Nevertheless, no policy initiatives were adopted to bring in foreign domestic workers so as to encourage more Japanese housewives to work outside the home. The idea was not even discussed. Instead of bringing in foreign domestic workers so that housewives could join the labor force, the Japanese government opened the "back doors" to meet the demand for unskilled labor. The new immigration law of 1990 allowed *Nikkeijin*—mainly Brazilians and Peruvians of Japanese descent—to enter the country legally and engage in unskilled work. At first, most of these workers were men, but many started bringing in family members; today in Japan, many women from these countries are working in factories or as caregivers in nursing homes.[70]

Another "back door" for unskilled immigrants is the technical training program, which allows people from other Asian countries to stay in Japan for three years to "get trained," mainly in the manufacturing and construction sectors. While there are some "training" components involved, this scheme mostly serves to supply migrant workers for "3D" (dirty, dangerous, and difficult) jobs in small and medium-sized enterprises. Many of these trainees are women. Foreign students are yet another significant portion of the foreign workforce. Many of them are actually "workers," since they work more than twenty hours a week, which is the legal limit set by the immigration law. Half of these "students" are women, and work in the service sectors, typically as waitresses, dishwashers, and cleaners.

Why has Japan not accepted foreign domestic workers in order to encourage more local women to enter the labor force? The answer to this question relates partly to state policy which bars unskilled foreign labor. Another answer has to do with gender ideology: the general view among Japanese is that a woman's place is in the home. The state strongly supports this ideology through its policies which imply that Japanese women should handle domestic work by themselves and should not need foreign domestic workers. Throughout the modern era of industrialization, the Japanese government has encouraged women to be a *ryosai kenbo*—good wives and wise mothers—and to raise children to become productive workers. Women were supposed to serve as "*jugo no mamori*"—shields behind male soldiers; that is, they were supposed to provide material and psychological comfort to their husbands. This state ideology emerged during World War II and remains in place to this day among some families.

Such gender ideology was further reinforced in 1961, when the Ikeda Administration emphasized the importance of mothers to child development and began encouraging them to stay home.[71] Notwithstanding the lack of data, a senior state official declared that a mother who does not spend enough time with her children for the first three years might be having a detrimental effect on their physical, psychological, and intellectual development. The Ministry of Health and Welfare initiated this campaign, which became part of the country's human resources policy, as reflected in Prime Minister Ikeda's words: "The foundation of human resources development is that good mothers give birth to good babies and raise them as good children."[72]

Various studies indicated that this position had no empirical basis, yet this "myth of the three-year-olds" has penetrated the society as a result of political and media propaganda. According to the recent White Paper, most Japanese women still believe that women with small children should not work, and 70 percent of women actually quit working when their first child arrives.[73]

Gender equality has been promoted by the Koizumi Administration in recent years; even so, gender ideology is still being supported through various state policies, especially those relating to taxation and social security. The Japanese government has long encouraged housewives to stay home by providing tax incentives to those earning less than 1.03 million yen (US$9,740) per year. Although these incentives were reduced in 2004, there is still a spouse deduction scheme in place for those below this income level. Furthermore, the social security system implicitly encourages housewives to stay home by excluding them from free eligibility for social security and health insurance if they earn more than 1.3 million yen (US$12,300) per year. If they earn 1.41 million yen per year, they are subjected to a high income tax.[74] At the same time, workplaces enforce their own penalties. Most Japanese companies provide benefits such as "spouse allowance" if the spouse (usually the wife) earns 1.03 million yen or less. This discourages many Japanese housewives from earning above that threshold.

At least for the immediate future, foreign domestic workers are highly unlikely to take root in Japan, because many Japanese women continue to internalize traditional gender roles. In a small unpublished study, most married Japanese women said they would not consider hiring even Japanese domestic workers. The reasons vary: many of them did not want strangers in the house, and some did not like the idea of eating an outsider's cooking. Generally speaking, many seemed to believe that housework was their duty or something personal that they did not want outsiders to get involved with.[75] The average Japanese working woman with at least one small child spends 5 hours and 26 minutes a day on child care and housework, whereas the average Japanese working man spends only 26 minutes a day.[76]

Another problem is the lack of housing space. In Singapore and Hong Kong, many apartments are constructed with quarters for domestic workers. In Japan, by contrast, modern houses and apartment buildings tend to be small, and often lack extra rooms to accommodate live-in domestic workers. In theory, these workers could live on their own and commute; however, most governments—including Japan's—do not want to take this approach because it would make it more difficult to keep track of migrant workers.

Various types of household help have become available in Japan in recent years. Many municipal governments have begun to provide "family support services"; that is, they serve as brokers between those who require child-care assistance and those who are willing to "volunteer" for a few hours each day. Although officially categorized as mutual-support systems, these services are actually very close to employment arrangements in that the "volunteers" are paid about US$7 an hour. Local cooperatives are establishing a similar system called *kurashino tasukeaino kai* (associations for helping one another's lives); these co-ops cover not only child care but also regular housework (cleaning, cooking, shopping, and so on) for US$6–7 an hour. Besides these "volunteer" systems, specialized private companies are now offering professional cleaning and housework services for fees ranging from US$15 to $40 an hour. Some women—those who can afford it—rely to some degree on household help or child-care arrangements. Arranging part-time help makes more sense to many women because it enables them to maintain their identity as a "good wife and mother"—they are not liberating themselves entirely from domestic and caregiving work. Many also think they are maintaining their privacy and autonomy by not hiring a live-in domestic worker.

TOWARD MORE OPEN POLICIES?
AGING AND IMMIGRATION

Low birth rates and an aging population in Japan, however, brought such immigration policies into question. Japan is now one of the world's fastest-aging countries. The record-low fertility rate of 1.29 in 2003 is expected to exacerbate the labor market situation and shake the foundations of Japan's social security system. According to one estimate, the percentage of the Japanese population over sixty-five will increase from 17.2 to 25.8 percent by 2015, making it by far the highest in the world.[77] A study by the UN Population Division projects that the Japanese labor force will decline from 87 million in 1995 to 57 million by 2050. At the same time, the dependency ratio will decrease from 4.8 in 1995 to 1.7 in 2050, placing a heavy burden on the social security system. The same study reveals that Japan will have to accept 609,000 immigrants every year until 2050 in order to maintain the working population at its 1995 size; furthermore, it will have to receive as many as 10 million immigrants per year in order to maintain the dependency ratio at its 1995 level.[78] According to the International Monetary Fund (IMF), Japan's population decline is going to reduce its real GDP per capita growth by 0.8 percent, which will have a severe impact on the economy.[79]

Now that Japan's life expectancy has become the highest in the world, and that the proportion of families with two working parents is increasing, it is becoming extremely difficult for family members to take care of elderly parents. To meet the growing needs of many families, in 1999 the government launched a nursing care insurance system, the aim of which was to increase the number of care providers from 157,000 to 350,000 over the following five years.[80] Yet even this number has been criticized as insufficient to meet the demand. The Ministry of Justice expects that the number of elderly who require nursing care will double from 2.8 million to 5.2 million in 2025; this means that the number of workers required to provide nursing-care services will also increase, from the current 520,000 to about 1 million. Yet of the 500,000 people who have completed the training to become caregivers, only 170,000 have actually taken employment in that field, partly because of the unfavorable working conditions.[81]

In response to this reality, in March 2000 the Ministry of Justice released the Basic Plan for Immigration Control. Besides proposing an increase in foreign technical professionals in information technology and telecommunications, the plan stated that "the government will consider the introduction of foreign specialists in view of the shortage of nurses for the elderly."[82]

In November 2004, the Japanese government finally declared that it would begin to accept nurses and caregivers from the Philippines in 2006 under the framework of the Economic Partnership Agreement as part of an overall free trade agreement. This agreement allows Filipino nurses and caregivers to stay in Japan for three and four years respectively. After six months of language training, they will be able to work in Japanese hospitals and nursing homes as trainees. Once they pass appropriate national exams in Japan, they will be able to continue working at their workplace as official employees while renewing a permit every three years. The agreement also created another scheme which admits Filipino university graduates with no professional care experience to receive training and Japanese language. Once they pass a national exam, they will also be able to work as caregivers in Japanese hospitals and nursing homes on a permit-renewal basis.[83]

It is noteworthy that the Japanese government categorized caregivers as skilled workers while most industrialized countries regard them as unskilled. It was of course due to the basic tenets of its immigration policy that officially shuns unskilled foreign labor. To maintain policy consistency, the government decided to accept only caregivers with a university diploma or nursing college certificate. Recognizing caregivers as skilled workers can be regarded as a positive move as long as their wage and working conditions will be secured. However, it also limits opportunities for many other competent caregivers with less education.

The actual impact of this agreement on the care sector will remain minimal for a while as the annual intake of these migrants will not be large. While the actual number of nurses and caregivers to be accepted is still under negotiation, the authority does not envisage the total inflow of more than 200 per year.[84] The Japanese government has not yet perceived the acceptance of Filipino nurses and caregivers as a major solution to its aging problem at least for now. This opening of the care sector was partly used as a political compromise to proceed with the bilateral economic partnership that would serve Japan's overall interests in trade and investment. In fact, the Philippine authority sees little employment prospect for Filipino caregivers in Japan in the foreseeable future due to its "lack of market access."[85] The new agreement, at least as it stands now, provide little economic opportunity for most Filipino women who are in desperate economic situations.

It remains a question, however, how long Japan can keep its immigration gates narrow for caregivers. Japan has been challenged by a rapidly aging population and thus it seems inevitable that it will eventually have to accept foreign caregivers on a much larger scale. There is a serious shortage of care workers for the elderly, and many Japanese hospitals and nursing homes have already asked the government to liberalize its immigration policies so that they could hire foreign nurses and caregivers.[86] In the same regard, public opinion has been shifting to a more favorable one especially with regard to caregivers. A 1999 survey of 3,600 respondents, 90 percent of whom were women, found that nearly 80 percent opposed increasing the number of occupational categories open to foreign workers.[87] Yet a recent survey in 2004, found that most respondents (71 percent of men and 52 percent of women) agreed that the Japanese labor market should be open to foreign caregivers, and 57 percent supported the idea of extending foreign nurses and caregivers permanent-resident status.[88] On the other hand, the same respondents showed less support for accepting foreign workers in other sectors, which implies that the Japanese have begun to recognize the gravity of the aging problem and are becoming more accepting of migrant workers in the care sectors.

Given such growing public support, it would be possible for the government to further expand the new immigration scheme in the future. Increasing the number of nurses and caregivers could be one option, and extending the partnership to other countries could be another. For this, the successful implementation of the current scheme would hold a key. Providing decent working conditions for migrant women and gaining support from the society—including Japanese elderly, their families, medical institutions, and the public—would be of absolute necessity. In any case, considering the present situation, it seems a matter of time that Japan will become a major receiver of migrant caregivers from Asia.

WEST ASIA (MIDDLE EAST) [89]

Economic development in West Asia (the Middle East) has been quite distinct from that in East and Southeast Asia and has resulted in different immigration patterns. West Asia's economic growth has been driven mainly by the oil industry, which early on required a substantial number of construction workers to build the oil fields and their related infrastructures. The economies of these countries have been diversifying in recent years by developing various other sectors such as tourism and banking; their manufacturing sectors, however, are chronically weak. As a consequence, they have been demanding different types of migrant workers than Japan and the NIEs. Because their economic structures are different, so are the factors that bring in migrant women. This section examines the third pattern of economic development that has led to international female migration.

West Asia is the world's largest destination of foreign migrant workers. In 2000 there were 19 million migrants in this region; that represented 43 percent of Asia's total migratory population and 11 percent of the world's.[90] There were 7.4 million migrant women—short-term and long-term—in the region. The total number of these migrants has exceeded that of native populations since 1990; in this region there are now more foreign migrants than native-born people.

It should be noted, however, that not all West Asian countries are major receivers of foreign migrant labor. West Asia can be divided into countries that are endowed with oil and those that are not. The former include Bahrain, Kuwait, Oman, Qatar, Saudi Arabia, and the United Arab Emirates, which form the Gulf Cooperation Council (GCC). These oil-rich GCC states are strong magnets for migrant labor from Asia. West Asian countries without oil, such as Syria, Lebanon, and Yemen, have by contrast been *sending* workers to the GCC countries. While they have begun to receive some migrant workers in recent years, they are not major destination countries.

Immigration to Saudi Arabia and Kuwait started in the 1930s, almost immediately after oil was discovered. However, full-scale oil production did not begin until World War II.[91] Until 1973 the inflow of migrant workers into the oil-endowed Gulf States was on a relatively modest scale in terms of sheer numbers and range of nationalities; even so, by that year there were already 880,000 migrant workers from neighboring countries, including Egypt, Oman, and Jordan.

To fully understand the high levels of labor migration in West Asia, it is important to recognize that region's distinct sociodemographic characteristics. First, the oil-rich GCC countries have small populations; except for Saudi Arabia and Libya, they were all under 1 million in 1975. Even Saudi Arabia, which is the largest country in the region, had fewer than 5 million people on its territory in that year.[92]

Second, the labor force participation rates in the oil-rich countries have historically been low. By tradition in this region, women were discouraged from working outside the home. Around 1970, at the time of the economic "take-off," their labor force participation rate was only 3.3 percent in Bahrain and 5.2 percent in Kuwait.[93] Labor force participation among men has also been lower than in other Asian countries. For instance, in Bahrain in 1971, 49.0 percent of men were economically active, compared to 63.2 percent in Japan and 54.8 percent in Hong Kong. This was partly because there were still almost 400,000 Bedouin living traditional nomadic lives and thus not very well suited to wage employment. Furthermore, the Bedouin were not especially willing to work in the formal sector because the government provided them with subsidies.[94] In addition, many nationals were simply not used to working in industry. In 1975 in Saudi Arabia, 51.7 percent of nationals were still working in agriculture or the fisheries; this meant that the domestic supply of skilled labor was insufficient to keep up with oil-led development when it began to accelerate in the early 1970s.[95] As Table 2.2 shows, labor force participation rates in oil-rich countries were quite low.

This shortage of skilled labor was related to the third distinctive characteristic in this region—low levels of literacy during the initial stages of economic growth (Table 2.2). According to Birks and Sinclair, this was partly due to the particular nature of traditional school systems in the region. At Quranic schools, which normally accommodated boys only, religious leaders in the community taught little but the reading, writing, and recitation of the Quran. A graduate of a Quranic school typically could not read a newspaper easily, nor do arithmetic.[96] Quranic schools were later replaced by "Western schools"; even so, the earlier system's legacy persisted into the early 1970s, which led to a dearth of skilled workers in oil-rich GCC countries. As a consequence, these states have had to rely on other countries to supply both skilled and unskilled workers for their economic development.

After the oil price hike of 1973, the sources of migrant workers changed. With their rapidly increasing revenues, the oil-rich GCC countries and the Libyan Arab Jamahiriya began financing large-scale construction projects. The demand for labor in the Gulf region also grew explosively, triggered by

TABLE 2.2
Population, Labor Force, and Literacy Rates in West Asia, Early 1970s

Country	Population (millions)	Labor Force (millions)	Literacy Rate (%)
Oil-Rich States (GCC)			
Bahrain	0.21	0.05	47
Kuwait	0.47	0.09	55
Oman	0.56	0.14	55
Qatar	0.07	0.01	33
Saudi Arabia	4.59	1.03	33
United Arab Emirates	0.20	0.05	14
Oil-Poor States			
Egypt	37.36	12.52	40
Jordan (East Bank)	2.62	0.53	62
Lebanon	n.a.	n.a.	68
Syrian Arab Republic	7.34	1.84	53
Yemen	n.a.	1.43	10
Democratic Yemen	1.66	0.43	10

SOURCE: Birks and Sinclair (1980).

increases in investment and business activity. Between 1973 and 1975, with the region's economy taking off, the number of migrant workers rose from 880,000 to 1.8 million.[97] Once the labor pools in the neighboring Arab states had been depleted, the oil-rich countries had to turn elsewhere. This is how the source countries of migrant workers became more diversified.

The oil-rich countries had already expanded their search for workers to more distant Arab countries such as Yemen, Sudan, Lebanon, Syria, and Iraq as well as to the Palestinian Territories. After 1973 they looked even farther, toward non-Arab countries, especially in South and Southeast Asia. They recruited many workers from India and Pakistan because they were geographically close and were willing to work for low wages. Diversification accelerated in the 1980s and 1990s; the migrant labor force now included Filipinos, Bangladeshis, Sri Lankans, Thais, and Indonesians. In the 1970s and 1980s, South Korean workers also came to the region; they left in the late 1980s, however, drawn home by economic growth and rising wages.[98] Although regional data are not available, the figures solely for Saudi Arabia provide a good indication of the diversification trends in the region. The number of South, Southeast, and East Asians in that kingdom increased from 38,000 in 1975 to 2,094,140 in 1990, by which year they comprised 61.5 percent of the total migrant workforce.[99]

This diversification of the 1980s and 1990s was in part a result of deliberate state policies. The oil-rich Arab states have small populations and low birth rates; that is why most of their workers have been foreigners. In 1990, foreigners were 91.6 percent of Qatar's workforce, 89.3 percent of the UAE's,

and 86.1 percent of Kuwait's.[100] In these countries there are now more foreigners than there are locally born. This is becoming a serious concern, because foreigners who are not happy with their social and economic lot have
the potential to rise up against the minority ruling class. The various states
perceive them as threats to both national security and the social order, although the region requires foreign labor.

This is why many GCC countries have adopted policies to control the
origin countries of migrant workers; the goal is to prevent groups of those
workers from taking unified action against the state. Specifically, the GCC
countries have been using nationality quota systems as bargaining chips vis-
à-vis the developing states. A given quota can be reduced or increased (as a
punishment or a reward), depending on the temperature of the relations between the GCC country and the migrant-sending country. Since almost all
migrant-sending countries want the receiving countries to set larger quotas
to increase remittance levels, they cannot take too tough a stance against
GCC countries on other economic and political issues. In other words, the
nationality quota system provides GCC countries with diplomatic and political leverage.

FEMINIZATION OF MIGRATION

In the Gulf States, immigration policies for women have been relatively
open. In the 1960s, family migration was allowed and many wives of migrant men—mainly from neighboring Arab countries, but some from Asia
—worked as domestic workers.[101] In Kuwait, not until 1979 was family migration reduced and was the settlement of foreigners prohibited. Since then,
women have started arriving as contract workers in their own right.[102]

In the late 1970s the types of the migrant workers became diversified along
with the source countries. There was an increase in the demand for migrant
women—specifically, for domestic workers from other parts of Asia. This
reflected the changing lifestyles of the oil-rich countries. Although men still
outnumbered women with regard to the total number of migrant workers
in the Middle East, the rate was soon increasing faster for women than for
men. The number of migrant women in the oil-rich countries increased
forty-seven times between 1960 and 2000 whereas the number of men increased only forty-one times.[103] As Table 2.3 shows, the numbers have been
especially high in Saudi Arabia, Kuwait, and the United Arab Emirates. According to a *Gulf News* article published on April 21, 2000, 50 percent of
UAE citizens were employing foreign domestic workers—an average of two
per household.

One of the peculiar characteristics of female migration to Arab countries
is that it has not been linked directly to the increasing labor force participa-

TABLE 2.3
Migrant Women in GCC Countries

	1960	1970	1980	1990	2000
Bahrain	7,425	11,346	25,718	49,349	85,398
Kuwait	23,037	176,201	361,825	609,175	342,950
Oman	6,625	8,373	37,683	94,167	142,697
Qatar	3,021	16,348	40,493	89,091	105,596
Saudi Arabia	22,997	103,163	577,066	1,267,310	1,770,803
United Arab Emirates	329	10,972	179,515	442,664	538,995
Total	63,434	326,404	1,222,300	2,551,756	2,986,438

SOURCE: UN (2004).

tion of local women, although in recent years this link has started to appear. As Table 2.4 shows, the labor force participation rate among Arab women in GCC countries was very low until the mid-1970s, when Asian domestic workers began arriving. This was in stark contrast to the high labor force participation rate among women in Singapore and Hong Kong at the time. In West Asia's oil-rich countries, many households began hiring domestic workers in the context of the conspicuous consumption that was emerging in this time of rapidly increasing oil wealth. As overall incomes rose, many households began employing domestic workers for household chores. The levels of wealth in GCC countries rose to the extent that Arab employers now lived in palatial homes with eight to twelve rooms. A recent study indicates that the number of small children in a home was not a significant determinant for employing domestic workers.[104] In other words, hiring domestic workers became "necessary" as a consequence of lifestyle changes and the yearning for more services. Domestic workers also evolved into a status symbol; one's wealth was measured in part by how many of them one employed.

This trend eventually reached non-GCC Arab countries. In Jordan— which used to be a major migrant-*sending* country in the region—people began hiring domestic workers with the money they earned in the oil-rich GCC countries. Jordanians watched their employers in Kuwait and Saudi Arabia hiring domestic workers and began to equate domestic workers with conspicuous luxury. Asian domestic workers soon became a "fashionable item of consumption for the new national and immigrant working class."[105]

The employment of domestic workers accelerated in the 1980s and the 1990s once the labor force participation rate among Arab women began increasing (see Table 2.4). In Southeast Asia most local women were concentrated at first in the manufacturing sector; by contrast, Arab women in oil-rich countries have been working mainly in white-collar jobs because the economies of GCC countries are based on oil production and related services, and the jobs in oil production are already occupied by male migrant

TABLE 2.4

Women's Labor Force Participation Rate in GCC Countries

	1970	1975	1985	1990	2000
Bahrain	4	10	n.a.	18	24[a]
Kuwait	11	15	n.a.	24	30[b]
Oman	6	n.a.	n.a.	9	7
Saudi Arabia	5	5	7	9	n.a.
Qatar	5	n.a.	n.a.	17	21[c]
United Arab Emirates	9	10	n.a.	18	19[d]

NOTES: *a* = 2001 data; *b* = 1998 data; *c* = 1997 data; *d* = 1995 data; n.a. = not available.
SOURCES: ESCWA (1997a; 1997b); ILO (2004).

workers. In 1993, 49.0 percent of Kuwaiti female workers were in professional/technical fields, 44.3 percent in clerical service, 4.7 percent in other kinds of services, and 2.0 percent in other sectors.[106] However, it should be noted that most local Arab women stay in the labor force for a relatively short time since the public sector—in which most of the local workforce is concentrated—offers generous and early retirement. In Kuwait, public-sector workers are entitled to 75 percent of their salary after twenty years of service, and women over forty and men over forty-five can obtain a loan to start a business. Married women can even retire with full benefits after fifteen years of service. Such a policy does not give local women (or men) an incentive to stay long in the labor force.[107] In 1992, 90 percent of the national workforce worked in the public sector, which offered higher wages and more generous social security benefits than the private sector.[108]

NATIONALIZATION OF THE LABOR FORCE

Owing to slow economic growth and security concerns, many GCC countries have begun announcing policies to replace foreign migrant workers with nationals. The authorities in these countries did not want migrants —who are the majority of the national populations—to unite and carry out strikes or riots. However, these nationalization policies have had little effect since local workers are unwilling to take "migrants' jobs" which pay poorly and bear a social stigma. In addition, most nationals already work in the high-paying public sector. This situation has been changing over the past decade; an economic slowdown across the region has led to a decrease in public-sector jobs and more menial jobs became available to nationals. However, they are still reluctant to take such jobs, while not many are qualified for highly skilled and professional jobs either. As a consequence, a strong "Kuwaitization" or "Saudization" of the labor force has yet to materialize. In fact, despite the "Saudization" policy of the past decade, 150,000 to 200,000 Filipino workers have continued to arrive in Saudi Arabia each year.[109] The UN projects that the high ratio of migrant workers in the region is not likely to change in the near future.[110]

National Stereotypes and Selectivity for Migrants

As noted earlier, the demand for foreign migrant labor has risen across Asia over the past three decades. Most migrant women have been slotted into feminized occupations—as domestic workers, floor-level factory workers, entertainment-cum-sex workers, and so on. Although these sectors involve some men, gender selectivity is clearly operating in favor of women in the labor market, reflecting and perpetuating existing gender stereotypes. In particular, care work and housework are often perceived as women's work, with women being viewed as "better suited than men" for such work by both employers and recruitment agencies.[111] Women are also preferred as factory workers because of their presumed docility, obedience, and manual dexterity.

Migrant female labor is not monolithic. With regard to women, levels of demand and the wages paid are determined not by individual qualifications but rather by national stereotypes. When studying patterns of international female migration, it is important to examine the processes whereby this selectivity operates in the destination countries at the political, economic, and social levels. In this section, I focus on domestic workers and analyze how Asian women are selected on the basis of national stereotypes and other factors.

POLITICAL SELECTIVITY

The immigration policies of many countries involve some preference for migrants of certain nationalities. The reasons are both political and diplomatic. The governments of destination countries "do favors"—offer large immigration quotas—for the governments of particular origin countries. Historical factors such as colonial legacies sometimes play a role in this preferential treatment. In this time of increasing globalization; however, some countries are turning their immigration policies into political tools for economic partnership. Malaysia, for instance, used to adopt a policy that allows only Filipina and Indonesian women to enter the country as domestic workers; this was part of an economic cooperation agreement signed by Malaysia, Indonesia, and the Philippines.[112] Because of this preferential treatment, other major sending countries such as Sri Lanka could not even send one domestic worker to Malaysia through official channels until 1997.[113] In the most recent case, Japan singled out the Philippines as a source country of nurses and caregivers in the context of economic partnership agreement. Japan used it as leverage for bilateral negotiations in tariff reductions in various economic sectors. As Chapter 3 will discuss in more detail, many developing countries work to obtain preferential status for immigration quotas in order to increase migrant remittances. This is why their labor ministers pay so many official visits to migrant-receiving countries, requesting that more of their citizens be accepted as migrant workers.

The political selectivity for migrants can entail a religious component, especially in Muslim countries. In Malaysia, regulations allow Muslims (mostly Malays) to employ Muslim (mostly Indonesian) domestic workers. For the same reason, the Gulf States show a similar strong preference for Muslim migrant women. Many Arab families contend that their children would be "vulnerable to many psychological disorders because of the clashing values" if they were tended by Catholic Filipinas or Buddhist Sri Lankans.[114]

Ethnicity is yet another factor in immigration policies. In multiethnic countries such as Malaysia,[115] an influx of migrant workers from India or Sri Lanka or China would be a great concern for the state because of the effect it could have on the existing ethnic balance and domestic politics. For this reason, migrants from these countries are carefully monitored to ensure that the overall population structure is not undermined. In the same vein, immigration policies in GCC countries have been established with the goal of diversifying the nationalities of migrant workers; this is to prevent migrant workers from developing the sort of solidarity that could result in political unrest against the authorities. In many parts of the world, this political selectivity significantly affects the overall level of immigration flows.

SOCIAL SELECTIVITY AND NATIONAL STEREOTYPES

At the micro level, within ranges set by governments, employers and recruitment agencies play a key role in selecting migrants. Their preferences determine the market wage rates. Generally speaking, Filipinas enjoy the highest wage levels throughout Asia. My fieldwork in Hong Kong suggested that most Filipina domestic workers were paid the official minimum salary of HK$3,670 (US$470) a month in 1999; this was reduced to HK$3,270 (US$420) in 2003. However, many other nationalities did not receive the same treatment. An official of the Indonesian government reportedly mentioned that 90 percent of Indonesian workers in Hong Kong were paid below the official minimum wage, and a local NGO survey confirmed that the average Indonesian domestic worker received HK$2,310 (US$300) a month or less in 1999.[116] My own interviews with Sri Lankan domestic workers indicated that the market rate for a Sri Lankan was even lower—HK$2,000 (US$270). Most Sri Lankan domestic workers I interviewed in Hong Kong had good qualifications such as a high school diploma and excellent command of English, yet it was hard for them to find an employer who was willing to pay them the official minimum wage, since the "market rate" for Sri Lankans was HK$2,000. Indian domestic workers (there were fewer of them) received the lowest wage, sometimes HK$800–1,000. All of these domestic workers have been receiving HK$400 (US$51) less than the previous market wage since the official minimum wage was reduced in 2003. Employers who underpay their domestic workers face a fine up to HK$200,000 and conceivably a one-year jail term, yet most of them continue to pay below the official minimum wage for domestic workers from Indonesia, India, Sri Lanka, and Thailand. Such differential wages exist everywhere in Asia.

These market rates are determined separately for each nationality by employers' preferences; they are then communicated by recruitment agencies to potential clients. The rates are not related to individual qualifications; rather, they reflect stereotypes and prejudices relating to the overall qualifications of particular nationalities. These stereotypes and prejudices are reinforced by the media, recruitment agencies, and employers' personal networks. One of the most important qualifications for domestic workers is a language—specifically, English proficiency. English is becoming the common language among Asians of different language backgrounds. Because of the British colonial influence, most employers in Hong Kong, Singapore, and Malaysia speak English. They find it easier to communicate with Filipina domestic workers, many of whom have a fairly good command of English. Even when employers speak little or no English, such as in the case of Taiwan, they prefer to hire English-speaking domestic workers so that family members can receive "free language lessons" from them.[117] My field research suggested that Filipinas with less than a high school education did not speak English very well; even so, the demand for Filipinas is high because on average they speak and understand English better than Sri Lankans, Indians, Indonesians, and Thais. Even in the Middle East, many Arab employers also speak English: almost 90 percent of my Filipina respondents in the United Arab Emirates stated that they communicated with their employers in English. Arabic is often preferred, and most migrant women bound for the Middle East learn basic Arabic during predeparture orientations. Overall, however, English is still the dominant language in Asia, and thus Filipinas are preferred because of their proficiency in it.

Yet another selectivity factor, related to the previous one, is education. Many employers expect domestic workers not only to do housework but also to take care of children; this includes helping them with their homework. In other words, a domestic worker is at various times a cleaner, a cook, a nanny, and a governess. Filipinas are in the highest demand because on average they are better educated than domestic workers from other countries. Many surveys have shown that the average education level of Filipina domestic workers is indeed the highest among all nationalities. About one-third of Filipina domestic workers have some college education. My field research showed that most of these women had spent only a year or two in college before being forced to drop out by marriage or poverty. In the primary labor market in the Philippines, a few years of college education do not add much value to human capital. Most employers prefer to hire college *graduates*, and women without a college diploma are treated as the same as high school graduates, no matter how many years they spent in college. This dynamic changes for those who want to work as domestic workers abroad. One or two years of college education add value to their human capital, since very few foreign domestic workers from other countries have attended college. Although more than two-thirds of Filipina domestic workers are actually high school graduates, the image of "highly educated Filipina domestic workers" prevails among employers. Higher education, which is almost synonymous with a good command of English, also meets the needs of many Asian parents. Most middle and upper-class Chinese parents in Hong Kong, Singapore, and Taiwan want to educate their children in an English-speaking environment because English proficiency will help them enter a better school and land a better job. Because they bring with them all these extra benefits, well-educated domestic workers enjoy higher status among employers in these countries and are more in demand.

Employers' selectivity also entails many other complex dimensions, both social and cultural. Skin color, hygiene, and appearance matter to many employers. Filipinas, Indonesians, and Sri Lankans are all "Asians," but Japanese and Chinese employers never see them as belonging to the same group as themselves; rather, they see sharp racial and class differences. Even so, they do not want their domestic workers to be "too dark" or "too different." In their view, the ideal domestic worker is "a little dark" so that employers can feel somehow superior to them, but is concurrently "civilized" and "Westernized" in terms of hygiene and culture so that they will have little trouble sharing residential space with her. A domestic worker should also look reasonably attractive and "Westernized" in neighbors' eyes, but not to the extent that female employers feel jealous or threatened.

It is important to note that these selection criteria do not arise "naturally" among employers; in fact, they are largely established and reinforced by "maid agencies" in destination countries. Often it is these agencies that inform the employers about differential wage rates among the various nationalities—differentials that are actually illegal. They also promulgate stereotypes of each group by placing glossy advertisements in newspapers and on

websites and by informing prospective employers in person. When I contacted several "maid agencies" in Hong Kong, the agents made the following remarks:

> Indonesians are not good. They don't speak good English. . . . There are not many
> Sri Lankans in Hong Kong. There are lots of Filipinas—more than 140,000. But
> not Sri Lankans and . . . [pause] . . . They [Sri Lankans] don't look nice. They
> have dark skin, you know. Filipinas look much more pleasant. They are well
> dressed. They know everything about how to take care of you. Filipinas are the
> number one choice for our clients.[Hong Kong Chinese agent—1]

> They [Sri Lankans and Indians] are slow and have a strong smell that [East] Asians
> normally don't like. . . . Indians and Sri Lankans put very strong perfume oil on
> their body.[Hong Kong Chinese agent—2]

> I know it's awful. It's not that *we* do [discriminate]. . . . My business is providing
> domestic workers, and I don't care what color, race, or creed. But the Chinese
> don't tend to like terribly dark-skinned people. It's a funny thing, you know, but
> this is what I find. [A British agent]

The vice-chairman of the employers' association believed that the level of
Westernization and sharing of a common religion (Catholicism) are also
important:

> I think [the most preferred characteristics of Filipina domestic workers are] be-
> ing Westernized and living habits. Also, Philippine [*sic*] are Catholic or Christian.
> A lot of people in Hong Kong are either Catholic or Christian. Religion is quite
> an important factor. . . . I am not criticizing Islamic [*sic*]. I am just saying that
> there is a difference between Islamic [*sic*] and Christianity.

Religion did not surface very often during my conversations with other employers in Hong Kong; however, it may be a facet of the integrity and hon-
esty that employers seek in domestic workers. Of course, being Christian
does not guarantee ethical behavior; that said, Christianity in Asia is partly
related to Westernization because the Western colonial powers converted
many Asians to Christianity in the past. Therefore, even when their domestic worker is not a devout Christian, employers at the very least feel that they
still share the same "Western" values. These values are also related to the
shared common sense. A British agent who owns a company that caters to
foreign expatriate families in Hong Kong emphasized the level of "common
sense" among Filipinas as a reason why many employers choose them over
other nationalities.

> They [Filipinas] have got initiative and common sense. . . . And to be honest with
> you, if I had to put good Filipinas against the other races, I would have to choose
> Filipinas because, in my opinion, their attitudes are very much in a more com-
> mon-sense area [for Westerners]. . . . When you are putting children to be looked

after by somebody, you want the best you can get. . . . If there is a problem, they [Filipinas] know how to telephone you, they know how to handle it, and they could take messages as well. A lot of employers are businesspeople here. They go away and they need them on their own. It is important to have somebody who has got that common sense. I don't put down other races, but it's just that there aren't enough good ones [domestic workers] in relation to Indians and Sri Lankans.

Humphrey's research on foreign domestic workers in Jordan buttressed my findings regarding employers' preferences for Filipina domestic workers in Hong Kong. Humphrey found that foreign domestic workers in Jordan were ranked according to categories such as race (lightness versus darkness of skin), communication skills (English versus no English), education (high versus low qualifications), attractiveness (beauty versus ugliness), and presentation (fashionable versus unfashionable appearance). He contends that Filipinas are preferred because they are better educated, are more familiar with English, have fairer skin, and dress like Westerners. In Jordan the rate for an educated Filipina domestic worker in the late 1980s was US$250 per month; for an uneducated Sri Lankan it was US$70–100.[118]

Generally, Filipinas are perceived as Westernized and as similar to the employer with regard to education, hygiene, and level of common sense. Yet this strong preference for Filipina domestic workers does not necessarily translate into good treatment. Verbal and physical abuse of Filipina domestic workers is common and is no less significant than it is for Indonesians and Sri Lankans. Some employers—especially those without higher education— feel insecure about themselves and downplay their domestic workers' education and English skills; this helps them to legitimate the low salaries they pay and to maintain existing power imbalances.[119] Especially in the Gulf States, many employers have less education than their domestic workers; in some cases they become abusive in order to show who's boss and to ensure that the employee does not end up controlling the household. Employers want "capable domestic workers" but not if it means they cannot exert their power and authority.

The selection criteria do not necessarily remain static; they are subject to change. Recently, for example, more and more employers in Hong Kong have been hiring Indonesian domestic workers because they are less expensive (in terms of market rates) and are perceived as more docile and subservient than Filipinas. Filipina domestic workers are now becoming perceived as relatively outspoken and aggressive. This is partly because they have formed several labor unions and NGOs since the late 1980s and have been organizing political campaigns and rallies to protect the rights of Filipina and other Asian domestic workers in Hong Kong.[120]

The numbers of Sri Lankans and Indonesians are increasing in the United Arab Emirates and Saudi Arabia as well, reflecting the economic downturn in the region. A diplomatic source in the UAE noted that Arab families in the lower-middle-class were trying to reduce their household expenditures by hiring low-cost domestic workers from Sri Lanka and Indonesia; middle- and upper-middle-class families still preferred Filipinas.

Conclusion

Economic growth and state policies in the migrant-receiving countries have shaped the patterns of female migration in Asia. However, the demand for foreign female labor has emerged in different ways in different countries in the region. In Southeast Asia, rapid export-oriented industrialization pulled both single and married women from households into the labor force in the formal sectors. As the labor market tightened as a consequence of strong economic growth, these states decided to open the immigration doors to foreign domestic workers from the Philippines, Indonesia, and Sri Lanka, the point being to "free" local women to enter the labor force.

Japan, by contrast, has maintained strict immigration policies for un- skilled foreign labor. Its government has not allowed foreign domestic work- ers into the country even though there is a severe labor shortage. This is largely due to the continuing social perception that the wife should take care of the family and household chores. In Japan, migrant female labor is re- stricted mainly to the entertainment industry, including the sex industry, which local women vacated as their education levels rose. The new immi- gration scheme for caregivers will also be limited in its impact, at least as it stands now.

In the oil-rich countries of West Asia, the participation rate of local women in the labor force has always been very low, which signals that the demand for foreign domestic workers did not emerge because of any labor shortage. Rather, it resulted from a sudden increase in oil-based wealth, which raised levels of conspicuous consumption while heightening the lo- cal populations' status concerns. In recent years, more local women have be- gun entering the workforce and the demand for foreign domestic workers has been increasing. Overall, however, conspicuous consumption still drives much of the demand for foreign domestic workers.

Across Asia, states often indicate preferences for specific sources of mi- grant labor. Such preferences can derive from pre-existing colonial or cul- tural ties but more recently reflect political relationships especially with re- gard to economic agreements. Such *political selectivity* often defines the set of available nationalities of migrants in the country.

On the other hand, individual employers also exert their own preferences in the form of *social selectivity* based on existing racial and national stereotypes. Filipinos often fare better than other nationalities because of their positive image associated with Westernization and high education. In the cases where there is little political selectivity imposed (e.g., Hong Kong and Singapore), social selectivity can be a major market determinant, influencing the level of demand for migrant women from each country and affecting the wage levels of those women.

Despite the differences, all of these state policies shared one aim, which was to maintain the existing gender division of labor. None of the NIEs and the Gulf States has considered exploring alternative approaches—for example, promoting more equal sharing of household responsibilities between men and women. Similarly, expansion of state welfare services for child care and eldercare has not been considered as an alternative to bringing in foreign domestic workers. Japan is even further behind; its government does not even promote women's labor force participation by allowing the entry of foreign domestic workers. The state gender ideology still designates women's place to be the home.

Migrant-receiving countries play a major role in international female migration through their immigration policies which reflect both political and social selectivity. This chapter has presented a gender dimension of labor demand and immigration policies, with the goal of highlighting the pull factors of international female migration. However, pull factors alone cannot explain the patterns of international female migration. The state and employers can choose workers only from the available pool in the international labor market; they have no control over the pool itself. Why, then, are women of some nationalities available as migrants, whereas others are not? To understand the overall patterns of international female migration, it is important to examine the supply-side factors—the situations in migrant-sending countries. The next two chapters will analyze emigration policies and their impact on international female migration.

CHAPTER 3

Value-Driven Emigration Policies: The Role of the State in Countries of Origin

GLOBALIZATION IS often associated with the declining role of states and heavier reliance on free markets. Capital and goods move around the world much more easily today than in the past. With economies becoming more liberalized, states are becoming less significant. Yet with regard to the movement of people, little liberalization has occurred. Through their migration policies and border controls, states continue to play a key role in the international flows of people. While irregular migration and human trafficking have been increasing, states have not at all abandoned their efforts to control migration. In fact, they are attempting to regain control they have lost, mainly due to socioeconomic and security concerns.[1] Especially for citizens from developing countries, immigration controls have become tighter.

Migration control is, however, not monopolized only by industrialized countries. Just as many of them use their immigration policies to control the inflows of people, many developing countries also have emigration policies to control the outflows of their citizens. This is especially the case in Asia. The most striking aspect of emigration policies in Asia is that they do not treat men and women the same.[2] Many emigration policies in Asia restrict the cross-border movements of women while allowing men to leave the country almost freely. Even though the demand for migrant women is high in the international labor market, some countries still try to prevent women from emigrating or impose restrictions on them. These restrictions vary in their severity, and some of them also apply to men. Overall, however, women face more emigration restrictions than men.

This chapter examines the role of migrant-sending states in international female migration with the focus on the gender dimensions of emigration policies. First, it briefly explains why states are often involved in international labor migration in general and elucidates the economic implications of migration. Second, it presents an overview of gender-differentiated emigration policies in Asia. In particular, it touches on the general policy environment that prompts states to restrict women's emigration. Third, it provides historical accounts of the emigration policies of three countries—the Philippines, Sri Lanka, and Bangladesh—and shows how "value-driven" policies have been developed in each. As explained earlier, these countries have been chosen for the distinctive characteristics of their policies toward international female migration. In the Philippines the state has played an active role in international migration through its policies. At least initially, those policies aggressively promoted migration through institution building as well as through media campaigns. The Philippines' policies toward women's migration have generally been open except for occasional temporary bans. Their actual effectiveness aside, those migration policies have been second to none in terms of sophistication. By contrast, Sri Lanka, another major sending country, was noteworthy until recently for its laissez-faire approach to female migration. At least officially, the state never strongly promoted female migration, but neither did it strongly discourage it. Bangladesh is different from both of these countries: fewer Bangladeshi women emigrate, and the state has actively discouraged women's overseas employment by imposing many restrictions on it—most recently, outright bans.

How have gender-differentiated emigration policies been developed? This chapter provides a detailed answer and tries to highlight the differences and similarities among the three above-mentioned countries. The determinants of these policies will then be analyzed in Chapter 4.

The Role of the State in International Migration

Why do many states in developing countries favor international migration? Although the brain drain is a major concern, they believe that overall, international labor migration brings net economic benefits. Besides alleviating domestic unemployment, migration helps the economies of low-income countries through the remittances that migrant workers send home.[3] These remittances are an important source of foreign currency; in most developing countries they help improve the balance of payments.

Migrant remittances even have a significant impact on the world economy. Between 1970 and 2002, the annual flow of remittances worldwide increased from $2 billion a year to $111 billion.[4] In terms of trade values, remittances constitute the largest flow in the world; they exceed the international trade in crude oil and coffee. Table 3.1 shows that remittances are a

TABLE 3.1
Migrant Remittances in Major Countries of Origin, 2001

Country	Migrant Remittances (US$ millions)	Net ODA[a] (US$ millions)	Migrant Remittances as % of Total Exports	Migrant Remittances as % of Total GNI[b]
Philippines	6,155	577.7	14.7	7.5
Sri Lanka	1,169	276.3	18.0	7.1
Indonesia	1,046	1,731.0	1.8	0.7
Bangladesh	2,104	1,171.5	31.9	4.3
India	8,245	1,487.2	12.9	1.7
Pakistan	1,461	702.8	14.8	2.4

NOTES: a = 2000 data. b = gross national income (GNI), referring to the total domestic and foreign value added claimed by residents. GNI comprises GDP plus net receipts of primary income from nonresidents.
SOURCES: IMF (2003); UNDP (2002); World Bank (2003).

major component of developing economies. Furthermore, in all of these countries except Indonesia, the value of remittances exceeds that of official development assistance (ODA). In the Philippines the amount of migrant remittances is more than ten times greater than the net ODA; in India it is more than five times greater; in Sri Lanka it is twice as great. In the case of Indonesia, the proportion of remittances to the gross national income is rather small. This is partly because the state has not made enough efforts to channel remittances through itself; also, there are many undocumented Indonesian workers overseas who send their remittances home through unofficial channels.[5]

Given the economic benefits that may accrue, many states have been promoting international labor migration and have been working strategically to maximize its benefits. In the 1990s, Indonesia made significant efforts to upgrade its vocational schools with the goal of increasing the number of Indonesians working abroad to 2 million by the year 2000. (In 1995, there were 1.2 million.) It was hoped that this would boost remittances to $12 billion a year.[6] While it could not meet the goal, the Indonesian government continues to locate labor migration as part of its economic strategy.

Differential Reponses to Female Migration in Asia

It is clear that international migration brings economic benefits to developing countries which have solid economic incentives to promote it. That explains why states play a key role in international migration through their policies. The issue here is that in pursuing their national interests, states often treat men and women differently. More to the point, states generally intervene more heavily in women's immigration than in men's. Few restrictions

TABLE 3.2

Emigration Restrictions on Female Migration in Asia, Circa 2000

Country	Restrictions
Bangladesh	Ban on recruitment of female domestic workers. Ban on recruitment of entertainers but not on nurses, doctors, and engineers.
India	Women must be at least thirty to work as domestic workers in western Asia or northern Africa, with exceptions made on a case-by-case basis. Ban on recruitment of female domestic workers to Kuwait.
Indonesia	Women must be at least twenty-two. Restrictions regarding countries of destination for domestic workers and male/female ratio recruited by authorized agents may be lifted under certain conditions. Temporary ban on domestic workers to the Middle East.
Nepal	Women must be at least eighteen. Selective ban on employment according to the country of destination.
Myanmar	Ban on recruitment of female workers, except in the case of professionals.
Pakistan	Women must be at least thirty-five to work abroad as domestic workers. Ban on recruitment of nurses.
Philippines	Domestic workers: Women must be at least twenty-one (for some countries the age requirement is higher; for others it is lower—the minimum working age is eighteen). Entertainers: Women must be at least eighteen; selective ban on employment according to the country of destination; must complete required academic and skill testing, possess Artist Record Book, and undergo predeparture showcase preview. Nurses: Women must be at least twenty-three; must possess B.Sc. in Nursing and have one year of work experience in the Philippines.
Sri Lanka	Women must be at least twenty to work as domestic workers. Ban on recruitment of entertainers.
Thailand	Ban on recruitment of women except in the case of selected countries of destination. Entertainers must hold a diploma from a school of arts and a license, and must not perform in nightclubs.

SOURCES: Abella (1995); Lim and Oishi (1996); IOM (1999); and the author's field research in 1999.

are placed on male migration; by contrast, female migration is subject to many official restrictions, as Table 3.2 indicates.

Restrictions on female migration vary significantly across the region. India, Bangladesh, and Pakistan are quite restrictive regarding women's overseas employment. Bangladesh officially banned women from migrating abroad as domestic workers several times. The most recent ban was lifted recently, but even then, the migration process is still difficult and complex for women because the state monitors it so closely. India banned the migration of domestic workers to Kuwait in the late 1990s; this ban was lifted a few years later, but there is still a minimum age—thirty—for women working abroad as domestic workers.[7] In Pakistan, the state banned female migration in the 1980s. This ban is no longer in place, but the country imposes the highest minimum age restriction in the region—thirty-five years.[8] These restrictions are intended to discourage female migration; women are usually married and have many children to take care of by the time they reach the ages 30 to 35.

Other countries have more open emigration policies for women, who face fewer restrictions and a lower minimum age.[9] In Indonesia, the Suharto administration actually promoted female migration as part of its developmental plan. Indonesia's Fourth Five-Year Plan (1983–88) set a target of 225,000 women to be sent abroad; this was increased to 500,000 in the 1989–1994 plan.[10] Although that target was not attained, between 1983 and 1993 the number of migrant Indonesian women increased more than tenfold, from 12,000 to 130,000.[11] Other states have not promoted female migration as blatantly as this, but many actively seek overseas job opportunities for both men and women. The state agencies and embassies of the Philippines and Sri Lanka regularly conduct research on the international labor market to identify potential niches, and send "recruitment missions" to industrialized countries to win job contracts for their citizens. These efforts do not specifically target female workers; in effect, however, they promote female migration since the international demand for female workers—especially in domestic services and manufacturing—has grown much larger than male workers in the construction sector, which has been declining.

The important point is, however, that most of the states in Asia restrict the emigration of women in one way or another, while allowing men to migrate almost freely. There is a minimum age requirement for all emigrants, but for men, it is the same as national minimum working age: workers do not have to be older than that to emigrate abroad. The only other restrictions for men relate to certain destination countries in times of war or civil conflict. Otherwise, men are basically free to go anywhere. By contrast, women are often subject to more emigration restrictions. For them, the minimum age for overseas employment is often higher than the domestic minimum age for employment. State officials often explain that this is because women need to be "mature" if they are going to work abroad, in order to be able to protect themselves from abuse and harassment. Yet the same is not required of men. Some states also place other restrictions on women in terms of occupational types, qualification requirements, and destinations.

External Policy Environment

These restrictions on female migration reflect a certain external political reality—specifically, the weak leverage of migrant-sending states vis-à-vis receiving states, and also the lack of an effective suprastate regime to protect migrants. Developing countries are not in a strong position politically because the international labor market is basically a buyers' market. There are only a limited number of unskilled jobs available in the world; the developing countries must all compete with one another to find spaces for their unskilled workers.

This imbalance in the labor market has led inevitably to a situation of unequal political power between sending and receiving states. This has had several repercussions. First, it is extremely difficult for sending states to address the plight of their citizens working abroad. Even when there are problems such as maltreatment (which includes violence and abuse), non-payment of wages, and violations of contracts, the officials of sending states often find it difficult to confront receiving states in a forthright manner, let alone compel them to investigate the problems and punish employers who are mistreating migrant workers. There are too many other developing countries seeking to expand their niches in the migrant labor market. A sending state that responds too forcefully against a receiving state can easily find its immigration quota cut, and lose "job orders" to other sending states.

Yet this does not mean that sending states take no action. Whenever possible, they attempt to sign bilateral agreements with receiving states to secure large-scale quotas and to ensure that their migrant workers will be protected from abuse. This is of course a difficult task. These sorts of official agreements would allow sending states to make cases against the receiving ones. Although such cases are only a minor irritant to the receiving states, they prefer not to place themselves in an awkward position in the first place. Furthermore, according to many state officials, these agreements are "toothless." Destination states find it extremely difficult to protect the migrant workers they have accepted. One official in Hong Kong noted that her government lacked sufficient time and resources to thoroughly protect even local-born workers, let alone migrants. Thus bilateral agreements, even after they are reached, do not guarantee that migrant workers will be protected. And given how difficult it is to guarantee protection for workers, receiving states prefer to avoid making any commitments on the matter. As a compromise, states often conclude bilateral agreements in the form of memorandums or notes that do not entail any legal liabilities. These basic agreements between sending and receiving states at least provide a frame of reference to which both parties can turn when problems occur; however, they do not necessarily protect migrant workers. Moreover, as will be discussed in Chapter 7, existing international conventions have not been very effective in protecting migrants because so many destination states have not ratified them. All of this has been extremely frustrating for migrant-sending states.

Faced with these political constraints and with other domestic factors (which will be addressed in Chapter 4), many states in developing Asia have restricted female migration in order to "protect women." Furthermore, emigration policies reflect particular social perceptions of women's role. Emigration policies for men are driven almost solely by economic factors; by contrast, emigration policies for women are more complex and arise from the need to strike a delicate balance between economic necessity and social values as they relate to women. In the case of female migration, social values sometimes override economic imperatives. These "value-driven emigration policies" strongly affect the patterns of female migration in Asia. The following section presents an overview of emigration policies and their gender implications in the Philippines, Sri Lanka, and Bangladesh.

Value-Driven Emigration Policies: A Historical Overview

PHILIPPINES

International labor migration from the Philippines dates back to the beginning of the twentieth century. The country was devastated by its defeat in two liberation wars against Spain and the United States. In particular, the rural subsistence economy suffered under American colonial policy, which was geared toward export agricultural production rather than domestic consumption. In the 1930s, to escape poverty, Filipino farmers began migrating to Hawaii and California to work on plantations.[12] Many of them (they were mostly men) became permanent residents or American citizens. Even after independence in 1946, Filipinos continued to immigrate to the United States and Canada on a permanent basis.

Temporary labor migration from the Philippines started in the 1950s, when the state initiated overseas employment programs.[13] However, the state involvement in migration was still minimal, because the brain drain was a concern. Only after President Ferdinand Marcos took office did the state begin to involve itself heavily in labor migration. In 1974, Marcos launched an overseas employment program to send Filipino workers abroad; it was hoped this would help solve domestic economic problems such as growing national deficits and high unemployment. Marcos's strong initiative in effect institutionalized the entire emigration process. His intention was to increase the number of emigrants systematically and then redirect their remittances through official channels so that the amounts could be recorded officially and would thus improve the national balance of payments. Marcos emphasized the goals of the state labor program as follows:

> For us, overseas employment addresses two major factors: unemployment and balance of payments position. If these problems are met or at least partially solved by contract migration, we also expect an increase in national savings and investment levels.[14]

Marcos issued the Labor Code—also known as Presidential Decree 442—in 1974. This created an institutional framework for overseas employment. The Labor Code mandated the establishment of administrative bodies such as the Overseas Employment Development Board, the National Seamen Board, and the Bureau of Employment Services. These institutions were made responsible for recruiting, marketing, and placing workers, for operating public employment offices, and for regulating private employment agencies.[15] The Labor Code also banned the direct hiring of workers; Marcos wanted his government to dominate the recruitment industry for overseas employment and thereby maximize its economic returns.[16] The Labor Code itself did not reflect any particular gender distinctions, nor did Marcos himself specifically encourage either men or women to work overseas. This is partly because he and his policy makers assumed that most of the migrants would be men. At the time, the labor demand was overwhelmingly for male construction workers in the Middle East as a result of the oil boom. The state policies for overseas employment were seen as applying mainly to male workers and as actively promoting the international labor migration of men.

The demand for Filipino migrant workers has grown rapidly. The number of migrant workers increased more than tenfold between 1974 and 1984[17] and has continued to increase since then. In response to this, Marcos strengthened and bureaucratized its oversight of labor migration by merging two organizations to form the Philippine Overseas Employment Administration (POEA). With this institutional support, the number of Filipino migrant workers (including seafarers)[18] increased significantly. It is estimated that there were 7.8 million Filipinos working in 192 countries and territories in 2003.[19] At first, most Filipino migrants took jobs in the oil-rich countries of West Asia; since then, however, over the past thirty years, they have been finding work in many other countries besides. As Table 3.3 indicates, Filipinos also work in Southeast Asia, East Asia, and many other parts of the world.

The gender dimension of migration became articulated after Corazón Aquino replaced Marcos as president in 1986. In general, she followed Marcos's line, promoting overseas employment as a whole. She referred to migrant workers as the country's new heroes and heroines, and in 1988 she proclaimed December "the Month of Overseas Filipinos" in recognition of their vital role.[20] However, the protection of migrants, especially of migrant women, soon became a serious concern for her administration as emigration from the Philippines became increasingly feminized. Between 1980 and 1987 the percentage of women among migrant workers more than doubled, from 18.0 to 36.3 percent.[21] This was accompanied by a rise in cases of abuse and exploitation, which were widely reported in the media. Although the official number of "welfare cases"—a euphemism for cases of abuse and ha-

TABLE 3.3
*Major Destination Countries of
Filipino Migrant Workers, 2003*

Country	Number
Saudi Arabia	169,011
Hong Kong	84,633
Japan	62,539
Taiwan	45,186
United Arab Emirates	49,164
Singapore	24,737
Kuwait	26,225

SOURCE: POEA (2004).

rassment—is unavailable for the late 1980s, my review of local newspapers showed that the number of articles reporting the situation of migrant women started rising drastically after 1985. Concern for the plight of migrant women was growing across the nation; by the time Aquino took office in 1986, feminists and activists were pressing the government to address this issue.[22] In response, in 1987 Aquino ordered the Department of Labor and Employment to conduct a fact-finding mission to Hong Kong, Singapore, Malaysia, and the Middle East.[23] In 1988 the Pakistani government decided to halt the emigration of female domestic workers; the Aquino administration followed suit the same year, placing a worldwide ban on the deployment of Filipina domestic workers. Aquino was hoping to force the governments of destination countries to negotiate with the Philippines about improving the situation of Filipina migrant women.[24]

This comprehensive ban yielded some positive results. Many countries immediately requested exemptions, at the same time making offers of assistance to improve the lot of Filipina domestic workers. Within six months, sixteen governments, including the United States, Canada, Hong Kong, Singapore, and major European countries, signed bilateral agreements specifying working conditions and some protective measures for migrant women. However, these countries were already providing relatively decent working conditions. Those with which the Philippines wanted to conclude agreements did not come forward to negotiate. Some governments even retaliated by slowing down the processing of visas for all Filipino nationals seeking employment. This affected so many Filipino professionals and skilled workers that the Aquino administration was forced to reconsider its policy.[25]

It is ironic that the ban, which was initiated in part by Filipina feminist groups to protect "fellow" Filipina migrant women abroad, met with protests from the women it was meant to protect. Migrant women's groups in Hong Kong (representing mainly Filipina domestic workers) got quite upset, claiming that the government was taking away the right of Filipino women to seek employment abroad. Twenty-two migrants' organizations created a coalition, "United Filipinos Against the Ban," to press the Aquino administration to repeal its decision.[26] The government finally acceded to this demand and exempted Hong Kong from the ban without any concessions, on the basis of its "good record," which domestic workers were not willing to contest.[27] A similar protest took place when another ban was placed on Singapore. Feminist groups in the Philippines were trying to "protect" fellow Filipino women by imposing the ban; however, their efforts were not serving the interests of the migrant women themselves whose immediate concern was to keep their jobs so that they could feed their families back home. As will be discussed in a later section, class difference is an important issue that affects emigration policies as well as the reintegration processes of migrant women.

On another occasion, the Philippine government took action after the media reported that several Filipino women, while working in Japan as entertainers, died in suspicious circumstances. In response to the public outcry, in November 1991, President Fidel Ramos prohibited entertainers under twenty-three from going to Japan. The number of Filipino entertainers dropped from 59,000 to 10,000 within two years, with serious consequences for both sides. The entertainment business in Japan depended heavily on Filipino entertainers, who at the time comprised 88.9 percent of foreign entertainers in that country.[28] Furthermore, about 90 percent of Filipino entertainers were bound for Japan, and the prohibition was taking their jobs away. Recruitment agencies, which had been making enormous profits from this sector, also lost business. Inevitably, both sides immediately began pressuring the government to lift the ban. Recruitment agencies in Japan created a fund to lobby the Japanese government to break the deadlock; soon after that, Japanese politicians visited the Philippines to pressure the government. These external and domestic pressures led to the eventual lifting of the prohibition. However, in response to public anger, the government established a minimum age requirement. A former cabinet member recalled:

> It is politically acceptable to ban entertainers [from going abroad]. . . . People liked it. Taking a ban off induced indignation from the public. Thus the government put more restrictions [on age, occupations, etc.]. When and where to handle the public is a difficult question.

The most dramatic case — one that rocked the country and forced the government to take strong action — involved the execution of a Filipina domestic worker in Singapore. Flor Contemplacion, a mother of four, was charged with a double murder and hanged by the Singaporean authorities in 1995. Her pleas for clemency were in vain, as were President Ramos's direct appeals that her life be spared. When she was executed, the Filipino public exploded with anger. Most of them believed that her trial had been unfair and that she had been coerced into giving false testimony. Not only that, but just before her execution two witnesses had come forward to testify that she was innocent. The Ramos administration, the Department of Foreign Affairs, and the Department of Labor and Employment were all sharply criticized for mishandling her case. This forced the top officials of both departments to resign. The case also soured diplomatic relations between Singapore and the Philippines. Ramos downgraded the Philippine embassy in Singapore to a consulate and recalled his ambassador. The Singapore government responded almost immediately by recalling its ambassador to the Philippines.[29]

The Contemplacion case had a strong impact on government policy in the Philippines. Besides appointing a presidential commission to investigate the case further, the Philippine government temporarily forbade Filipina domestic workers from migrating to Singapore. The government then began paying closer attention to protecting migrant workers abroad. Most notably, in 1995 a new law—the Migrant Workers and Overseas Filipinos Act (Republic Act 8042)—was passed. This act, which is now often referred to as the "Magna Carta for Migrant Workers," included a number of positive initiatives for protecting women. For example, it established Migrant Workers and Other Overseas Filipinos Resource Centers in diplomatic missions; and it strengthened the "country team approach" by consolidating the efforts of various state agencies, NGOs, and recruitment agencies; all of these were now to cooperate actively in order to ensure that migrant workers were protected.[30] The same act also ensured that Philippine diplomatic missions would extend their assistance to undocumented migrants as well as documented ones. RA 8042 was intended to show the public that its government was determined to protect its citizens abroad.

The Ramos administration was confronted with major challenges requiring strong political action because of all the high-profile cases involving migrant women. In 1995, on the heels of the Contemplacion case, the case of Sarah Balabagan surfaced to upset Philippine society yet again. Sarah Balabagan was a sixteen-year-old domestic worker in the Untied Arab Emirates who stabbed her employer to death and then claimed he had sexually assaulted her. At her first trial she was sentenced to seven years in prison; then an Islamic Court condemned her to death. After Ramos and the international community pleaded for her life, the president of the UAE intervened, and her sentence was reduced to one year's imprisonment and one hundred lashes. While the dead man's family was to be paid US$41,000 in compensation, a wealthy Filipino businessman donated the money and Sarah Balabagan returned to the Philippines where she was welcomed as a national heroine.[31]

The Ramos administration decided to maintain the "paradigm shift" it had begun in 1992: it admitted that migration was here to stay and that the country's emigration policies would have to be reframed accordingly. Past administrations had treated overseas employment as a temporary measure to relieve economic strain. Under President Ramos, however, the government officially started perceiving migration as something it should try to "manage" rather than control.[32] According to a former cabinet member, the Ramos administration took the official position that although it would not promote the labor migration of men and women, it would facilitate it while trying to protect Filipino migrants from abuses. The minimum age requirements the government established fit well with this policy. The course the Ramos administration set has largely been followed by successive governments. It is only recently that President Gloria Macapagal-Arroyo began to promote migration more openly. She reportedly encouraged a Filipino migrant to stay abroad in a televised telephone conversation as follows:

> Jobs here are difficult to find and we are depending on the people outside the country. If you can find work there, and send money to your relatives here, then perhaps you should stay there.[33]

She has also referred to migrants as "Overseas Filipino Investors," emphasizing their economic contribution to the country.[34]

Most state officials, NGOs, and scholars now agree that bans are not an effective way to protect migrant women. Bans do not stop people from migrating but only deflect them into illegal channels where they are even more vulnerable to abuse and exploitation. Furthermore, bans—and the increases in "irregular" migration that result from bans—strain diplomatic relations between the Philippines and migrant-receiving states. Having had many years of experience with migration policy, the Philippine government realizes the importance of "managing" migration rather than "controlling" it. It has decided to manage female migration by establishing age restrictions and by working harder to protect Philippine citizens through its diplomatic missions.

SRI LANKA

Under British rule, Sri Lanka (then called Ceylon) was more experienced with immigration than with emigration. The British authorities had been bringing in Tamils from India to work on plantations in central Ceylon right up until the country gained independence in 1948. Sri Lanka's experience with emigration began slowly in the late 1950s. Once the government decided that the official language would be Sinhalese and that the languages of school instruction would no longer be English, Europeans and the British-educated Sri Lankan elites began leaving the country.[35]

The real exodus did not begin until the 1960s when the country's economic problems became acute. Political conditions were part of the problem. Under a socialist regime between 1956 and 1977, the country had adopted an import-substitution industrialization strategy as well as a closed economic policy. However, import substitution did not succeed in Sri Lanka any more than it had in most other developing countries. On the contrary, it actually undermined the Sri Lankan economy, and as a consequence, thousands of professionals and skilled workers left for Europe and North America every year. This brain drain impeded economic development and became a serious concern within the government. Following a series of Cabinet meetings, the government introduced legislation that established compulsory service for doctors and engineers trained in public institutions.[36] In 1971 it also passed the Passport and Exit Permit Act which tightened emigration controls by requiring any professional employed in the public sector to obtain an exit permit from the prime minister before leaving the country.[37]

Sri Lanka moderated both its emigration policy and its overall economic policy in the mid-1970s. However, it was not until after the United National Party (UNP) won the 1977 election that the economy underwent fundamental liberalization and that the "population embargo" was lifted. The new government soon began exploring the possibility of sending semiskilled and unskilled workers to the Middle East to take advantage of the economic boom there. The government recognized that in order to compete with migrant workers from other developing countries, it would have to make a systematic, state-level effort to promote overseas employment. The Department of Labor had been functioning as a recruitment agency as early as 1976, at a time when the previous regime was taking the first steps toward liberalizing the economy; in 1977, after the UNP took power and began thoroughly liberalizing the economy, that same department expanded its operations as a labor recruiter. Around the same time, the government further bureaucratized emigration processes and began promoting overseas employment on a large scale. The Foreign Employment Bureau was established within the Department of Labor in 1978. The legal framework for overseas employment was erected by the Foreign Employment Agencies Act of 1981 and by the Sri Lanka Bureau of Foreign Employment Act of 1985. The 1981 legislation was in part a response to the growth of unregistered recruitment agencies and their shady practices, and was designed to monitor those agencies and thereby ensure that workers were protected. The purpose of the 1985 legislation was to strengthen the capacity of the Sri Lankan Bureau of Foreign Employment (SLBFE) by transferring more institutional autonomy to it from the Department of Labor.

The government succeeded well at promoting overseas employment, and the number of migrant workers increased rapidly. In 1978 only 8,082 Sri Lankan workers left for the Middle East; the following year, 20,980 did.[38] Today, Sri Lanka sends more than 200,000 workers a year through official channels; it is estimated that 970,000 Sri Lankans are now working in nearly forty countries.[39]

In Sri Lanka, the level of male emigration was not very high from the beginning. By 1983 there were 200,000 male Sri Lankans working in the Middle East; this counts as rapid growth, yet in raw numbers there were still far more workers in that region from India and Pakistan—930,000 and 800,000 respectively.[40] Sri Lanka has a small population and hence a small labor force, but this is not the entire reason. Sri Lankan men had difficulty finding jobs in the Middle East's construction sector. This was largely a problem of timing: by the time Sri Lanka entered that region's labor market, Indians, Pakistanis, Bangladeshis, and even Koreans had already carved out their own niches and had already established networks with local employers and recruitment agencies.

But there was still a strong demand for migrant women in that region, mainly for domestic workers. India, Pakistan, and Bangladesh had either forbidden women to work abroad or placed restrictions on them doing so; this meant that a niche was available provided new entrants were willing to provide domestic workers. Sri Lankan recruitment agencies began actively hiring women to fill this niche. Since the late 1970s, a large number of Sri Lankan women have been leaving for the Middle East as domestic workers. The demand for unskilled male labor began decreasing in 1982 as construction projects were wound up in the Middle East; however, the demand for migrant women continued to grow.

The proportion of women among Sri Lankan migrant workers has risen significantly over the past two decades. The 1978 statistics provide no gender breakdown; however, the data on domestic workers provide a sufficiently accurate picture. They indicate that the proportion of domestic workers— the vast majority of whom were women—among Sri Lankan migrant workers increased from 17 to 43.6 percent within one year; moreover, women outnumbered men by 1980. This predominance of women peaked at 79 percent in 1994, but women are still a significant majority today, accounting for 65.3 percent of all migrant workers.[41] Table 3.4 shows the main destination countries of Sri Lankan migrant workers.

The Sri Lankan government has been relatively lenient toward female migration. Unlike other migrant-sending states, it has not comprehensively banned women's overseas employment. Its emigration policy sets the minimum age of domestic workers at eighteen—the lowest in the region. It prohibits the emigration of entertainers, but the impact of this on female migra-

TABLE 3.4
Major Destination Countries of
Sri Lankan Migrant Workers, 2002

Country	Number
Middle East	
Saudi Arabia	325,000
United Arab Emirates	138,000
Kuwait	165,000
Lebanon	80,000
Europe	
Italy	60,000
Cyprus	15,000
East/Southeast Asia	
South Korea	4,000
Hong Kong	2,500
Malaysia	2,000
Other Asia	
Maldives	14,000

SOURCE: SLBFE (2003).

tion flows is minor; a large majority of Sri Lankan migrant women prefer domestic work because of the strong social stigma that is attached to "entertainers." Some women emigrate as tourists and then work illegally as singers and dancers, but according to a senior government official, their number is not significant. In any case, Sri Lanka's emigration policy for women has been quite open compared with those of other major migrant-sending states in Asia.

However, this lenient policy should not be taken to mean that Sri Lankan migrant women face few problems. In 2002 there were more than 6,545 complaints filed by migrant women relating to harassment, abuse, and non-payment of wages.[42] The real numbers are probably higher, given that many women are too ashamed and embarrassed to report such cases. The government has been concerned about the well-being of Sri Lankan women working overseas ever since female migration started increasing in the 1980s. According to David Soysa, a former director of the SLBFE and current president of the Migrant Services Centre, the Sri Lankan government attempted to ban the emigration of unskilled women to Lebanon and Kuwait in 1989.[43] The ban on Lebanon was in place for both men and women because of the civil war and was lifted after the war was over. The ban on Kuwait was only for domestic workers and arose after a number of abuse and "welfare" cases and the Kuwaiti government's failure to take action. However, this ban never took effect, since the Gulf War began right after it was issued, at which point the ban lost its meaning, since most of the Sri Lankan migrant workers in Kuwait were repatriated once the war started.

The Gulf War was fortuitous for Sri Lanka for two reasons. First, the government did not have to implement the ban after all and thus did not have to strain its diplomatic relations with Kuwait. Second, Sri Lanka offered to help Kuwait with its postwar reconstruction by sending workers. This initiative succeeded: out of gratitude, the Kuwaiti government took in more Sri Lankan male workers than before. It also promised to make efforts to provide better working conditions for Sri Lankans, although this promise did not last very long.

Many scholars and NGOs have noted the plight of Sri Lankan domestic workers. According to a study by the Migrant Services Centre, close to 90 percent of them have faced some kind of problem, be it abuse, harassment, or non-payment of wages. Even so, the government does not intend to end female migration. A former labor minister, John Seneviratne, made this comment while he was still in office:

> I accept that some of our Sri Lankan ladies when they go to the Middle East and other countries, they face some problems—sometimes, sexual harassment, et cetera. But I should say that there are about five percent. Others—more than ninety-five percent—are having a peaceful and happy life, and when they come back to Sri Lanka, they invest their money in fruitful ventures, like buying a new house or further [the education of] their children, or self-employment ventures. So I should say there are [abused women], but they are not that represented [*sic*], only five percent. But merely because of this five percent, are we to stop—to make a full stop sending migrant women workers to the Middle East and other countries?[44]

The lenient policy toward female migration reflects the reality that international migration is now indispensable to the Sri Lankan economy. Migrants' remittances amounted to US$1.2 billion in 2002[45]—almost one-third of the country's foreign exchange earnings. This income has made a huge contribution to the balance of payments and to the national economy as a whole. And about 60 percent of the remittances come from Sri Lankan migrant women working abroad.[46] Some researchers estimate that out of the total population of 19 million, 2.5 to 3 million Sri Lankans are supported by remittances from family members working overseas.[47] This figure rises to almost 4 million if the migrants themselves are included. This means that about one fifth of Sri Lankans are financially dependent on labor migration. This dependency has become so strong that the government would find it very difficult to declare an outright ban on women's overseas employment. This in turn has weakened the government's bargaining power vis-à-vis the governments of receiving countries. A former state official deplored the situation:

Philippine [*sic*] never goes as a beggar like we do. They are a good negotiator and when they can't accept something they say that straightforwardly [to migrant-receiving countries]. Our government can't do that. We are so weak.

In response to growing concerns about the welfare of migrant women, a Presidential Task Force on Migrant Women was established in 1997. The main purpose of this body was to investigate female migration from Sri Lanka and assess its impact. According to local scholars, it is not clear whether this presidential initiative was ever intended to help protect migrant women. Some even argue that the real reason for it was to pacify the public—that is, it was a public relations exercise by the government. If so, it disguised its real motive—to continue to promote female migration. One of the members of the task force admitted that after three extensive surveys were conducted to examine the impact of female migration, the subsequent recommendations were scarcely implemented because there was no institutional will.

The Sri Lankan government has never made a clear policy statement on female migration. In 1999 Labor Minister John Seneviratne said only that there was no declared policy of discouraging women from going abroad.[48] According to a senior director of the SLBFE, the government's basic stance can be described as follows: "We don't push them [women] as such but don't discourage them either. For those who wish to go, we let them go and provide help and protection."

By contrast, the government has started actively promoting male migration in recent years. One recent labor minister stated that the government would prefer that more men left the country to work. During his visit to Singapore and South Korea in April 2000, he actively sought job opportunities specifically for male workers. His discussions with Singapore's labor minister resulted in job orders for male construction workers; it was also agreed to establish a training center in Sri Lanka to train construction workers, who would then be sent to Singapore.[49] His successor made a similar attempt in 2003 when he concluded a memorandum of understanding with the Malaysian government. This agreement promised at least 50,000 jobs for Sri Lankans, mainly for male construction workers.[50]

This shift suggests the re-emergence of traditional gender ideology in the Sri Lankan society. As many social problems arose such as growing divorce rates, alcoholism, and children's school dropout rates, migrant women have been taking the blame for family disintegration. In actuality, most of these problems are caused by husbands' extra-marital affairs, heavy drinking, gambling, and neglect of children.[51] Nevertheless, instead of questioning men's misbehavior, migrant women are held responsible for having abandoned their family. Women's Affairs Minister Hema Ratnayake reportedly said that women "should think not twice but thrice before leaving their young ones." She also urged women "not to desert their children for foreign jobs as this can lead to a breakup in the family and other problems."[52] Even local women activists argue that these "social ills" have been "arisen as a result of women seeking unskilled jobs abroad."[53]

These repercussions in the society have led the government to encourage more men to work abroad. However, in promoting male migration, the government still does not have a clear policy to reduce female migration. Rather, it is promoting overseas employment in general, and this implicitly maintains and even promotes female migration, given the high demand for unskilled female workers in the Middle East and Southeast Asia. Almost every year, the labor minister visits migrant-receiving countries and asks their governments to accept more Sri Lankan workers. In this respect, the lack of policy on female migration in Sri Lanka can be understood as a strategic decision. The government wishes to increase the level of remittances to further its economic development, but is also aware that the international demand for unskilled labor is greater for women than for men. Growing public concern is making it difficult to overtly encourage women to work abroad. Having no clear policy on female migration is a convenient approach to maintaining the status quo and even to allowing such migration to increase as much as the market will bear.

BANGLADESH

Bangladesh, a small country with a large population, is a major source of migrants in Asia. Yet major migratory outflows did not emerge there until the 1970s. Very few Bengalis[54] emigrated before the 1950s. In the 1950s and early 1960s only several thousand Bengalis emigrated annually, and most of them were bound for the United Kingdom.[55] These early emigrants were mainly professionals and skilled workers who were being allowed to work in Britain under the British Immigration Act. By the early 1970s, this flow had virtually stopped as a result of stricter British immigration laws. At that point the destination for Bangladeshi migrants shifted from Europe to the Middle East, where the demand for labor was growing. However, unlike Indians, Pakistanis, and Filipinos, who had started entering the overseas labor market by the late 1960s, Bangladeshi workers could not emigrate to that region until 1976. One factor in this was Bangladesh's struggle for independence from Pakistan. After it gained independence in 1971, most Arab states did not recognize the new country immediately, perceiving its independence as a rejection of Muslim identity.[56]

In 1974, after vigorous diplomatic efforts by the Bangladeshi government, the new nation finally obtained political recognition from the Organization

TABLE 3.5

Numbers of Migrant Women from Bangladesh

Year	Total Number of Migrant Workers	Number of Migrant Women	Women's Share in Migrants (%)
1991–98*	1,814,090	13,039	0.72
1996	211,714	1,567	0.74
1997	381,077	1,389	0.36
1998	267,667	775	0.29

NOTE: *Only aggregated data are available from 1991 to 1997.
SOURCE: BMET.

of Islamic Countries. This enabled the Bangladeshi government to launch a labor migration project that mainly targeted the Middle Eastern countries. The Bangladesh Bureau of Manpower, Employment and Training (BMET) was established in 1976 within the Ministry of Labor to "manage and monitor skills training as well as national and international employment promotion."[57] Then in 1982 the Emigration Ordinance (which replaced the 1922 Emigration Act) established the legal framework for labor emigration from Bangladesh. The Emigration Ordinance proclaimed that the government would be promoting the overseas employment of its citizens while controlling and regulating the flows as necessary.

Like the Philippines and Indonesia, Bangladesh approached overseas employment as part of its development plans. All of its five-year plans have promoted labor emigration.[58] The Second Five-Year Plan (1980–85) stated clearly that one of its major objectives was "to substantially raise the annual manpower export."[59] The Third Five-Year Plan (1985–90) took the same stance, even emphasizing the importance of remittances and the need for more institutional support. The Third Five-Year Plan set a target of 60,000 workers to be sent overseas annually. With the state's strong support and the increasing demand for migrant labor, this target was easily met, and annual flows of workers continued to increase until they reached 268,000 in 1998. Between 1976 and 2000, Bangladesh's total migrant workforce grew from 9,000 to more than 1.9 million.[60] The Middle East has been their main destination: Saudi Arabia, the United Arab Emirates, and Kuwait. However, more and more Bangladeshis are working in Southeast Asian countries such as Singapore and Malaysia.

In stark contrast to Sri Lanka and the Philippines, emigration from Bangladesh is still largely a male phenomenon. According to the Ministry of Labor, around 12,000 women were legally employed abroad in 1999; that was only 0.8 percent of all Bangladeshi migrant workers. As Table 3.5 shows, between 1991 and 1998 only 13,049 women emigrated overseas, whereas

TABLE 3.6
Major Destinations of Bangladeshi Migrant Women ★

Country	Number
United Arab Emirates	3,923
Malaysia	845
Bahrain	625
Kuwait	199
Saudi Arabia	198

NOTE: ★Those who went through recruitment agencies.
SOURCE: INSTRAW and IOM (2000, 15).

1,814,090 men did.[61] The drop between 1997 and 1998 was a result of two factors: a ban on the emigration of female nurses and domestic workers, and the Asian financial crisis. In 1999, about 70 percent of Bangladeshi migrant women worked in the UAE, the rest mainly in Malaysia, Bahrain, Kuwait, and Saudi Arabia (see Table 3.6).[62]

Note that these official figures do not give the whole picture of female migration. For instance, it is estimated that 32,000 undocumented Bangladeshi women, most of whom are assumed to be domestic workers, were working in the Middle East in 2000.[63] Also worth noting is that these women comprised only a small percentage of the 330,000 undocumented migrants from Bangladesh.[64]

The large majority of Bangladeshi migrant women are unskilled or semi-skilled workers. Only a small percentage of them are professionals—mostly nurses. Even during the years when the government placed a ban on women's emigration as domestic workers, it was still legal for professionals to work for Bangladeshi expatriates in foreign countries, and some chose to emigrate through this channel.[65] However, some more unskilled women followed unofficial channels in order to work as domestic workers abroad.

Female migration has always been a minor phenomenon in Bangladesh, but this is not because the government has always banned it. In fact, at first the government made a limited attempt to promote female migration. It did not succeed. According to a former head of the BMET, in 1976 as an experiment the government dispatched about fifty female domestic workers to Iraq. Seven months later it was compelled to halt this initiative, primarily because the BMET received too many complaints from these women. He recalls of their departure:

> When we went there—I went there myself to visit them after three months—it was clear that our girls were not psychologically ready for working in Iraq. . . . Unlike the Filipina, our girls don't know English. . . . Secondly, we didn't have many women who could use modern household gadgets. . . . The complaints

were mainly about too much work, sometimes of sexual harassment, and also [the] type of food which was not to their liking. We gave all of them an option to go back [to Bangladesh]. We just felt that maybe it was premature for us to send women to domestic job[s].

The migration of unskilled women was banned after this attempt.[66] Professional and skilled women were still allowed to work overseas, but there were very few of these—they constituted 1 percent or less of the total migrant workforce.

This comprehensive ban on unskilled women was lifted in 1991 on the initiative of the labour minister. He recalls how this came about:

> In 1991, I convinced then Prime Minister Ziaur, saying, "If you believe in gender equality, women should be allowed to go [overseas to work]. [Job] offers are there for women." [The] prime minister accepted it. It was not necessarily an easy process since it was already known that the job offers were manipulated by agencies, et cetera. The issue of language barrier was still there except in Kuwait and UAE where some people speak Hindi. However, he [the prime minister] was convinced when I said, "Indians and Nepalese are working [overseas]. If our women can perform well, why not?"

After lifting the ban, he was criticized in several newspapers for placing Bangladeshi women in vulnerable situations. But this criticism did not grow any stronger, and other government officials never raised the issue with him. The decision to lift the ban was thus maintained.

The former labor minister contended that his initiative arose purely from his egalitarian views; some, however, suspect otherwise. One NGO report contends that female migration was liberalized in response to the Kuwaiti government's need for reconstruction help following the 1991 Gulf War.[67] Perhaps this was the case, but the most fundamental reason was probably the economic downturn in Bangladesh in 1990. When the Gulf War broke out, 62,000 workers had returned from Kuwait and Iraq. Since migrants' remittances were worth almost 70 percent of the country's total exports, this repatriation rocked the Bangladeshi economy. It is estimated that this reverse exodus cost Bangladesh at least US$106.5 million in remittances.[68] Estimates are that the total impact of the Gulf War on Bangladesh exceeded US$400 million after the costs of emergency repatriation, increased oil prices, and export losses to Kuwait and Iraq were all included.[69]

Some government officials recall that one important reason for lifting the ban on the migration of unskilled women was to help balance the economic losses incurred when the male migrants returned. The Ziaur administration hoped that the remittances from migrant women from abroad would help solve the country's balance-of-payments problems. Furthermore, a significant number of undocumented migrant women were working overseas; the government realized this and hoped to divert their remittances to official channels by legalizing female migration.

Yet even after the ban was lifted in 1991, women faced various restrictions for emigration. The minimum age requirement was one of them. While all men above eighteen could emigrate freely regardless of skill levels, women had to meet higher age requirements. Professional and skilled women had to be over twenty-one to work overseas and unskilled women had to be over thirty-five. My interviews with government officials suggested that such differences in minimum age requirements indicated the assumed "maturity levels" of workers in the eyes of state elites. In other words, these requirements clearly illustrate the existing bias that women are less mature than men simply because they are women. Even women with education are considered as "less mature" than men with no education. According to the officials, state controls were especially tighter on unskilled women largely in order to protect them: the vast majority of these women took domestic work, which has a high risk of abuse and exploitation.

Emigration policies also stipulated that Bangladeshi women who applied for domestic work abroad had to get the approval of a male guardian, be it their husband or father or even son. The same rule does not apply to men; men require no approval from a guardian. Again, this is another gender-differentiated policy for emigration. As will be shown in the next chapter, such requirement symbolizes a traditional gender ideology—the perception that women belong to men. Despite these restrictions, 13,039 Bangladeshi women legally went overseas to work between 1991 and 1998. Of these, 55.8 percent were working in the Middle East as nurses, cleaners, domestic workers, and garment workers, and 41.3 percent were working in factories in Malaysia.[70]

In 1998, after seven years of liberalization, female migration was again halted. That year, on July 21, after some reported cases of abuse and exploitation in the Middle East, the Cabinet Committee on Employment of Bangladesh Nationals in Foreign Countries decided to ban the emigration of domestic workers and nurses.[71] This time, however, civil society did not remain quiet. The National Association of Diploma Nurses (NADN) and various women's NGOs, human rights NGOs, and recruitment agencies protested this ban. The NADN argued that Bangladeshi nurses were working in many countries and were doing very well. An umbrella group of NGOs, including Ain-O-Salish Kendra (ASK), the Refugee and Migratory Movements Research Unit (RMMRU), the Christian Commission for Development of Bangladesh (CCDB), and the Welfare Association of Repatriated Bangladeshi Employees (WARBE) wrote joint letters to the Ministry of Labor and other high-level government officials, and even visited them to express their concerns. The president of the Bangladeshi Association of International Recruiting Agencies also published a long letter in the main national newspapers, in which he appealed to the government to lift the ban. He met the prime minister and the ministers of foreign affairs, labor, finance, and home affairs to argue that it was inhumane to ban women from going overseas and that the right to emigrate is a basic human right.

As a result of these protests, especially the ones from the recruitment agencies, the ban on nurses was lifted in late 1998. However, the ban on domestic workers remained in place for some time longer. Some NGOs continued to fight it, but many of the women's and human rights NGOs did not, at least initially. Soon after this, regulations on the emigration of single women professionals and skilled workers were imposed that were even stricter than the ones they replaced. The point of them was to prevent the shadow recruitment of domestic workers by foreign employers. Before being cleared to leave the country, all unmarried women were required to produce documentary evidence of their employment status as well as a guardian's consent letter. For Bangladeshi nurses, permission to travel would be granted only after a check had been made of the clinic or hospital where they would be working.[72]

In September 2003, the ban on the migration of domestic workers was finally lifted. According to a local scholar, this change was made after the Saudi king made a pointed request for it; he wanted to bring more Muslim maids into his kingdom. However, the policy remains extremely restrictive: Bangladeshi domestic workers, their employers, and the recruitment agencies themselves must meet a number of terms and conditions. For instance, the migrant woman must be over thirty-five, preferably married, and accompanied by her husband, and the promised monthly salary must be over 400 Saudi riyals (about US$107).[73] If strictly enforced, this policy change may not increase the number of migrant women by very much, since few married women over thirty-five wish to work abroad (see Chapters 5 and 6). The rule that husbands must accompany their wives sounds like a good idea, since it could increase employment for male Bangladeshis and possibly prevent employers from abusing women. In reality, however, this policy is unrealistic. A similar attempt by the Indonesian government did not work because most migrant women's husbands did not have the skills that overseas employers seek, such as gardening and driving.

EMIGRATION POLICIES IN OTHER COUNTRIES

There are many other Asian countries from which a large number of workers emigrate on a temporary basis. In the 1990s, Pakistan sent 138,000 migrant workers overseas in an average year.[74] More than 1.2 million Pakistani workers resided overseas at the end of the 1990s.[75] India is another major origin of migrants; almost 400,000 workers leave India for overseas jobs every year; today, 15 million Indians are working abroad.[76] In both countries, women are only a very small fraction of the migrant labor force.

Both of these countries have adopted value-driven emigration policies. In Pakistan, women's migration was banned from the late 1980s to the early 1990s. Although this ban has been lifted, women are still discouraged from working overseas on their own. The top official of the Bureau of Emigration and Overseas Employment (BEOE) stated that Pakistan's general policy was to promote labor migration and to "send as many workers as possible," whether on a contract basis or as part of permanent migration, in order to alleviate unemployment and gain foreign currencies. However, he also stated clearly that female migration was *never* encouraged. The Emigration Rules have gender-specific regulations relating to age and occupation; in addition to this, the state has internal procedures in place to restrict female migration. The state agencies select only married women who emigrate with their husbands. Furthermore, women must visit the state emigration authorities for an interview before they can leave.[77]

India has taken a similar stance on female migration. According to the head of the government's emigration division, India's state policy is "not against female migration but does not promote it either." In practice, its regulations are quite restrictive. Women under forty cannot go overseas even as tourists without a "sponsor declaration certificate." In addition to this, women's emigration to Kuwait as domestic workers was banned between 1999 and 2001, after a large number of domestic workers complained to the Indian Embassy in Kuwait about maltreatment and abuse. The ban was intended to pressure the Kuwaiti government to improve the situation of Indian domestic workers.

A senior director of the Indian government contended that the best way to protect Indian women from abuse is not to let them go in the first place. According to him, the ban was intended to protect women. "We don't promote female migration at the expense of women workers," he said. At the time of the Kuwait ban, women were permitted to work as domestic workers in any other country provided they met three conditions: (1) the work contract had to be attested by the Indian Embassy of the relevant country after the local employer's credentials had been verified by the embassy; (2) if unmarried, the women had to submit a "no objection clearance" signed by her parents in front of a magistrate; (3) if unskilled, the woman had to deposit a return airfare with the protector general in case repatriation was necessary. Men did not face conditions like these. India's emigration policies, like those of Bangladesh and Pakistan, entailed stark gender differences.

In Southeast Asia, Vietnam prohibited the emigration of female domestic workers for quite some time. Until the Berlin Wall came down, Vietnamese women were only allowed to work in East European countries; this reflected solidarity among the world's socialist states. At the time, thousands of Vietnamese women were working in Eastern Europe, mainly in factories. Once Vietnam began liberalizing its economic policies, it loosened restrictions on overseas employment. The ban on female migration was lifted in 1999, although only for a limited number of destination countries. Since that year, a large number of Vietnamese women have begun working abroad. In 2001, Vietnam signed an agreement with Taiwan on the emigration of female domestic workers. As a result, the number of Vietnamese domestic workers in Taiwan increased from a mere 33 in 1999 to 40,397 in 2003.[78] All of this indicates that in the case of Vietnam as well, the key determinant of international female migration has been state policy.

Conclusion

International migration yields significant economic benefits: it reduces domestic unemployment, earns foreign currencies through remittances, and improves a country's balance of payments. These are the reasons why the governments of many developing countries promote migration, at least the migration of men. However, the emigration of women is generally more restricted and sometimes openly discouraged or banned. Women are subject to more controls in the emigration process. This is because policies for female migration are largely driven by values whereas those for male migration are by economics. Value-driven emigration policies reflect the social and economic status of women. The actual effectiveness of restrictions on female migration is debatable; the point here is that value-driven migration policies are a distinctive characteristic of international female migration.

This chapter has discussed how value-driven migration policies have developed in Asia. It has highlighted the similarities among developing countries with regard to how women are treated in international migration. It has also addressed the differences: some governments prohibit or restrict female migration whereas others leave their emigration gates open for women. This leads to a question: Why do countries differ in their policy responses to the demand for migrant women in the international labor market? The next chapter analyzes the determinants of value-driven emigration policies and how these determinants are linked to national identity.

CHAPTER 4

Why Gendered Policies? The State, Society, and Symbolic Gender Politics

FOR SCHOLARS IN political science and political sociology, understanding policy-making processes has been one of the major goals. For many decades, scholars have been analyzing policy-making processes in terms of relations between states and societies. Some have viewed the state as an arena in which various public conflicts play out and have examined the power resources of social actors and the impact of those actors on policy outcomes. Others have perceived states as independent actors that do not necessarily reflect the interests of their societies: a "strong" state has its own autonomy and is endowed with the capacity to act in its own interests. In recent years a concept called "state–society synergy" has emerged that attempts to synthesize these two approaches.[1] Here, the state is still considered "strong"; however, it also acts in relation to society. The new "institutionalist" approach has further emphasized institutional structures and administrative capacities as explanatory factors.[2] According to this approach, state structures and policy legacies play a significant role in shaping interests, the possibility for political action, and the capacities that each class possesses.

Both the "state–society synergy" approach and new institutionalism tell us much about policy formulation processes. Yet the making of migration policy has other dimensions besides these. William Brubaker, for instance, addressed the importance of nationhood and national self-understanding to the development of immigration policies. According to Brubaker, differences in the ways that nations understand themselves have resulted in two distinctive policy outcomes in Europe: "state-centered and assimilationist" immigration policies have been followed by France, whereas "Volk-centered and differentialist" policies have been followed by Germany.[3] While these two types of policies have gradually converged in recent years, the differences in fundamental policy orientation still exist in the world.

The policy-making process for female migration in Asia has similar components. I would extend Brubaker's argument to analyses of emigration policies for women. In the case of emigration policies in Asia, national self-understanding has a strong gender dimension that reflects social and cultural values relating to women's employment. Both society and the state are perceived as responsible for protecting women's sexual purity, and this affects emigration policies for women who are exposed to sexual harassment and abuse by foreign employers. The making of policies for female migration involves processes that I refer to collectively as *symbolic gender politics.*

To understand the determinants of gender-differentiated emigration policies, I begin by discussing political and institutional factors such as policy legacies, institutional structures, and civil society; all of these factors have affected emigration policies for women. Then I turn to the role played by national identity and explain how a nation's self-understanding and self-image are reflected in policy-making processes. After that, I integrate some relevant literature from policy and gender studies in order to clarify the complex nexus between the state, gender, and migration in the gender-differentiated outcomes of state emigration policies.

Policy Legacies and State Structures

Past state policies for economic development have a significant impact on present state policies for international migration. The nature of development policy is important because migration policy is often formulated within the framework of economic development plans. In Sri Lanka the state followed a strategy of import substitution industrialization—in simpler terms, a closed economy—in an effort to defend itself against the industrialized world. This involved establishing strong state control over trade, exchange rates, and population movements. As a result of the state efforts to halt the brain drain, very few Sri Lankan workers migrated overseas between 1971 and 1975. When the United National Party (UNP) took power in 1977, it immediately liberalized economic policies and eased emigration restrictions. Soon after that, in 1976, it began promoting labor migration in an effort to revive its deteriorating economy. As a consequence, the number of migrant workers has increased dramatically since then.

A state that actively promotes emigration tends to be what Johnson calls a "developmental state"—one that takes strong initiatives in economic development and that pursues an export-oriented strategy in cooperation with the private sector.[4] Many developmental states in Asia have encouraged their nationals to work overseas by institutionalizing the migration process. As discussed earlier, the Philippine president Ferdinand Marcos established a manpower export program within his development plan by merging and strengthening the state emigration capacities. Overseas employment, he asserted, would be an important part of national economic development. President Corazón Aquino, who succeeded him, did not try to reduce the overall level of overseas employment, although her administration banned female migration for a short time. President Fidel Ramos also pushed forward with robust economic reforms, but even he recognized the importance of labor migration to the Philippine economy. In a speech on November 16, 1992, Ramos declared:

> Overseas employment remains a strategic development program of our government. I say 'development' because the overseas employment program is a major pillar of national development. It does not only help ease the employment situation in our country but also generates invaluable foreign exchange which is necessary to fund development projects and strategic programs in our country.

Indonesia, another developmental state, has pursued a similar approach, actively promoting international labor emigration. Like the Philippines, it perceives overseas employment as a generator of foreign currencies and as a means to improve the country's balance of payments.

Aggressive emigration policies have often reflected a centralized state structure. In the Philippines the entire overseas employment program was established under the dictatorial Marcos regime. Marcos issued eleven Letters of Instruction and eight Executive Orders relating to overseas employment; Aquino issued only three Executive Orders which were of minor importance in terms of content.[5] Marcos's top-down rulings, although far from democratic, helped establish the institutional framework for promoting labor emigration on a large scale.

Strong state initiatives have important consequences for female migration. Even when such initiatives do not specifically target women, they amount to official endorsements and thereby legitimate overseas employment in general. In the Philippines, the mass media and the state's own publications often depict migrant workers as national heroes and heroines who are making substantial contributions to national development. During the Christmas season, the president makes a point of greeting returning migrants on a red carpet at the airport. International migration, both men's and women's, is now admired and encouraged by Philippine society.

Development policies are key to understanding emigration policies, but other social policies are also worth examining. Even when the state promotes overseas employment for nationals, this does not mean that labor migration will follow automatically. Before they can find jobs abroad, workers must possess skills or certain qualifications that are in demand on the international labor market. States have been important actors in this respect. In the Philippines, the American colonial authorities followed liberal education policies, which helped Filipinos establish an equal and comprehensive school system after independence.[6] In the decades since independence, the Philippines' education policies have been quite inclusive, offering compulsory education to both girls and boys up to the secondary level. In addition, the state decision to keep English as a main language of instruction has given Filipinos a comparative advantage over other Asians when it comes to finding employment abroad. Curricula have also been important: many schools, both public and private, are attuned to the particular demands of the overseas labor market, such as for nurses and caregivers. This egalitarian education policy with strategic links to overseas labor demand has helped increase labor migration from the Philippines. By contrast, over the same decades, Indonesia's education system was not as advanced. Attempts by the Suharto administration to send more than 50,000 nurses to the United States failed in 1988, largely because Indonesian women lacked the necessary professional qualifications as well as language proficiency.[7]

The impact of state policies becomes clear when we look closely at migration outcomes. In the countries that have adopted a laissez-faire approach to labor migration or that have never especially promoted overseas employment in general, emigration levels are not very high. For instance, emigration was never officially promoted in India, and as a consequence the percentage of Indian migrant workers is quite small relative to the national labor force as a whole, although the absolute number of migrants is large and migrant information-technology workers often catch the media's attention. Migration of Indian women as independent workers is particularly uncommon. Even in the state of Kerala, a major source of Indian migrant women, women still comprise only 9.3 percent of emigrants.[8]

The state structures also affect migration flows to a degree. The key players in this regard are of course the state agencies specifically in charge of overseas employment, such as the Philippine Overseas Employment Administration (POEA), the Sri Lanka Bureau of Foreign Employment (SLBFE), and the Bangladesh Bureau of Manpower, Employment, and Training (BMET). These institutions were established to help workers emigrate, to safeguard their rights, and to monitor their working conditions. Today they actively promote overseas employment by "marketing" workers and exploring job opportunities in various parts of the world. They do so because their institutional performance is largely measured in terms of the number of employment contracts they process. In other words, if the number of emigrants were to go down, the institution would be perceived as failing to do its job and exposed to public criticism. It could also lead to a decline in position within the government. These agencies are often subsidiaries of the Ministry of Labor which has rather limited resources compared with other ministries. In order to secure and increase their budgets, they attempt to send as many migrant workers as possible to foreign countries. Once established, these state agencies are obliged to maximize emigration levels.

State—Society Relations: The Role of Civil Society

The relationship between the state and civil society also affects how policies are developed. According to Skocpol, it is important to examine not only "the resources and instruments that states may have for dealing with certain problems but also particular kinds of socio-economic and political environments populated by actors with given interests and resources."[9] For instance, when we analyze the evolution of economic policies, we find that they were developed within a network of state and society actors, including business communities and labor unions.[10] Indeed, the strength of these interest groups and their involvement are important determinants of emigration policies. Their degree of strength and involvement vary, however, reflecting historical factors.

State—society relations are crucial in policy-making processes for overseas employment. Emigration policies are not just affected by interest groups; they helped *create* those interest groups when the government first began promoting overseas employment. Many governments have encouraged the private sector to set up recruitment services. As a result, many recruitment agencies have sprung up and the number of unregistered agencies has increased significantly. In Sri Lanka there were only 125 registered agencies in 1978; two years later there were 525. These private agencies, which handle recruitment, training, and the processing of visas, now constitute a large-scale "migration industry" as well as a powerful lobby group.

Non-governmental organizations[11] (NGOs) also play an important role in formulation processes of emigration policies. They constitute a diverse group. Some NGOs were established by migrants themselves or returned migrants. They specifically focus on helping one another, protecting their rights, and lobbying against policies that affect their situation. Other NGOs were established by local activists, but are also working on migration issues. I call all these organizations "migration NGOs." Besides these groups there are NGOs that specialize in human rights, labor issues, and women's issues. They share some common ground with migration NGOs and thus get involved in policy debates and advocacy work relating to migration issues. All of these NGOs often accuse state agencies of corruption and inability to protect citizens abroad. They also criticize recruitment agencies for charging exorbitant fees and not providing enough support services for migrant workers abroad.

These NGOs operate both on sending and receiving sides. Except in the Middle East, where NGO activities are severely limited, most destination countries have migration NGOs. In countries of origin, these NGOs are also active in addressing the specific needs of migrants, both prospective ones and returnees. The following section will examine their role in emigration policies in each country.

PHILIPPINES

The involvement of migration NGOs is the strongest in the Philippines. This is not surprising, since the Philippines has one of the most vibrant civil societies in Asia. In 1995 there were already 65,000 NGOs operating across the country, and the general "tone" of the society is amenable to the activities of civic organizations. The "people's revolution" of 1986 ousted Marcos and helped establish a democratic regime; since then, the state–society relationship has been stronger than in other Asian countries. The 1991 Local Government Code stipulates that local governments must promote the establishment and operation of NGOs as active partners in forging local economic policies.[12] In addition, all state agencies are required to consult with relevant NGOs and other sectors of the community before implementing any program.

The development of migration NGOs is a natural outcome of the fact that the Philippines has the largest number of citizens working abroad—7.8 million—as well as many returnees.[13] These people have been organizing themselves to speak in a united voice. There are at least forty-one migration NGOs in the Philippines.[14] They do more than engage in advocacy; they provide various services. Some offer predeparture and pre-employment orientations for prospective migrants; others assist migrants on site through various NGO networks.

There are also migration NGOs established in destination countries that assist Filipino migrants. Many of them are funded and operated by religious institutions such as Catholic churches, but some are funded and operated by the migrants themselves. Such migrant associations even attempt to reach out to migrants of other nationalities with the goal of jointly addressing common issues. A typical example is the Asian Domestic Workers Union in Hong Kong which was organized by Filipina domestic workers before evolving into a multiethnic organization representing Indonesian, Thai, and Sri Lankan domestic workers. Furthermore, Filipino migrants have been taking steps to form a regional network of migration NGOs. The Asian Migrant Centre in Hong Kong and the Migration Forum in Asia in the Philippines are the focal points of this regional advocacy for migrants.

NGOs became visibly involved in the making of migration policy only after the People's Revolution of 1986. However, they were not entirely powerless under the Marcos regime. For instance, when Marcos issued Executive Order No. 857 (EO 857), which was intended to force Filipino migrant workers to remit a large portion of their salaries through the national banking system,[15] the workers protested quite strongly in Europe, the United States, Hong Kong, and the Philippines.[16] After these protests caught the attention of international organizations which voiced their criticism, Marcos repealed the most punitive sections of EO 857 concerning forced remittances.

Recently, migration NGOs in the Philippines have been more active and vocal than ever and have been playing a crucial role in the policy-making arena. The POEA is in regular contact with these migration NGOs and invites their representatives to policy discussions. Whenever a major change in policy is being considered, migration NGOs always involve themselves in the process, although their views are not always incorporated. The Migrant Workers and Overseas Filipinos Act of 1995 (Republic Act No. 8042) acknowledges the role of NGOs and encourages their steady involvement in crafting policy. As seen in the recent enactment of legislation to enable absentee voting by migrants, migration NGOs have strongly influenced state policies through their effective lobbying both in the Philippines and internationally. In the rest of developing Asia, this degree of civic activism is more limited.

SRI LANKA

Migration NGOs in Sri Lanka are less developed than those in the Philippines. There were more than 40,000 NGOs operating in the country in the mid-1990s,[17] but few of them dealt with migration issues until recently. Even today, there is only one NGO that devotes itself specifically to the needs of prospective and returned migrants. The National NGO Council of Sri Lanka describes the government's attitude toward civil society as rather "regulative" and contends that "there has been no opportunity for people's participation in recent Sri Lankan history, except to attend government functions and provide applause at political party meetings."[18]

However, the main reason why migration NGOs have not established themselves in Sri Lanka is that the migrants themselves have not shown much interest. Sri Lankan migrant workers (both prospective and returned) are less active than Filipinos have been in addressing their rights and getting involved in policy-making processes. Perhaps this reflects the fact that most returned migrants are housewives with very little past exposure to grass-roots movements. In addition, many of them have small children and must struggle to make ends meet once they return. Apart from participating in micro-credit programs, returned migrant women have not made it a high priority to organize their cause and advocate for their rights. In this regard, the situation in Sri Lanka is very different from the one in the Philippines and Bangladesh, where many of the migration NGOs were founded by re-turned migrants with high education and white-collar backgrounds who ac-tively engage in civic activism.

This explains why the only migration NGO in Sri Lanka—the Migrant Services Centre (MSC)—was not in fact established by former migrants. The MSC was founded by a former director-general of the SLBFE, David Soysa, under the auspices of a trade union, the National Workers Congress. The MSC has been offering two main programs for migrant women. One is predeparture orientation courses for prospective migrant women. With fi-nancial assistance from the government, the MSC equips these women with necessary skills such as cooking, basic Arabic, and operation of household appliances (such as vacuum cleaners, microwave ovens, and TV/VCRs, which most of these women do not possess at home). These orientations also pro-vide general information about life overseas, including the realities of work-ing for foreign employers. Some participants decide not to emigrate once they understand what overseas employment entails. Most of them, however, cannot afford to back out because by the time they have attended the ori-entation they have already paid their migration fees.

The second important program the MSC offers involves helping returned migrants organize themselves for better economic reintegration. The MSC has helped establish Migrant Workers Associations (MWAs)[19] and operates micro-credit programs for returned migrant women through them. Accord-ing to Soysa, these programs help returned female migrants become more fi-nancially secure so that they will not have to leave their families again. Through these programs and other MWA activities, the MSC is trying to foster leadership skills among returned migrant women. It also disseminates information to them and communicates their needs to the state.

Besides operating these programs, which are designed specifically for mi-grant women, the MSC engages in advocacy for migrant workers in general. For example, it campaigns for the ratification of international conventions on migrant workers as well as better protection policies. Recently it has also been addressing the issue of suffrage, pressuring the government to extend voting rights to Sri Lankan migrants working abroad.

In Sri Lanka, other grass-roots initiatives to support migrants have been launched mainly by labor unions and women's organizations. An American-funded labor NGO, the American Center for International Labor Solidarity (ACILS), has been quite active in addressing the plight of Sri Lankan migrant women and has already convened a number of workshops and meetings focusing on the protection of migrant workers overseas. The Center for Women's Research in Sri Lanka (CENWOR) has conducted various studies on female migration. In recent years, more and more NGOs in diverse fields, such as education and training, have been launching programs for migrant workers. In 2000, twenty-three of these local organizations established the Action Network for Migrant Workers (ACTFORM) in an attempt to link society, the state, and the media to work together on this issue. These groups focus on raising awareness of violence against women, on training women to counter workplace harassment and abuse, and on disseminating information on HIV/AIDS.[20] Not all of these programs are specifically designed for migrant women; some are meant to reach all working women. Yet most of these organizations are actively addressing the rights of migrants abroad as well as the need to protect them. None has ever called for a ban on female migration in order to protect women—the way some women's NGOs did in the Philippines in the 1980s.

The increasing involvement of NGOs and the emergence of ACTFORM signal that civil society is beginning to take root among Sri Lankan migrant workers. However, plenty of challenges still face this endeavor. State agencies and international NGOs have not shown much interest in funding projects on female migration except trafficking; as a consequence, the large majority of NGOs still lack sufficient resources to make this issue a main priority. The involvement of NGOs in policy-making processes remains extremely limited compared to the situation in the Philippines.

The most significant challenge is to find ways to encourage more migrant women to organize themselves. As mentioned earlier, most of the migration NGOs in Sri Lanka have been established by people who themselves have never been migrants. As a result of the MSC's work, many women have begun to join MWAs in order to receive financial help and address their concerns. However, these women have not immediately taken leadership roles in those groups. In fact, some of these groups are run by local community leaders who have no migration experience. Nevertheless, participation in such group activities will help migrant women develop leadership and organization skills among themselves as they acquire experience in planning and implementing programs. Such leadership building and further financial support would be indispensable in enhancing the role of civil society in the future migration policy-making in Sri Lanka.

BANGLADESH

In Bangladesh, migration NGOs have not been well developed either. This is rather strange in that the country is well known for its vibrant civil society. In response to Bangladeshi's severe economic problems exacerbated by frequent natural disasters, a large number of international NGOs have entered the country to provide social and economic assistance over the past several decades. With the strong financial support from Japan, the United States, Canada, and other European countries, the number of international and local NGOs in Bangladesh has significantly increased. In 1995 there were around 15,000 NGOs, and 950 of these were international NGOs.[21] The state recognizes the role of civil society and has become more supportive of it in recent years. State agencies collaborate with the NGOs on many projects, such as immunization and forestry programs.[22]

Why, then, have migration NGOs not been well developed in Bangladesh despite its large migrant population abroad? The answer relates to the particular structure of civil society in Bangladesh. Non-governmental, non-profit organizations are extremely well developed in Bangladesh, but their mandates and priorities are influenced by the interests of the Western donors who support them. In order to receive funding to sustain themselves, many local NGOs tend to work on the issues that interest their donors in industrialized countries. Most of these donors are interested in health, education, agricultural development, and women's issues, but not much in migration. The trafficking of women and children has begun receiving much attention in recent years, but donors still do not consider labor migration very important. This may be because migration has been a politically sensitive issue. In addition, those who can afford to go abroad for employment are perceived as fortunate; the truly destitute, by this logic, are the ones who cannot even pay the migration fees.

The class difference between NGO staff and poor women in rural areas is another barrier. Many women's and human rights NGOs were keen to lift the emigration ban on nurses, but not so concerned about the ban on domestic workers. The only exceptions include the Bangladesh National Women Lawyers' Association (BNWLA) and Naripokkho (a women's NGO), both of which have argued that the ban violates the fundamental rights of women.

One reason why most women's NGOs do not raise the issue of migrant women's rights is that the educated female elites find it difficult to identify with poor women who are desperate enough to emigrate; this makes it hard for them to represent the interests of these women. This is not to suggest that the elite women do not care about poor, uneducated women. Of course many of them do, and see it as their mission to protect women who are in a weaker social and economic position. Yet just as in the Philippines, where women NGOs initiated the first ban on female migration, many elite women in Bangladesh favor the ban in the belief that it is protecting poor, uneducated Bangladeshi women from brutal abuse and exploitation by foreign employers.

This view is prevalent not only among state officials but also among people in the main NGOs, who constitute the elite class of Bangladeshi society. The president of one large local NGO believes that unskilled poor women should be treated differently from men. He contended that the ban was necessary for such women:

> In a number of ways, they are children. They are very poor, [and] illiterate. . . . As a society, we have to, sometimes, take certain measures and decide whether this is the right time for women to go [abroad] or not.

This kind of attitude is common among elite Bangladeshis. One scholar recalled that a friend asked him to join the campaign to stop the emigration of Bangladeshi women by saying:

> *They are our women.* They cannot handle themselves [overseas]. They will all end up as prostitutes! (author's italics) [23]

The elite feel that they know what is the best for the poor. Many NGO staff, academics, and state officials, both male and female, often use the term "our women" when talking about poor, uneducated women. This patriarchal attitude is quite common in many other countries. In fact, patriarchy is often exercised not only by male but also by female elites. The elite women's sense of protection is very similar to that of men—they feel that it is the duty of the more educated and powerful ones to "protect" the country's poor, uneducated women. They almost always mean well by this. Yet the elite women do not necessarily understand the real needs of poor women or share common interests with them.

Migration NGOs in Bangladesh emerged only recently, when some male Bangladeshi migrants returned from the Middle East and began organizing themselves to address the needs of Bangladeshi workers abroad. The first migration NGO, the Welfare Association of Repatriated Bangladeshi Employees (WARBE) was founded in October 1997 with the help of two local grass-roots NGOs. The WARBE was the first migrant-initiated association in Bangladesh; it has nine *thana*[24] committees in the Dhaka district and has been expanding across the country. It has more than two thousand members, most of whom are male, which reflects the fact that few women emigrate from Bangladesh. Besides holding meetings and organizing activities for returned migrants, the WARBE provides awareness programs, conducts information campaigns, and holds predeparture orientations for prospective migrant workers. It also coordinates with other NGOs in speaking out against the ban on female migration and advocating for the rights of migrant workers. The other organization, the Bangladesh Migrant Centre, was established in 1998 by Bangladeshi migrants returning from South Korea and now operates in both Korea and Bangladesh. It monitors the treatment of Bangladeshi workers in Korea and observes how the labor laws are being applied to them there. Overall, however, it operates on a smaller scale than the WARBE.

However, none of these NGOs offers programs targeting migrant women. The situation is similar in other NGOs. Some NGOs began to work with migrant workers on a temporary basis, whenever programs were funded, but have never targeted migrant women as their main constituency or worked on the advocacy for their rights.

The most influential actors—although not civil society organizations—are the recruitment agencies in Bangladesh. These agencies were also against the ban, although in their case, this was for business reasons. The demand for Muslim domestic workers has been quite strong in the Middle East, and these agencies were missing out on a golden business opportunity. The president of the Bangladeshi Association of International Recruiting Agencies (BAIRA) insisted that migration was part of human rights, and thus the government had no right to stop women from going abroad whether they were unskilled or illiterate. He criticized the government, arguing that they were treating women like children:

> An eighteen-year-old is an adult. She has a right to vote and you [politicians] were elected by them. . . . Who will provide food and accommodation for those desperate women [if you do not allow them to work abroad]?

Overall, however, except for recruitment agencies and a few NGOs, most civil society organizations in Bangladesh kept silent on the ban on female migration. They are still not interested in migration issues—especially those of female migration, except in the context of trafficking. Bangladeshi civil society is still in the very early stage of involving itself in migration policy. Nevertheless, some positive changes have been made, albeit slowly. For instance, the Refugee and Migratory Movements Research Unit, a research institute at the University of Dhaka, has been increasingly vocal on various migration issues and is involving more NGOs into their advocacy work and policy recommendations. At conferences and consultation meetings, it also addresses the issue of female migration. It played an important role in convincing the government to lift the ban on female migration in 2003. With such initiatives, it is likely that NGOs will develop their voices and capacity in migration-policy making in the near future.

National Identity and Emigration Policies

Another important determinant for emigration policies is national identity. In recent years, scholars have been highlighting the fact that an immigration policy is not just a simple response of the state to domestic labor demand; it is also the product of national identity—the way in which the nation perceives itself. An industrialized nation carefully chooses which groups to let in; its decision depends on how it understands itself as a nation and how it perceives certain groups within its identity framework. For instance, Rogers Brubaker[25] has argued that historically, France has had lenient immigration policies because its nation-building process was not rooted in a particular racial or ethnic group's nationalism; rather, it emerged from the battle for freedom and liberty. That nation's founding values—"Liberty, Equality, Fraternity"—apply not only to the French but also to those who are not French. In this sense, French national identity has been based on political values rather than the identity of a particular group.[26]

Brubaker's argument about national identity is also applicable to the opposite mindset which is discernible in some major destination countries in Asia. In Japan, for instance, beliefs about racial purity and cultural homogeneity shape national identity, even though those beliefs are based on myth rather than reality. This national identity has helped create the general understanding that Japan exists for the "Japanese" people, however contested "Japanese-ness" might be. This identity has resulted in immigration policies that allow the descendants of Japanese emigrants—*Nikkeijin*—to enter Japan. Many of these *Nikkeijin* are third- and fourth-generation Brazilians and Peruvians and thus do not speak Japanese and do not necessarily share the culture; however, the fact that they are of Japanese ethnic origin has been sufficient for the government to grant them special immigration status. In the same way, Germany's immigration policy allows the long-dispersed "*Aussiedlers*" (ethnic Germans) to return to their homeland from Eastern Europe and the former Soviet Union, based on the similar idea that the country should accept those who share the same racial origin.[27] Such self-understanding of the nation based on ethnic identity has a significant impact on immigration policies.

This principle is not limited to immigration policies; it similarly applies to emigration policies. Many states try to control the emigration of their citizens, and do so partly on the basis of national identity. For instance, during the Cold War, the communist and socialist states strictly controlled the emigration of their citizens in order to "protect" them from capitalism, but also in order to protect their own communist or socialist ideologies. As will be discussed in the later sections, national identity affects emigration policies in many developing countries as well.

With regard to emigration policies, national identity is largely concerned with democracy, human rights, and gender. As discussed earlier, most states in Asia grant more freedom of movement to men than to women. Emigration policies for women often differ from those for men; this is because emigration policies for women are not only economically driven but also "value-driven." This value is derived partly from the state political philosophy and from deeply rooted social norms that constitute the foundations of national identity.

The Philippines and Sri Lanka identify themselves as democratic states and place importance on human rights. Neither country sees a comprehensive ban on migration as a legitimate option any more. The educated elites in both countries recognize the right to emigrate as a human right. Many state officials and NGO staff whom I interviewed repeatedly mentioned that freedom of movement is a constitutional right of their nationals, both men and women, and that the government cannot stop them from going overseas to work. When I asked why the country has never banned female migration, a senior official of the Ministry of Labour in Sri Lanka said: "Women have a right to work and right to migrate. The government is not supposed to stop them. If we do, that's against democracy."

Philippine officials have learned from experience that the bans did not necessarily have the desired effects. For instance, when the Aquino administration banned the migration of domestic workers to Kuwait and Saudi Arabia in 1988 because of frequent maltreatment by employers, some women still entered Kuwait through Bahrain, Oman, and other countries. When the ban was lifted in 1997, an estimated 14,000 Filipina domestic workers were working in Kuwait.[28]

In Bangladesh, by contrast, the ban on the emigration of unskilled women has been generally accepted as a means of protecting vulnerable women, even though the Bangladeshi constitution acknowledges freedom of movement as a right of all citizens. This state policy is noteworthy, given the country's difficult economic situation. Bangladesh is one of the poorest countries in the world; its per capita GDP was US$1,700 (less than half of Sri Lanka's) and its total national debt was US$11 billion (much higher than Sri Lanka's US$7.7 billion) in 2002.[29] If labor migration policy is driven purely by economics, one would have expected Bangladesh to massively promote female migration in order to generate more remittances. Given the strong demand for Muslim domestic workers in the Middle East, the migration of Bangladeshi women would almost certainly have contributed greatly to the Bangladeshi economy. Yet an opposite policy has been followed—the country has banned women from working abroad as domestic workers. Although the ban was lifted in 2003, the current administration still tries to control female migration and places many restrictions on the emigration of female domestic workers.

To understand state emigration policies for women in Bangladesh, one must understand that the protection of women has strong social implications for national identity. The national identity of Bangladesh has multiple dimensions, one of which is related to religious values. Many policy makers referred to the Islamic teachings which state clearly that men should protect women. Indeed, Verse 4:34 of the Holy Quran declares: "Men are the protectors and maintainers of women, because God has given the one more (strength) than the other, and because they support them from their means."[30]

The idea that women must be protected is widely accepted in Bangladeshi society, and from this has arisen the norm that a woman should not leave her house without a man to "guard" her. According to a male official of the Ministry of Labour,[31] a devout Muslim man should ideally be able to say: "My wife never sees the sun." Of course, the reality is different. In the modern era, when more women work outside the home, it is difficult to maintain such ideals. Especially among poor households, women cannot afford to stay home. Even so, the view that women must not be given free rein is shared by the government elites and by other influential organizations. When referring to the ban on female migration, a senior director of the BMET argued the following:

> From the religious point of view, women are not allowed to go out to work. They should be in *purdah*.[32] But this does not mean that women cannot work [overseas]. If the safety and security are there, women can work [but since they are not there, women should not work abroad]. We get the remittances of seven thousand crore[33] taka [US$1.4 billion] from male workers [every year]. It's not necessary that women workers go [overseas].

More importantly, the idea that men should protect women has gone beyond the family context that the Quran seems to have implied originally. It has been extended to include the role of the state. In principle, every state is indeed responsible for protecting its citizens, both men and women, but the urge to protect women is undeniably strong in Bangladesh. Most state officials believed that the state was the supreme "protector" of women, whether they were consciously or unconsciously internalizing Quranic teachings. Faced with the difficulty in providing effective protections for migrant women overseas, the Bangladeshi Cabinet decided that the most effective way of protecting them from abuse and exploitation by foreign employers was to forbid them to go abroad.

Of course, the Bangladeshi authorities do not entirely ignore the economic aspects of female migration. The Ziaur administration lifted the ban in 1991 in the hope of benefiting economically from migrant women's remittances. Overall, however, economic concerns have taken a back seat when priorities are being set for emigration policies for women. The policies for female migration are much more value-oriented than for male migration. The state well understood that migrant women could bring in more remittances and much-needed foreign currencies, yet the ban on female migration remained until 2003, and many restrictions continue to apply. The labor minister announced a clear policy: "Earning foreign exchange *at the cost of the honor of our women* abroad is not acceptable." (author's italics) [34]

The senior director of the state recruitment agency, Bangladesh Overseas Employment and Services, has emphasized that the policy restricting female migration is driven by Bangladeshis' social values rather than by economic benefits:

Money is not everything. We are poor, we know. But we have got the social values for women that we don't sell for money. . . . They [other labor exporting countries] are exporting them [women] as products. . . . As far as we are concerned, we are very religious. What *their ladies* can do, *our ladies* can't do. [The] social system is different. *We have a social value which respects women.* (author's italics)

According to state officials, the ban on female migration is meant to respect Bangladeshi women. They harshly criticize some other Asian countries for not respecting women—that is, for profiting from women's remittances while exposing them to abuse and harassment by foreign employers. Many policy makers see promoting female migration as no different from exporting women as commodities. In fact, many state officials and NGO staff distinguish Bangladesh from other labor-exporting countries such as Thailand and the Philippines in terms of social values. They declare proudly that their society is more moral than others. "Not being like them" engenders a strong sense of pride among Bangladeshi policy makers and intellectuals, reaffirming their national identity and dignity. One official's statement clearly reflected this:

If you ban [female migration], you bring a value and dignity to your country. Money doesn't give you dignity. . . . That sort of money [remittances from migrant women] we don't require—selling one's value, dignity, and status. . . . *Once men or society loses our dignity and status, what will you do with the money?* (author's italics)

His remarks exemplify the patriarchal attitudes that are quite typical of Bangladeshi policy makers. "Men" and "society" are often viewed as synonymous, which indicates that men are considered as the primary actors in the society. If "their" women's safety were to be threatened, both "men" and "society" would lose their dignity and status. Dignity and status comprise important components of their national identity. The state assumes the role of "protector of women" and projects such an image to the public. The same attitude even exists among female policy makers. A female senior official supported the ban on female migration, contending that the state must protect poor women. "Setting moral values straight" is important for Bangladeshi state officials. Even if the ban were to increase illegal migration and render women more vulnerable, banning female migration was still considered worthwhile. The ban helped articulate the values that the state considered desirable for the society. In this sense, the ban successfully projected an image of the state as a "bearer of morals" as well as a "protector of women."

Of course, every policy has multiple dimensions, and it is possible that the ban on female migration served other purposes. First, the ban helped the state avoid public criticism for not extending migrant women enough protection. If the media reported any cases of abuse of Bangladeshi migrant women abroad, the government could conveniently argue that the women themselves were responsible because they had violated the rules. Politicians and state officials would not be blamed and would not be exposed to any political risks. Second, by significantly lowering the number of Bangladeshi migrant women overseas, the Ministry of Foreign Affairs could avoid diplomatic strains with the governments of destination countries. According to a local scholar, an official of the Ministry of Labour told him it was officials in the Ministry of Foreign Affairs that had suggested a ban on female migration. This same source reported that the Ministry of Foreign Affairs had been finding it difficult to negotiate with the governments of destination countries on the protection of Bangladeshi women. They were apparently reluctant to deal with this issue, especially because most destination countries are important trading partners for Bangladesh. Wherever the government's true intentions lay, the ban on emigration of unskilled women served various purposes.

The value dimension of emigration policies does not necessarily represent religious values alone. *Islam as a religion does not always lead to the restrictive policies for female migration.* As I pointed out earlier, Indonesia, a Muslim country, is a major source of female migrant labor. What matters most for emigration policies is the perceptions of policy makers and elites with regard to women and their role in economic development. In the case of Indonesia, the Suharto administration strongly promoted export-oriented industrialization, which increased women's labor force participation in factories, both inside and outside export processing zones (EPZs). In setting out to globalize the Indonesian economy, Suharto recognized that he would have to promote the emigration of both men and women in order to increase remittances and thereby increase its foreign currency holdings. His determination to increase emigration was reflected in the official development plan for 1989–94, which set a goal of "exporting" 500,000 Indonesian women workers abroad.

Indonesia is a Muslim country; however, the national identity that the Suharto administration held to was not that of an "Islamic state" but rather that of a "developmental state"—one in which the state would play a strong leadership role in economic development within global capitalism. However, after Suharto stepped down and a democratic regime took power, Indonesia's national identity began to shift in the direction of emphasizing democracy and human rights. The Megawati administration followed in Suharto's footsteps in promoting the emigration of both men and women, but it also paid more attention to the plight of Indonesian migrant women. In fact, it banned further recruitment of domestic workers for the Middle East in 1998, albeit only as a temporary measure.[35] The purpose of the temporary ban was to ensure that recruitment agencies in receiving countries registered all contracts at an Indonesian embassy. In this way the government could strengthen its control of labor migration and better protect migrant women.

Emigration policies reflect national identity and social values. National identity is especially important for the governments of developing countries, which have found themselves overwhelmed by economic globalization. These countries have no choice but to open their economies and promote export-oriented industrialization. This, however, exposes them to the powerful influence of "Western" values and cultures. In this context, government restrictions or outright bans on female migration can be interpreted as forms of resistance to economic globalization and to the "moral degradation" associated with it. By "setting the values straight," Bangladeshi policy makers were trying to retain their national identity and dignity in the globalization process. For them, this had to involve restricting women's right to movement. Protecting women represented the core of the value dimension of state policies, despite its negative consequences for women.

The Symbolic Gender Politics

The policy-making process for female migration also entails what I refer to as "symbolic gender politics." I define symbolic gender politics as political practices whereby women are used as symbolic tools of the state to serve its interests. As McClintock notes, in nationalism discourse, women often are constructed as the symbolic bearers of the nation and biological reproducers of the members of national collectivities.[36] Thus, sexual abuse and harassment against women by foreigners is not only a disgrace for the individual victims but also a humiliation for the state and nation. This is partly related to the fact that sexual abuse and rape have commonly been written in law as a crime against male property rather than against women's personhood.[37] In this context, the abuse, rape, and harassment of migrant women abroad mean violations of male property and of *the symbolic property of the nation.*

This does much to explain why sexual crimes and violence against women so often take place during wars and other conflicts: women are symbols of authenticity and of national or ethnic identity.[38] In such conflicts, rape is often used by male groups as a means of displaying their power or dominance over their enemies. A typical example of this is the war in Bosnia; during the months and years of "ethnic cleansing," countless Muslim women were systematically raped by Christian Serbs. These Muslim women were viewed as the inner sanctum of the patriarchal homeland of Muslims; for the Serbs, their mass rape was symbolically of a piece with the seizure and destruction of Muslim property.[39] The rapes by the Serbs were also meant to prevent the "mothers of the nation" from reproducing a "pure" Muslim nation in that these women were the symbols and bearers of Muslim purity and the national lineage.[40] Many similar cases have been observed in other parts of the world. In South Asia there was a systematic rape of 30,000 Bengali women during the war between West Pakistan (the present Pakistan) and East Pakistan (the present Bangladesh).[41] According to Siddiqi, the rapes signified a violation of East Pakistan's territory and honor and showed that the state was unable to protect its land and women.[42] Women indeed represent a national space and territory vis-à-vis foreign enemies; in this sense they constitute the symbolic foundations of nationalism.

Women's symbolic nature affects the emigration policies of many developing countries. It is because women are not a value-neutral workforce: they symbolize a nation's dignity and constitute the foundations of nationalism and national identity. The public tends to be more sensitive to their abuse and exploitation than to that of men. The Contemplacion case in the Philippines was the very case in point. The execution of a Filipina domestic worker, Flor Contemplacion, by the Singapore authorities tremendously enraged Filipinos back home.[43] As Gonzales remarked, her death triggered the explosion of "the migration volcano." President Fidel Ramos observed that he had never seen the Filipino people so angry since the assassination of

Senator Benigno Aquino in 1983.[44] A member of Ramos's Cabinet explained it to me this way:

> Women are an emotional issue. When Flor Contemplacion was hanged, many Filipino men thought it could have been their wife or daughter. You know, the Philippines has this macho culture and men get very emotional about women getting hurt.

The Contemplacion case involved more than the death of a woman who might have been innocent. She had been executed by "the Other"—by *foreigners* who, in their view, had not given her a fair trial. This was what mattered to the citizens, especially male Filipinos.

Sexual abuse and the harassment of women are hardly uncommon *within* these countries; in fact, many news items about rape and sexual harassment appear in local newspapers. Yet incidents of *one's own women* being abused and harassed abroad by *foreign men* are perceived differently from such domestic cases. Abuses of women by foreigners arouse much more outrage and nationalism among the public because these are crimes against the nation's symbolic property. When such a public reaction occurs, the state often acts promptly to restrict or ban female migration in order to underscore its role as the "protector of women." Of course, as seen in the case of Bangladesh, these public reactions are not always necessary for the state to develop restrictive emigration policies for women. Nevertheless, even in Bangladesh, policy makers felt that the abuse of migrant women threatened their country's dignity. For Bangladeshi officials, it was crucial to protect the female workers themselves *and* to protect those women's sexual purity from foreign employers—for maintaining both national dignity and pride.

Furthermore, emigration policies for women carry an especially strong value dimension because of the limited enforcement and implementation capacities of the state. In a sense, these policies are symbolic means for the state to inject its own views and gender values into society. These policies also serve to buttress the state's image as a protector of women. Bans on the emigration of unskilled women are certainly examples of this.

In the Philippines, symbolic politics was in play in 1999 when the Ramos administration approved a phasing out of female migration. This policy was a response to recommendations made by a presidential commission that had been formed immediately after Flor Contemplacion was executed in Singapore. Nevertheless, no effective measures were actually taken to pursue this goal, and the number of women who left the country hit a record high in 1999. The "phasing-out initiative" was an expression of symbolic politics in that the state was informing the public that it wanted to discourage female migration instead of promoting it. This was a crucial strategy—especially in the wake of Contemplacion's hanging—because ever since the Marcos regime, the public had perceived the state as a promoter and exploiter of overseas employment. Policy makers must have known that a phasing out was impossible, yet they considered it important to establish such a policy as a way to make its intentions clear to the public. This policy was intended to change the state's image from that of an exploiter of migrant women to that of a protector. Although in the end the phasing out never took place, the policy was a useful strategic tool in that it symbolized the state's values and stance. The rushed passage of RA 8042 and the ratification of the UN Migrant Workers Convention were two other responses, the intention of which was to show Filipinos that their government was doing its best to protect its citizens abroad.

Conclusion

Emigration policies for women are value-driven because women are more than just a labor force. Women not only represent the values of the state but also embody national pride and dignity. In this sense, sexual violence against migrant women amounts to atrocities against the state and society. Protecting women is perceived as a responsibility of the state, and this affects policies for migrant women who are exposed to sexual harassment and abuse by foreigners. Restrictive emigration policies for women are the products of symbolic gender politics. Through emigration policies for women, the state projects its own stance and image as a "protector" of women, and puts forward certain social values about women that it wants to inject into society.

Like many other policies, emigration policies are outcomes of various institutional and political factors. For instance, they have some component of path dependency, tracing their existence to past policy legacies especially as they relate to economic development. Liberal economic policies with a strong export orientation and past strong promotion of male labor emigration tend to be associated with lenient policies for female migration. What is unique about emigration policies for women is that the degree of such path dependency is rather weak and unstable. It is easily jeopardized by other factors, such as reports by media and embassies about the abuse and exploitation of migrant women. Because these reports undermine national dignity, states tend to tighten their policies for female migration, placing further restrictions on women's emigration as a means to protect them.

Where civil society is well developed, as it is in the Philippines, strong controls and heavy restrictions on female migration by the state cannot be a long-term solution, because migration NGOs and recruitment agencies would immediately raise their voices and protest. It is alleged that in the Philippines, some powerful politicians own or have very close ties with recruitment agencies, and thus try to preserve their business interests by keeping the emigration gates open. Migration NGOs also exert some influence. The Aquino administration's ban on female migration was repealed after NGOs and business groups protested, arguing for women's freedom of movement and right to work. By contrast, in many other countries in Asia, migration NGOs are not well developed and thus have not been influential in ensuring women's freedom of movement and right to work abroad. In Bangladesh, where migration NGOs are relatively underdeveloped, some NGOs even endorsed the ban on female migration; they supported the state's goal, which was to protect "their" women from abuse and exploitation by foreign employers. However, the growing efforts by some NGOs in recent years helped repeal the ban on female migration in 2003.

Overall, emigration policies for women are not a simple outcome of political negotiations over conflicting interests, nor are they the result of simple economic calculations. Rather, they are an outcome of complex interactions between national identity and symbolic gender politics. In fact, emigration policies for women are often made high up in the political chain, often without parliamentary debate or public hearings.

The policies for female migration are also value statements, informing the society of the state's moral stance. Therefore, these policies are drafted by a small number of senior officials in the form of presidential or ministerial decrees and are penetrated into state agencies for implementation. Especially in developing countries with very modest budgets for public spending, the full or even moderate level of policy enforcement can be difficult. As a consequence, these policies tend to become symbolic banners that represent national identity and gender-related values instead of actually bringing about substantial results.

State policies always have a value dimension or a "public face." This is especially so with policies for female migration because of the values and symbolic meanings that women embody. Thus the policies become more oriented toward setting values "right" by restricting women's migration. Even if the policies do not function as they should, they sometimes exist in order to present the state's views on what the situation should be.

Although not perfectly enforced, however, value-driven emigration policies do affect the overall level of female migration. As was seen in Chapter 1, all of the major sending states of migrant women have adopted relatively open emigration policies for women, whereas most of the "non-senders" have adopted restrictive or closed policies. In the case of Bangladesh, restrictive emigration policies have helped block large-scale female migration. Emigration policies do make a difference in terms of setting an overall framework by legitimizing or delegitimating female migration.

Nevertheless, emigration policies are obviously not the only determinants of female migration. There are always some women who do not comply with policies, and the level of non-compliance varies between countries. In the Philippines, the ban on migration of domestic workers to Kuwait was not effective because women were willing to emigrate through unofficial channels, and a total of 14,000 of them ended up working there at the time of the Gulf War. By contrast, the number of Bangladeshi women who have gone against their country's comprehensive ban on domestic workers is relatively small. Even the NGO's estimate, which local scholars believe to be too high, suggests that there are only 40,000 Bangladeshi domestic workers in the entire Middle East region, including those who are legally employed by Bangladeshi citizens.[45] Given that the female labor force in Bangladesh is almost twice as large as that in the Philippines, this estimate indicates that many fewer women emigrate from Bangladesh than from the Philippines.

Economic indicators show that the Philippines fare much better than Bangladesh in terms of per capita income. Why, then, are more Filipino women willing to migrate than Bangladeshi women? To understand the patterns of female migration, microlevel analyses of female migration are essential. In the next chapter, I will examine migrant women by focusing on their socio-economic status and decision-making power within households.

CHAPTER 5

The Road from Home: Women's Autonomy, Migration, and the Trapping Mechanism

FOR MOST WOMEN in developing countries, the decision to work abroad does not come easily. Married women often worry whether their husband will stay faithful and whether their children will be well looked after and able to cope emotionally with their mother's absence. Single women worry about their elderly parents or younger siblings. The risks of abuse and harassment by foreign employers also cast a shadow on their decisions. In fact, most women perceive migration as a major life-changing event, and thus spend quite a long time contemplating it.

Once their mind is set, however, they become determined to go. Some women migrate over the objections of their parents or husbands. Others do not even consult with other household members. Miriam, a cheerful woman in her early thirties, did not tell her husband she was going abroad until the day of her departure because she thought he would object. With a laugh, she said: "I woke him up early in the morning and said I was going to Malaysia for two years on that day. He was shocked and was trying to stop me, but it was too late!"

While Miriam's was a rather extreme case, many accounts of migrant women revealed the importance of examining their autonomy in the analyses of international migration. In major source countries of migrant women such as the Philippines and Sri Lanka, most women made their own decisions about migration instead of passively accepting the decisions of others. By contrast, in Bangladesh, from which fewer women emigrate, women had less autonomy over their decision-making. Clearly, then, women's autonomy and decision-making power are central to the causal mechanism of international female migration. Indeed, as discussed earlier, macro-policies alone cannot determine patterns of migration because they cannot dictate individual behavior. Women do not simply subject themselves to state policies; they think and act on their own, sometimes in defiance of the state. Women's agency therefore has to be integrated into the analytical framework.

This chapter shifts the focus from macro-policies to micro-individuals and highlights the role of the migrant women themselves in emigration processes. First it examines the "faces" of migrant women by presenting their socioeconomic profiles and ideal types. Then it scrutinizes the socialization processes undergone by migrants. The roles that social networks play and the effects of "migration culture" on individual women are elucidated. The third section of this chapter analyzes the impact of women's autonomy on decisions to migrate. It discusses how gender roles and women's autonomy within households determine patterns of international female migration. Finally, this chapter puts forward a concept that I call "trapping mechanisms," which lead migrant women to extend their overseas stays, or migrate more than once, or both. Some migrant women return home before the end of the contract because of maltreatment or for other reasons, but the majority of them stay longer than they had initially planned, and take up another contract again to work abroad. The reasons why migrant women become "trapped" in the destination country or migrate repeatedly—the phenomenon called "circular migration"—will also be investigated.

Migrant Women: Who Are They?

The monolithic image of migrant women is that they are poor, rural, and uneducated. However, in actuality, they constitute a quite diverse group. They come from various socioeconomic backgrounds, with much depending on which country they are from and which one they are migrating to. Filipinas are at the top of the socioeconomic hierarchy of migrant women in Asia; they tend to be better educated and to have more professional experience, and as a consequence, they tend to make higher wages in their destination countries. By contrast, Bangladeshi migrant women occupy the lowest rungs in terms of educational and professional background and, it follows, wage levels. This section is based mainly on my field survey of 116 migrant women from the Philippines, Sri Lanka, and Bangladesh.[1] As discussed earlier, far fewer Bangladeshi women emigrate abroad than Filipina and Sri Lankan women. The ban on emigration of domestic workers was still in place at the time of my fieldwork. Hence, my sample for Bangladesh is very small—only eleven migrant women. For this reason, whenever relevant, I also include nine cases of "quasi-migrants" in the analyses of Bangladeshi migrant women: two were "prospective migrants" who were about leave the country; and seven were "attempted migrants" who paid the fees but could not emigrate because the agents cheated them and disappeared without providing jobs. Though not having actual migration experience, these women also provide significant insights for our understanding of international female migration.

DEMOGRAPHIC CHARACTERISTICS

Most migrant women were relatively young—a large majority were between 20 and 39 at the time of their migration. Regarding Filipinas, 59 percent of current and former migrants were in the 20–29 age group, and the mean age for all migrant Filipino women was 29.6. Sri Lankan migrants had a similar demographic profile: their mean age was 30.5. Migration scholars have generally assumed that Sri Lankan migrant women tend to be older; recent government statistics indicate they are not. Since the late 1990s, Sri Lankan migrant women have been getting younger. Since 2000, the number of migrant women in the 20–24 group has more than doubled.[2]

Migrant women from Bangladesh were the youngest, with a mean age of twenty-five; the great majority of them were in their early twenties when they left the country. Bangladeshi women tend to marry young—when they are eighteen on average[3]—and low-income Bangladeshi women marry even younger. This means they often need additional income during their early twenties as their children grow older. By the time they are forty, their children have already grown up and "married out" or become financially independent. The average Bangladeshi woman retires at forty-four.[4] When I interviewed slum residents in Dhaka, the capital city, women over forty said they had never thought of emigrating as domestic workers because they were "too old" to do the necessary hard work. In Bangladesh, where the average life expectancy is extremely low—only 59.4[5]—people over forty are normally not the primary workforce as far as the low-income population is concerned.

Most migrant women were married. Bangladeshis had the highest marriage rate: 60 percent were married and the rest were either separated or widowed; none of them was single at the time of emigration. This is due to early marriage and to the strong moral code that discourages single women from leaving home alone. For Sri Lankans, the percentage of married women was also high (52 percent), reflecting social mores similar to those of Bangladesh, although the degree of social pressure on women seems much weaker in Sri Lanka. Filipinas were rather divided: 44 percent of women were married whereas 40 percent were single at the time of emigration.

Previous studies have found a higher proportion of married women among migrants,[6] but this composition has been changing. The data from

Sri Lanka indicate that the presence of single women in international mi-gration has been increasing gradually over the past decade.[7] These changes in migrants' demographics—more young single women among migrants—are related to changes in social environment in the Philippines and Sri Lanka, which I will discuss in Chapter 6.

EDUCATION LEVEL

With regard to education, Filipina migrant women are the best educated relative to Sri Lankan and Bangladeshi women. However, this does not mean that all Filipina migrant women are well educated. Filipinas often de-scribe themselves as having a "college education," but in fact, most of them are college drop-outs. In my sample, only 13 percent had a college diploma; a further 15 percent attended college without completing a degree. Other studies have found that there are more college drop-outs than graduates among Filipina migrant domestic workers.[8] Many of them had wanted to continue their higher education but were compelled by financial difficulties to drop out and seek work. In a diploma-oriented society such as the Philip-pines, those without a college diploma are treated the same as high school graduates even if they have spent a few years in college. Furthermore, given the tight labor market, high-paying jobs in the formal sector are always al-located to the graduates of the top universities, not to those who have grad-uated from middle- or lower-ranked colleges unless the latter have strong family connections. Educated women who cannot find employment in the Philippines seek alternative opportunities abroad.

Sri Lankan migrant women tend to be less educated than Filipinas, al-though relatively well educated compared with women in most developing countries. Sri Lanka has long been known for its high literacy rate among women, which is a legacy of past socialist rule. The literacy rate for women was 80 percent as early as the 1970s and had increased to almost 90 percent by 2000; that year the average female literacy rate in *all* developing countries was only 66 percent.[9] In my sample, 6.3 percent of Sri Lankan migrant women had a college education; 10.4 percent had passed the "A level" exam (the equivalent of grade twelve); and 52 percent had passed the "O level" exam (the equivalent of grade ten). The percentage of college-educated women was not very high; even so, most women had at least a secondary education and had attained a sufficient literacy level. Yet it must be noted that high literacy and adequate education levels have not often worked to the advantage of Sri Lankan women who are employed overseas. My re-spondents with ten years of education did not understand or speak English well because they had been taught only in a local language, either Sinhalese or Tamil. Most of them could hold a simple conversation in English and read some words; but around one-quarter of them had been unable to read their employment contract and for that reason had signed many documents and bank checks blindly both before and after departure.

Bangladeshi women were the least educated of the three groups: only one of the eleven migrants and one of the nine "quasi-migrants" whom I surveyed had any formal education. And even they had completed only grade three and five respectively. The rest had no education at all and were completely illiterate; not one of them could even write her name, let alone read or write. It was entirely impossible for these women to understand the contract documents. All of this reflects the low education levels from which Bangladesh suffers in general. In 1980, when most of my respondents were of school age, only 26 percent of all Bangladeshi women had reached the education level of grade five.[10] The literacy rate for Bangladeshi women is still low. In 2002 it was only 31.4 percent for adults and 41.1 percent for youth—far below the average for women in developing countries.[11]

Education is a vitally important factor for the process of female migration. It does not directly affect women's decisions to migrate, but it does much to shape their mentality, life attitudes, and orientations for upward social mobility. In the Philippines and Sri Lanka, education helps women develop an interest in foreign cultures and languages. Education also empowers women by giving them the self-confidence to try new experiences as well as the courage to face challenges. Furthermore, it gives women motivation to seek better life. They know the importance of education in obtaining a high-paying job, and are thus willing to pay for quality education for their children or siblings. Such education, however, is often costly, and this compels women to work abroad.

In Bangladesh, by contrast, most low-income women are illiterate, which tends to make them passive as well as indifferent to the world in general. Low-income Bangladeshi women even lack general knowledge about their own society. During the interviews, I was often stunned that some women did not understand the difference between recruitment agencies and the government. Many women fear strangers outside their own village, let alone employers in foreign countries.

Women with little education are generally not interested in taking up new challenges to improve their lives. Upward mobility is often foreseeable for those with education. Bangladeshi women in slums and poor villages spend most of their lives in the "culture of poverty"[12] where education—a hope for upward mobility—is rarely available. They also never learn that hard work can be often rewarded. The lack of experience with success discourages them from developing ambitions or high goals. Most of them accept impoverishment as their destiny. Clearly, education shapes women's mentality and their motives for seeking overseas employment.

OCCUPATIONAL BACKGROUND

The three groups of women also varied greatly with regard to their past occupations. This reflected the differences in education. Most of the Filipina migrant women had worked in white-collar jobs: sales clerk, secretary, nurse, teacher, and so on. In my sample, only 15.1 percent had been housewives. By contrast, most of the Bangladeshi and Sri Lankan migrant women had been housewives—60 and 55 percent respectively—before taking employment overseas.

The results from my own study (and from others) belie the long-held assumption that many migrant women are young single women—often former production workers in export processing zones (EPZs). It was assumed that the employment practices of EPZs generated a pool of potential migrant women. EPZs hired a large number of young single women from rural areas who were easy to fire when they got old or became pregnant or when factories relocated elsewhere. Women who left EPZs then stayed in the urban area, where they joined the ranks of the unemployed because of the "cultural distance" from their communities of origin. It was hypothesized that these women comprised the pool of prospective emigrants.[13]

Perhaps some migrant women fit this description, but the empirical data show that the occupational backgrounds of migrant women are far more diverse than was previously assumed. Many case studies point out that only a small fraction of migrant women are former factory workers.[14] In my sample, only 17 percent of Filipinas, 8.5 percent of Sri Lankans, and 5 percent of Bangladeshis had worked in factories. Moreover, most of these workers had been employed mainly *outside* EPZs. As I will demonstrate later, EPZs indeed employ many women, but these women are still a very small percentage of the overall female workforce. My fieldwork also suggested that most former EPZ workers did not emigrate overseas but found local jobs instead. The EPZs have done much to increase acceptance of female labor force participation in general—a subject I discuss further in the following chapter—but the data show that there is no direct linkage between the EPZs and international female migration.

PROFILES OF MIGRANT WOMEN BY DESTINATIONS

As noted earlier, Filipina migrant women have the highest socioeconomic profile among the three groups, followed by Sri Lankans and then Bangladeshis. While these are general group characteristics, the profiles of migrant women can significantly differ by country of destination. For instance, migrants in Hong Kong tend to have a white-collar background and to be better educated than migrants in the Middle East. According to my survey, 57 percent of Filipinas in Hong Kong had attended college and 79 percent had been white-collar workers at one time. By contrast, only 8 percent of migrants in the United Arab Emirates had some college education and only 12.5 percent had a white-collar background. Similar differences were observed among Sri Lankan migrant women. Hong Kong apparently attracts migrant women with higher profiles because the wages are higher there and the working conditions are better. In addition, recruitment agencies tend to select women with higher profiles for Hong Kong because Hong Kong employers prefer better-educated workers with a good command of English (see Chapter 2). Many poor women choose the Middle East as a destination because jobs are easily available and the fees are lower. Filipinas need to pay only US$250–400 to work in Middle Eastern countries; to work in Hong Kong, they need to pay US$1,100–1,300. Sri Lankans pay US$250–$300 for the Middle East, whereas to work in Hong Kong, they must pay US$800–$925 in cash or $1,100–1,900 in salary deductions. Clearly, the Middle East is a more affordable destination for low-income women. Such affordability is an indication of unpopularity among migrants; educated ones especially prefer not to work in the Middle East because of its notorious working conditions (no holiday, long work hours, and high risk of harassment) and low wages.

This geographical stratification is not limited to Asia. In fact, female migration has become globally stratified. For instance, migrants [15] in the United States, Canada, and Europe tend to have the highest socioeconomic status—that is, the highest levels of education and occupational status prior to migration. This is partly a result of demand-side factors, but it is also a function of the migration fees that migrants must pay. When I interviewed recruitment agencies, I learned that they were charging more than US$7,000 per individual for positions in the United States and Canada, and US$3,000–5,000 for Italy. While the full amount was not due at the time of application, the migrant was required to pay a large cash deposit prior to departure. Many Filipinas—even those with a middle-class background—took out high-interest loans to pay such a deposit. Low-income women find it almost impossible to take out loans for this purpose because they do not have sufficient savings or collateral. Some people, of course, find ways around this problem—for example, they arrive in the destination country as tourists and seek illegal employment, or they find jobs through personal networks and thereby avoid having to pay fees (a system often called "direct hire"). In general, however, migrant women who work legally in North America and

Europe occupy the highest rung on the socioeconomic ladder among the world's migrant women.

By contrast, most migrant women in Asia are less qualified and belong to no higher than the lower-middle class. Many of the women I interviewed in Asia dreamed of going to North America or Europe but could not afford to do so. Migrant women in Hong Kong and Taiwan were relatively well educated and skilled, but because they lacked capital, they were unable to migrate to the United States, Canada, or Europe. Migrant women in the Middle East were the poorest and least educated. It is important to take such differences into account when analyzing the backgrounds and motives of female migrants.

Why Migrate? The Ideal Types of Migrant Women

Why on earth do women leave home for foreign countries? The primary reason is an economic one—all of them expect to earn money to support their family, build a house, purchase land, pay for their children's education, repay debts, and so on. However, it is not the only reason as the levels of economic need can vary. For some middle-class Filipinas in North America and Europe, migration tends to be a matter "of social mobility at the household level and of adventure and experience at the individual level." [16] Many migrant women in the Middle East, on the other hand, belong to the low-income class and migrate because their families are in serious financial need.

Given all this diversity among migrant women in Asia, it is difficult to generalize about motives for migration. These women's economic needs vary not only with the destination country but also with age, marital status, and stage in life. Nevertheless, I still think it useful to categorize the underlying orientations of migrant women. One way of doing this is to construct "ideal types." I use the Weberian term "ideal types" because they do not necessarily represent the exact situations of individual migrant woman. It is impossible to construct typologies into which all migrant women can be classified perfectly, since the motivations of human beings are so often complex. Having interviewed many migrant women, I can say that the reasons for migration are not simple and straightforward. Of course, the vast majority of migrants expect financial returns from working overseas and want to save money for themselves and their families. However, financial needs are sometimes mixed with or even superseded by factors other than economic ones, such as family problems. From this I conclude that the best way to clarify the underlying causes of female migration at the individual level is to extract the overriding motives of each migrant and mold these findings into ideal types that represent sets of *orientations* of migrant women.

Based on my fieldwork, I put forward five ideal types: (a) "adventurous women," (b) "dutiful daughters," (c) "good mothers and wives," (d) "distressed women," and (e) "destitute women." Because these are merely ideal types in the Weberian sense, some women may fit into two or more categories. In fact, I expect most of them fit multiple categories because individuals' motivations are so complex. Single "dutiful daughters," who say that they migrated mainly in order to help their family, often admit later that they also wanted to see a foreign country and experience a different culture. However, ideal types are still useful to highlight specific orientations of migrant women. Below I describe the five ideal types and give examples of each in the form of profiles of actual migrant women who seem to epitomize the orientation.

"Adventurous Women"

The first ideal type is "adventurous women." These are the ones who decide to work overseas to seek some adventure in life. Adventurous women fall into two groups. The first is comprised of young single women with a moderate level of education. It also includes college dropouts and graduates of minor colleges who have been unable to find a decent job locally. Younger daughters of large families of the lower-middle class fall in this category as well. These women became interested in working overseas while learning about foreign countries at school, or they heard exciting stories from their friends and relatives who had worked overseas. The second (and smaller) group includes older women who are unmarried and have no children. Some are separated, divorced, or widowed and live with their parents or siblings. Many of them are teachers, administrators, or sales clerks — white-collar jobs that pay little and offer limited career mobility. Although most women in both groups do not have any acute problems with daily survival, they belong to the lower middle-class and cannot afford to travel much even within their own country, let alone overseas. Overseas employment, which involves the opportunity to fly on an airplane and live in a foreign country, is appealing to them.

Most of these women are seeking a new experience overseas, but this does not mean they do not have economic motives. On the contrary, many of them dream about living the "middle-class life" so often depicted in the media — purchasing a nice house and stocking it with electronic appliances (a TV, a VCR/DVD, a stereo) and luxury goods (jewelry, cosmetics, designer clothes). Most young single women with no children have fewer financial responsibilities than married women and thus have a stronger orientation toward consumerism. They want more disposable income for conspicuous consumption. Older single women with no children share this tendency to some extent, but generally, they are most worried about financing their retirement and see overseas employment as a means of saving enough money to start a business. In developing countries where social security is limited, many elderly people depend financially on their children. Women without children need more financial resources for their old age. Elenita and Kanthi, whose life stories are described below, are typical "adventurous women."

ELENITA: A YOUNGER SINGLE "ADVENTURER"

Elenita is a charming young Filipina living in a village outside Manila. She worked as a dancer in Cyprus for two years. She was only nineteen when she left the Philippines. After she graduated from high school, she dreamed of going to Europe. A friend of hers was already working in Cyprus as a dancer and encouraged Elenita to join her there. Soon after that, a recruitment agent (a Filipino woman married to a Greek) came to her village to meet applicants. Elenita went to see her and learned that she would not have to pay any recruitment fees if she went to Cyprus as a dancer. Therefore, she decided to go there and signed a contract.

She arrived in Cyprus and began working four hours a day at a dance club, for which she was paid US$350 a month. Although she had a large family including a little brother, she did not often think about supporting them. Only a few times did she send them small sums of money. Nor did she save or invest any money for herself. When I asked her what she did with her salary, she laughed and said: "I bought CDs, appliances, and *lots* of jewelry!" When she returned to the Philippines, she had to sell all of her jewelry to pay the recruitment fees for her brother's migration to Saudi Arabia. What she earned in Cyprus is now all gone. "But at least it was an experience," she said. "I met many people from different countries. My colleagues [dancers] were Macedonians, Yugoslavs, Thais, and so on. I also sat with the customers of different nationalities—Arabs, Europeans, [and] Japanese. I learned a lot." She was very happy with her experience and is willing to work abroad again.

KANTHI

Kanthi is a Sri Lankan domestic worker in Hong Kong. She never married and is now forty-six years old. In Sri Lanka she had a good job as an administrator at a maternity hospital. She left that job and emigrated in 1982 because she "wanted some adventure." She emigrated first to Kuwait, and worked there as a domestic worker for three years. Then she moved to Jordan in 1986 to work as a caregiver for another two years. She came to Hong Kong in 1989 and had been there for ten years when we met. Her parents had passed away long ago, and her only sister was married, so for a time there was no one she needed to support. Then in 1989 her sister got divorced, and since then Kanthi has been supporting her and her five children. After working overseas for seventeen years, she took her savings and bought a house and a piece of land in Sri Lanka. "Now I really don't need money," she said. "People ask me why I work [in Hong Kong]. I say I am trying to learn many things. I have so many friends to take care of, too."

As an old-timer, Kanthi helps many young Sri Lankan domestic workers who have recently arrived in Hong Kong. Every Sunday she attends a gathering of Sri Lankan migrants in a downtown park; there, she listens to her friends' problems and offers them advice. She feels happy and fulfilled by helping them, and she enjoys being respected as a community leader. I asked her if she wanted to go back to Sri Lanka anytime soon. "Not for a while," she said. "I feel free here. In Sri Lanka, people ask me [too] many things." In Sri Lanka, the social pressure on women to get married is so strong that people ask her why she is not married and why she is working abroad. Kanthi does not want to confront those questions, nor does she want to face the stigma that is attached to single women working abroad. She feels much happier in Hong Kong where no one bothers her about these things. She said she wanted to live in Hong Kong as long as she could.

"Dutiful Daughters"

Many scholars have pointed out that women in developing countries are not necessarily more family-oriented than those in industrialized countries. Many of them do seek their own income, freedom from parental control, and new experiences.[17] I fully concur with these findings, but among some migrant women, filial piety and family obligations can still be the driver (at least the initial one) for migration. Women of this ideal type tend to be single and from a large family with many younger siblings or small nieces and nephews.

"Dutiful daughters" often say they migrated overseas mainly in order to support their parents or help with the education of their siblings. Sometimes they have family members who are sick and need expensive medications that the family cannot afford. So they consider it their duty to work overseas and earn money for everyone in the family, since they are single and have no one they need to take care of. They think they are in the best position to migrate overseas. Once they do migrate, they send home large sums of money (almost their entire salary) every month. However, this money is sometimes misused by family members, as I will describe in a later section.

Some single Sri Lankan women emigrate partly in order to assemble a dowry for themselves. Dowries have been legally abolished in most South Asian countries, yet the custom is still alive among all social classes. Typically, the dowry is provided by the parents for their daughter's marriage. In cases where parents cannot afford to offer very much, daughters will be under great stress and worry since too small a dowry (or none at all) can lead to problems in the marriage, to conflicts with in-laws, and sometimes even to physical abuse. In Bangladesh, despite the Dowry Prohibition Act of 1980 and the Cruelty to Women Act of 1983, the dowry is still the primary cause of violence against women. Dowry-related violence against wives has been on the rise in Bangladesh in recent years; this is considered a serious social problem.[18]

In Sri Lanka dowries need not be too high, but many people still believe that providing a sufficient dowry is important for securing a happy marriage and placing a woman on a good footing with her in-laws. A woman whose parents are poor or who has many sisters may have to either accept a dangerous marriage or prepare her own dowry. Some daughters take the latter course and migrate overseas to work. For example, Lalita, a twenty-three-year-old Sri Lankan woman who worked in Hong Kong, said she needed to earn 15,000 rupees (US$210) for her dowry and 25,000 rupees (US$350) for her future. Women who earn their own dowry are looking out for themselves, but they are also helping their parents who otherwise would have to work extremely hard to earn enough money for dowries. These women feel guilty that the entire family has to suffer because so much income must be set aside for dowries. In this sense, dutiful daughters have mixed motives: both self-serving and altruistic.

Filipina domestic workers do not have to worry about dowries because there is no such practice in the Philippines. However, many of them migrate mainly to support their parents and siblings. Amelia is a typical "dutiful daughter."

AMELIA

Amelia is a Filipina domestic worker in the United Arab Emirates. She is from a large, poor family. Before she went to the UAE, she lived with her parents, brother, sister, and two nieces. As soon as she graduated from high school, she looked for a job but without success. She recalled: "Even the places like shopping malls hired young college grads, not high school grads." Her father was a landless farmer and had been having a difficult time making ends meet. Her brother worked as a tailor and her sister as a beautician, but both jobs were part-time and poorly paid.

Amelia had cousins in Hong Kong and a niece in Saudi Arabia; all of them were employed as domestic workers. To her "they seemed pretty successful," and she developed an interest in working abroad. When one of her cousins came back from Hong Kong and started working for a recruitment agency, she told Amelia about her work experience and suggested that she apply for a job that was available in Singapore. "We were a poor family and [our] parents were old," she remembered. "I wanted to give them a good life before they died." In 1991, after consulting her brother, sister, and friends, she decided to take a domestic worker's position in Singapore for two years. She knew it would be a challenge for her since she did not even know how to cook, but she decided to try anyway. She did not tell her parents about her decision until the day before her departure. When she informed them, they were shocked but did not try to stop her. Amelia recalled: "My parents only cried and said, 'Sorry that we are so poor.'"

Amelia paid 7,500 pesos (US$180) to a recruitment agency as a fee down payment and went to Singapore. The rest of the fee was deducted from her salary over six months. Since she did not have any savings prior to leaving for Singapore, she borrowed money from her cousins. She worked hard in Singapore and remitted her entire salary to her sister, who was managing the family's finances. Her sister used the money for food, clothes, a television, and her own daughter's education. But she did not invest or save any of the money. By the time Amelia finished her two-year contract in Singapore and returned to the Philippines, all the money was gone, and the family went back to the same living conditions as before.

"Good Wives and Mothers"

Migrant women who belong to this ideal type are married and often have children. They want a better life for their family members, and they realize they are not earning enough to make ends meet or to provide good education for their children. Some of these women were forced to become breadwinners when the husband fell ill or lost his job. Most "good wives" and "good mothers" say they would never have migrated if circumstances had not required it. While foreign culture was appealing to a few, the vast majority of the "good wives and good mothers" never sought adventure or new experiences. Many of them looked upset when I asked if they were interested in experiencing a different culture. Typically they replied: "I am working here only for my husband and children's future, not for myself." They feel guilty about leaving their children at home and working overseas; yet they also have a strong desire to give their children a better future. By "better future" they often mean a private education in both high school and college. Especially in the Philippines, where the quality of public education is not considered very high, many people try to send their children to private high schools and colleges. In Bangladesh and Sri Lanka, a "better future for children" includes a large dowry. As discussed earlier, some daughters migrate to save money for their own dowry; in the same vein, some mothers work abroad in order to save for their daughters' dowries. When there are a number of daughters in the family, the mother may need to stay abroad for years in order to save up enough dowry money.

"Good wives" are also willing to help their husbands. Some of my respondents migrated in order to cover their husband's debts or medical bills. Many migrant women from the Philippines were entrepreneurial; they saved money for their husband to start a small business. Some of them purchased a jeepney (a converted jeep for local transport) or tricycle (a motorcycle with a covered passenger seat attached) for such purpose. Others started a *sari-sari* store (a small grocery shop) for themselves when they returned home.

"Good wives" in Sri Lanka were not as interested in starting a business. Generally, their goals were to meet the needs of their husband and children—to pay their husband's debts, to cover the family's living expenses, to buy a parcel of land, to build a house, to pay their children's tuition, to save for their daughters' dowries, and so on. Some used their overseas earnings to open a dress shop, but none of them helped the husband start his own business.

Bangladeshi women were the least entrepreneurial. None of them showed any interest in starting a business or investing money for themselves or their husbands. Their overriding goal was daily survival: to feed and clothe the family. The money they earned overseas was too little to start a business in any case, but their lack of entrepreneurship was perhaps due to the lack of education. Without basic education, it is difficult for anyone to develop the ability to set goals and plans in life. Most of my respondents could not think in terms of objectives and strategies. Dire poverty was also a major factor. Since all of them were landless, their first priority was buying a house and land so that they would not have to worry about paying the rent.

The following cases of Cecile and Amelia are typical examples of "good wives and mothers" from the Philippines. Amelia, who was described above as a "dutiful daughter," reappears in this section. Her case illustrates the process of circular migration and changes in migrant women's life stages.

CECILE

Cecile is a thirty-five-year-old Filipina migrant in Hong Kong. She has been working as a domestic worker for six years. She is married and has three children—one boy and two girls—who are waiting for her to return home. Cecile had a difficult time finding a well-paid job in the Philippines, partly because she did not have a college degree. She spent one year in college but could not finish her studies because of financial problems. After earning a secretary's certificate from a vocational school, she worked in a shoe factory in Quezon City for a while. Later, she found work with an NGO. However, her salary there was the minimum wage, and even after she added it to her husband's income, the family found it difficult to make ends meet.

Their financial situation deteriorated suddenly when her husband's business ran into trouble. With three friends, he had opened a store selling bamboo furniture. Since one of them was a local government official and community leader, Cecile's husband and the others trusted him completely and poured most of their savings into the business. Soon after they pooled their money, that person took it all to use for his own business, leaving the store bankrupt. Her husband and the other two partners tried to get the money back but did not succeed. In this way, they lost all their savings.

Cecile decided to work abroad to pay off her husband's debts and overcome the financial setback. Her two sisters were working in Hong Kong at that time, so she asked them to find a job for her. Some time later, one of them told her she had found one for her. Cecile immediately moved to Hong Kong and began working. "It was very hard to leave my family," she recalled, "but I had no choice." She was planning to work in Hong Kong for two more years. "By then, I will be able to save enough money for my family."

It is important to note that the goals of migrant women can change over time. Some single "adventurous women" and "dutiful daughters" turn into "good wives and mothers." After they get married, they emigrate again, but this time their goal is not to support themselves or their parents, but to support their own husband and children. In other cases, their family situation changes as their overseas stay is prolonged. Some women become separated or divorced because their long absence has strained their marriage (the most common cause of marital collapse is the husband's infidelity). At that point, they become the "official breadwinner" and their goal shifts to supporting themselves and their children. Amelia, whom I described earlier as a "dutiful daughter" who wanted to help her parents, made this transition.

AMELIA: FROM A "DUTIFUL DAUGHTER" TO A "GOOD MOTHER"

After Amelia finished her two-year contract in Singapore, she returned to the Philippines and got married. Soon after that, her husband decided to work as a waiter in Malaysia. Therefore, she followed him there and worked as a waitress from 1994 to 1997. They had a daughter in 1997. However, their relationship went through some turmoil, and they separated in 1998. Amelia faced financial instability and realized she would have to work overseas again.

Her goal had shifted from helping her parents and siblings to ensuring a better future for her daughter. She applied through the same recruitment agency as before and found a job as a domestic worker in Abu Dhabi in the United Arab Emirates. Amelia's mother tried to convince her not to work abroad again, saying, "Don't go. You stay here. You can just help your sister [with her work]." Her father had passed away by then, and Amelia thought that her mother probably wanted her to stay close by. Nevertheless, she left home because she wanted to earn more income to give her daughter a better education and a better life.

In Abu Dhabi, Amelia earned 740DH (US$185) a month, working from 5:30 in the morning to 11 at night. She was allowed no holidays. She slept on the floor because there was no bed in her room. Her employers gave her very little food—sometimes none at all. She could not stand these working conditions and ran away to the Philippine Embassy. Despite the hardships she encountered, she remembers her experience as a positive one. She feels that she became more independent and gained self-confidence. She wants to leave the UAE as soon as she can and apply for another job in Hong Kong, and to continue to save money for her daughter.

"Distressed Women"

"Distressed women" have emigrated in order to free themselves from problems at home. Some of them have problems with their in-laws and want to escape their bullying. Others have a husband who is abusive or alcoholic or who is having an affair or has multiple wives. In this last case, women often have to assume a breadwinner's role, since the husband is financially unable to sustain the family. Distressed women have tried in vain to resolve the situation. Thus they see working overseas as the best means to escape from their harsh reality. Often these women hope to save enough money to start a business, become financially independent, and leave their husband and in-laws for good. They see working overseas as a solution to many of their problems. Pacita and Mercedita were such distressed women working in the United Arab Emirates.

PACITA

Pacita is a twenty-seven-year-old domestic worker working in Dubai. She is originally from Manila and arrived in Dubai in October 1998. At the time of the interview she had been working there for just over a year. She is married and has two children, who are being taken care of by her mother-in-law in the Philippines.

Pacita left home to work overseas in order to escape her husband. Her marriage was difficult from the start. Her husband, a fisherman, lost his job soon after they married. After that, he worked at odd jobs and made some money, but never enough to support the entire family. For four years, Pacita worked in a garment factory in a neighboring village, where she made 130 pesos (US$3) a day. Their income was just enough to make ends meet. In fact, money was not really a major source of conflict for them. "I had lots of problems with my husband," she recalled. "He had many girls." In addition, he was sometimes abusive; he beat her whenever they had quarrels.

When friends told her that life was good overseas, she immediately jumped at the idea. She visited a recruitment agency where a friend worked and immediately found a job as a domestic worker in Dubai. Pacita only told her sister about her new job before she left home. "My sister was supportive of my decision, but I didn't let my mom know. She didn't know about it until I came here." She did not even inform her husband of her migration until she arrived in Dubai. When I asked her how he reacted to her working overseas, she said: "He said nothing."

MERCEDITA

Mercedita comes from a poor family. She started working in a garment factory in Manila when she was seventeen, as soon as she graduated from high school. She wanted to go to college, but her family could not afford the tuition. After working for a few years, she met her husband; soon after that, she got pregnant. After she gave birth to a son, she moved in with her husband and his family. At the time, he was still a student in the police academy; they were not yet married. They were only engaged, and married after he graduated.

Mercedita's parents-in-law gave her and her husband a small one-room house directly across from their own house. Her husband had four brothers who were already married and had children. They were all living nearby and often interfered with Mercedita's life. This gradually became stressful for her. Furthermore, her husband was a student whose only income was a stipend from his parents, which also caused problems. "My husband asked his parents [for money] whenever he needed something," she recalled. "I didn't like it because my mother-in-law did 'talk-talk-talk' [behind her back] with other in-laws about it and blamed me." Her in-laws thought she was spending too much money, even though the money she received was barely enough to cover basic needs.

Finally, she could not stand the situation any longer. "I thought I should earn money for my own family." When she told her husband she wanted to work overseas, he objected. "He said, 'I will marry another woman if you go to other country.' But I said, 'That's fine. Go ahead.' I didn't think that he would really do it." In fact, he did. After Mercedita went to Singapore, he married another women without telling her. She only found out when a friend wrote to her in Singapore and explained what happened.

"Destitute Women"

It has been generally understood that migrant workers are not the "poorest of the poor." [19] However, this assumption requires careful examination. For instance, the payment schemes faced by migrant workers have been chang- ing in recent years in ways that have altered the composition of the migrant workforce. Intense competition has driven many recruitment agencies to pursue a new labor supply—the destitute—in order to increase the num- ber of their clients. Aware that these women cannot afford high migration fees, the agencies demand only a small cash deposit, or none at all, for some destinations in Asia. They do not of course lower the total fees; they simply deduct those fees from the migrants' salaries, in the worst cases for six months or more. This turns these women into semi-indentured laborers. These salary deductions and loan schemes have enabled more poor people— including the poorest of the poor—to join the migrant workforce. Es- pecially in Sri Lanka and Bangladesh, the recruitment of the poor and the destitute has been accelerated by local "sub-agents." Some sub-agents are contracted by agencies; others operate independently. They approach desti- tute women in the neighborhood and lure them into migration by promis- ing high wages and a better life. They are known for charging exorbitant fees and for defrauding those who sign with them. Since most of them operate illegally, it is very difficult to control their activities. More and more desti- tute women have been resorting to them.

Destitute women emigrate to escape extreme poverty and because they lack other means to survive. Most of the destitute women I encountered were in Bangladesh; there were only a few in Sri Lanka and the Philippines. They were migrating in order to achieve a short-term goal—to feed them- selves and their children. None of them was interested in investing their in- come in a business, or in their own career development, or in private edu- cation for their children. In addition, many of them were separated, divorced, or widowed or had been abandoned by their husbands. In developing coun- tries, the lives of low-income working-class women are very difficult even when they are married. Their lives are even harder when they become household heads. It is extremely difficult for them to find employment op- portunities because of gender and age discrimination in the labor market. In Bangladesh, 96 percent of female-headed households live below the poverty line and 33 percent are chronically short of food.[20] The story of Salma is a common one among migrant women from Bangladesh.

SALMA

Salma is a thirty-year-old Muslim woman living in a small village south of Dhaka. She was an orphan and never attended school. She got married but was divorced fourteen years ago and has been raising three boys since then. Because she has no family or relatives, there was no one to help her financially. "I have no husband," she said. "I had no money or property to inherit. I had no savings. And I had to keep paying the rent for a small room. The life was hard."

At first, Salma did household work for a wealthy family in her village, but this did not bring in enough money to feed her children. She quit that job and began selling vegetables. She made 2,000–2,500 taka (US$40–50) a month, but it was still not enough. One day, she went to sell vegetables to a wealthy family in the village. The "madam" suggested that she consider working abroad and offered to introduce her to an agent. Salma immediately agreed and met the agent. He told her that the fee to secure a job as a domestic worker in Bahrain was 50,000 taka (US$1,000)—a lot of money. She borrowed it from a local moneylender at high interest, left her children with her ex-husband's mother, and left for Bahrain in 1996.

Having had no knowledge in Arabic, Salma had a difficult time communicating with her employer at the beginning. Her "madam" used to get angry and beat her whenever she was unhappy. The food was another problem: she could not eat the Arabic food because it was so different. She was only eating some bread every day. But after three months, she had learned some Arabic words and had grown accustomed to the local diet. She worked very hard, rising at four every morning and working until one the next morning. She was being paid only 3,000 taka (US$60) a month even though she had been promised 4,000 taka (US$80). However, her salary was raised to 4,000 taka the following year. She sent 3,000 to 4,000 taka home every three or four months and saved the rest for herself. She stayed in Bahrain for two years and seven months, until she fell ill. Because she had no health insurance and the employer would not pay her medical costs, Salma ended up paying 40,000 taka (US$800) for medical treatment. After paying the recruitment fee of 50,000 taka with interest, she had little money left. Although she wanted to continue working in Bahrain, her illness forced her to return home. She has since recovered from her illness and is planning to work overseas again.

Emigration Processes: Social Networks
and the Culture of Migration

As seen above, the profiles of migrant women are extremely diverse. However, the migration process itself—especially the ways in which prospective migrants find information about jobs—is quite similar: they find jobs overseas through personal networks or recruitment agencies. As many migration scholars have pointed out,[21] social networks play a major role in migration. The "harbingers" who emigrated earlier provide those still at home with information about employment opportunities abroad, and in this way link prospective migrants with destination countries.

In Sri Lanka, the majority of the migrant women in my sample (56 percent) found work through personal networks—through family members, relatives, friends, and so on. Even recruitment agencies, which are usually not considered social networks, have personal components. Among Sri Lankan migrant women who obtained a job through an agency, 73 percent had a relative or friend who worked there, and 15 percent knew someone who migrated through the same agency. All in all, only 12 percent of migrant women from Sri Lanka found work without any personal contacts.

In the Philippines, where recruitment agencies are thriving, a large majority (76 percent) of migrant women found work through a recruitment agency. But again, the majority of them had a personal connection with the agency staff. Only 17 percent of the respondents found work without any networks. Recruitment networks in Bangladesh exist as well, albeit to a limited extent: 25 percent of migrant women obtained their jobs through direct personal networks and 75 percent through sub-agents who knew them or a family member.

Most migrant women were acquainted with "harbinger migrants": 79 percent of Filipinas and 70 percent of Sri Lankans and Bangladeshis in my sample had friends or relatives who had worked overseas. Women in the Philippines and Sri Lanka were especially entangled in a broad, dense web of current and returned migrant women. At the time of the interviews, the vast majority of them had more than one family member and many friends who were working abroad or had done so in the past.

In the case of Ligaya, a twenty-seven-year-old Filipina domestic worker, both parents and an elder brother had been working in Hong Kong for fourteen years—her father as a factory worker, her mother as a domestic worker, her brother as a chauffeur. As a child in the Philippines, her uncle had taken care of her and her three siblings. "I was a mother, father, and big sister to all my two younger brothers and sister," she recalled. After finishing her training as a midwife, she began to think about joining her parents and brother. "I missed my parents so badly and wanted to be with them," she explained. "That's why I decided to move to Hong Kong." In 1992 her brother found a job for her as a domestic worker in the same house where he was working. Ligaya has been working there ever since. Although her salary is below the official minimum wage, she cannot complain; she is afraid that doing so might affect her brother's job.

Such networks can cross generations. Indrani, a twenty-two-year-old Sri Lankan woman, had a grandmother, an aunt, and three cousins who were working as domestic workers in Hong Kong. She became interested in joining them after one of her cousins found a job for her. Her father did not like the idea of her moving to Hong Kong, but the presence of these relatives softened his opposition and he finally agreed to let her go. Once she arrived in Hong Kong, however, Indrani's relatives, especially her aunt and grandmother, began controlling every aspect of her life. "They are much more powerful than my own employer," she sighed, "but at least I have some support whenever I get into trouble."

Over time, these family traditions of migration affect the values and behavioral systems of communities, forming a "culture of migration." As the number of migrants increases, migration "becomes deeply ingrained into the repertoire of people's behaviors, and values associated with migration become part of the community's values." [22] When migration was still dominated by males, young men perceived migration as a rite of passage to adulthood. [23] Later, as migration became more feminized in the Philippines and Sri Lanka, it also affected women's values and behaviors, and this forged a new culture of migration. In Bangladesh, where very few women emigrate compared to men, this culture has yet to develop.

Without necessarily providing a "rite of passage" to female adulthood, migration penetrates into the socialization process of girls. This is linked to heightened consumerism. During my fieldwork in a Philippine village, I found that girl children were already deeply embedded in and influenced by the migration culture. Nena, a nine-year-old whose mother is a domestic worker in Hong Kong, was already employed part-time as a domestic worker in her neighbor's house. According to the neighbor, Nena and her younger brother had not seen their mother for seven years. When I spoke to them, they said they liked their mother more than their father who lives with them. I asked them why. "Because mom buys me Hello Kitty," Nena answered. The neighbor explained: "Their mom sends them a lot of toys from Hong Kong and the kids love that." Sending many toys to children is a very common practice among migrant women. They try to compensate for their absence by fulfilling their children's material desires. Many migrant women admitted that this was not good for their children, but they still did it because they felt guilty about being away from home. They had few other ways to show their love. As Parreñas pointed out, this sort of "commodification of love" is the only way these transnational mothers can establish concrete ties of familial dependency with their children.[24]

Having been brought up with material comforts since early childhood, many children of "transnational families" associate migration with wealth and happiness. When I asked about her dreams for the future, Nena told me without hesitation that she wanted to become a domestic worker in Hong Kong like her mother because she could make a lot of money that way. Indeed, migrant mothers often become role models for their daughters. Yolanda, a returned migrant woman in the same village, has a daughter who is planning to work in Singapore as a nurse. The daughter has chosen to go to nursing school, expecting that a nursing diploma will enable her to find a job overseas like her mother. Yolanda is supportive of her, especially since her daughter plans to work as a professional nurse, not as a domestic worker. Most girl children of migrant women want to follow their mother's footsteps. They fantasize about the money they will be able to earn as migrants.

Materialism can have a strong impact on children's attitudes toward life. Children who are raised to be consumers tend not to incorporate lessons about working hard for the future. When the father and relatives in a migrant woman's household show little interest in education, the children often become disoriented and drop out of school—a serious problem in Sri Lanka. The attitude of the father as a role model can be another factor. A recent study found that remittances reduce the labor force participation of men left behind more than that of women left behind.[25] In other words, when a wife starts working abroad, the husband at home tends to stop working. Gamburd has observed that a wife's overseas employment poses a serious challenge to the masculinity of a husband, and to compensate, he indulges in drinking, gambling, and womanizing.[26] Such behavior of the father also leads to the loss of motivation for study and work among children.

Many children of migrants are aware that the material comforts they are enjoying will not last very long after their mother returns home, and that their standard of living cannot be maintained with the more modest earnings from local jobs. Often, the mother has only modest ambitions when she leaves home as a migrant worker; then she starts sending money back, and the children develop material desires and higher expectations that cannot be met without her overseas earnings. Hence, once grown up, they migrate overseas, which starts a cycle of intergenerational migration.

Decision-Making Processes:
Household Strategies versus Women's Autonomy

It is perhaps relatively easy for migrants' children, friends, or relatives to find work overseas, since information about migration is readily available to them and they learn about what migration entails. But not all migrants have such personal contacts. How did the idea of migration occur to these people? How did they reach the decision to migrate? To understand women's decision-making processes, we need to examine factors other than networks and migration culture.

The household strategy approach offers some insights about migration decisions. Here, the household is seen as the "primary decision-making unit" for both male and female migration.[27] It follows that migration decisions are made collectively rather than by individual migrants. According to the proponents of this approach, migration is part of a household strategy for its own survival; a household organizes and allocates its resources, taking into account the productive and reproductive roles of its members. As it was first conceived by economists based on the new household economics, this theoretical approach sees a household as an entity that is trying to maximize its collective utility.[28] The basic assumption is that the household decides who should migrate overseas to which country, based on its consumption needs and productive capacity. The decisions arrived at in this manner are supposed to serve the collective interests of the "household" as a whole.

However, this approach obscures women's agency by assigning too much weight to households as decision-making "actors." Many scholars have been questioning the very idea of "households" and the existence of "household strategies."[29] The main criticism to this approach concerns its two assumptions: one is that the "optimal reallocation" of a household's resources results from altruism and the voluntary contributions of its members; and the other is that the "group preference function" is identical with that of the altruistic household head.[30]

Critics of this approach contend that households are laced with conflict, inequality, and exploitation—things that do not necessarily comprise a collective utility or maximize the sum of individual utilities. The interests of the household or those of the household's decision-maker are not necessarily those of its less powerful members such as the women and children. The decision-making process often reflects power relations among household members. All of this means that it can be very problematic to assign a single utility function and decision-making role to the household as a collective entity. Furthermore, the household strategy approach blindly assumes that the household members are altruistic and unselfish. In this regard, many scholars in the past have portrayed Third World women as obedient daughters or caring mothers who work hard for their families. The recent literature suggests that such views are rooted in nostalgia or in the biases of Western researchers, and that many Third World women are autonomous and assert their own interests within the household.[31] Of course, many women *are* family-oriented and migrate for the sake of the family, but even then, the decisions they make on such a basis are not necessarily collective ones.

In fact, during my fieldwork I found no empirical evidence to support the tenets of the household strategy approach. I did not find a single case where the household members discussed who should go overseas and made a collective decision. On the contrary, the migrant women I spoke to had made their own decisions about migration. These women displayed much greater autonomy and decision-making power than is often suggested. More than 90 percent of Filipinas and Sri Lankans and 60 percent of Bangladeshis in my sample took the initiative to find out about overseas employment and then decided by themselves whether to go. Some women did not even consult their husband or parents: 30 percent of Sri Lankan women and 16 percent of Filipinas never discussed their migration decision with other household members. Moreover, 27 percent of Filipinas and 16 percent of Sri Lankan women left the country over the objections of their husbands or parents. Yapa surveyed one hundred Sri Lankan migrant women and found that these women have a lot of power to make their own decisions on migration.[32] Her study found that 85 percent of migrant women had decided by themselves whether to migrate and that 40 percent of these did not even consult other household members. More studies are needed for the Philippines and Bangladesh, but so far the available data suggest that women have much more autonomy than migration theorists have long assumed. Women are indeed the major decision-makers for migration.

Of course, from the finding that many women do not consult their parents or husband, and even migrate over their objections, we must not conclude that the household matters less to these women. In fact, most migrant women decided to work abroad for the sake of their family members—both immediate and distant ones sharing the same household.[33] The point here is that in the Philippines and Sri Lanka, women do not simply follow the "household strategy" or the suggestions of other household members. Most of them decide very much on their own whether to migrate. This leads to another question: Do a woman's overall role and her degree of autonomy within the household help determine whether she will migrate? The decision to migrate is one among many that women make in their lives. It follows that the processes whereby they make the decision should be placed in the context of their overall role and decision-making power within the household prior to migration.

There are many types of household decisions. Naila Kabeer listed twelve different decision-making dimensions ranging from daily household budgeting to children's education, family planning, and household financial planning.[34] Oppong and Abu found in their own study (conducted in Ghana) that women have seven roles in the household, in the workplace, and in the community.[35] To measure women's decision-making power in each of their roles would be a tremendously complex task.

While acknowledging such difficulty and complexity, I chose to focus on the dimension of household finance, which is generally considered one of the important indicators of women's autonomy.[36] By "the dimension of household finances," I mean not only women's decision-making power over daily expenditures but also their ability to make long-term decisions about allocating financial resources within the household. Other dimensions such as children's education and family planning are important indicators of women's decision-making power as well. However, I hypothesized from the literature that the financial dimension would be the best indicator of a woman's overall autonomy and decision-making power within the household. The migrant women I spoke to often referred to themselves as the "finance minister of the house." As Rae Blumberg suggested in her research, women's control of income and other resources is a major determinant of other variables such as family planning and overall power within the marriage.[37]

My survey found that most married migrant women were already playing a major role in financial decision-making before they emigrated. Among the migrant women in my sample, Filipinas had the highest level of decision-making power: 58 percent of married respondents actively participated in decisions about household finances. Of these, 93 percent were the sole decision-maker; the other 7 percent shared this power equally with the husband. As for married Sri Lankan migrant women, 46 percent had been making important decisions on household finances before migrating. Of these, 55 percent made such decisions basically on their own. As for Bangladeshi respondents—most of whom were very poor—the percentage was relatively high, partly because the husband was not a stable breadwinner and had less economic power. Thus, 42 percent of married Bangladeshi migrant women had at least some decision-making power over household finances prior to migration, and among these, 80 percent were the sole decision-maker. As I will discuss in a later section, these rates are extremely high compared with the national average in Bangladesh.

To my surprise, unattached women (single, separated, divorced, or widowed) in the Philippines and Sri Lanka enjoyed relatively less decision-making power. Only 39 percent of unattached Filipinas and 8 percent of un-attached Sri Lankans had decision-making power in household finances. The main reason was that most of them lived with their parents or siblings and were often financially supported by them; this placed them into a weaker position within the household. The vast majority of them said their father or mother or a sibling made most of the financial decisions within the household. In cases where a woman was the household head, that woman held all the decision-making power. This was true for all three countries.

In Bangladesh, unattached women enjoyed more decision-making power than attached ones: 55 percent made decisions entirely on their own. This was because they received relatively less financial support from their family (which was also poor and had a hard time ensuring its own daily survival). Widows and divorcées, who comprised about a half of the sample, admitted that their own parents and siblings did not welcome their return because it made a bad financial situation worse. Many of them were thus living alone with their children and struggling terribly hard to make ends meet. Ironically, then, their poverty allowed them more freedom and control over their lives and made them more self-reliant.

As many scholars have pointed out, women's decision-making power is related to their contribution to household income.[38] Many of the women in my sample had already assumed a breadwinner role prior to migration: 47.8 percent of Filipinas, 23.3 percent of Sri Lankans, and 40 percent of Bangladeshis had been engaged in wage employment as either sole or co-breadwinner. They had already been playing a major economic role within the household.

The economic role of women and their power to make decisions about household finances have important implications for emigration. Women with more decision-making power over household finances develop a strong sense of responsibility for making ends meet on a daily basis as well as for sustaining family life in the long term. They are the ones who are most aware of the general financial state of the household. In her study of Filipino families, Heinonen also found that women generally feel the effects of poverty and hardship in the household more directly than men because they are the ones who actually purchase what household members need.[39] Furthermore, many of them are educated enough to make long-term financial plans based on current expenditure patterns. In doing so, they grasp soon enough the benefits of earning extra income and thus are more likely to consider overseas employment as a means to fulfill the desires and dreams of their loved ones.

This observation helps us understand the cross-national differences in levels of female migration. In the Philippines, where the largest number of migrant women leave home every year, wives tend to have an equitable share of decision-making responsibility in most spheres. Yu and Liu studied 1,521 urban families in Cebu City and found that the wife exercised "almost absolute control" over spending money, family health care, and food preparation. With regard to financial planning, schooling, child care, and choice of leisure time activities, the wife and husband made decisions jointly.[40] Deano studied a national sample of 1,041 married women; 53 percent reported that decisions about budgeting and purchasing major household items were generally their domain.[41] In fact, this is not a recent phenomenon. Even during the pre-Hispanic era, Filipino women had "their own purse and were also custodians of the conjugal purse" and "could acquire property, often own and administer it, and dispose of its produce *without her husband's consent.*" (author's italics)[42]

Financial responsibility tends to push many married women in the Philippines toward wage employment. This is because they feel monetary needs more acutely as they make long-term plans for their family, especially their children. Eder studied Filipino women and reported the following comments: "I was supposed to be in charge of the money, but there was no money"; "If you just count on the earnings of your husband, it is not enough."[43] Filipinos tend to have large families and extended family systems, and this makes it easy for women to get help with child care when they work outside the home.

In Sri Lanka as well, married women have a fairly large share of decision-making power. According to a small-scale study by local researchers, 93 percent of married women in that country who were not living with in-laws made decisions about household finances by themselves.[44] Other studies have reported that Sri Lankan women enjoy a status almost equal to that of their male counterparts in various spheres of life.[45] According to Takakuwa, although traditional Sri Lankan society assumes that men are breadwinners and that women are housewives, social norms still call on women to manage the "home," and this often includes household budgeting.[46] In other words, it is the wife's responsibility to make ends meet, and if that is not possible, she herself is supposed to work in order to supplement the household income. The vast majority of Sri Lankan migrant women whom I interviewed fell into this category: they emigrated in order to meet their responsibilities as "household managers."

In Bangladesh, which sends far fewer migrant women overseas, the situation is rather different. Those who actually migrated abroad tend to have strong decision-making power, but generally speaking, Bangladeshi men control the household finances. Many of them even do the grocery shopping because they do not want their wives and daughters to mingle with men in the market. As a consequence, women often do not know how much money the household has. Financial decision-making is definitely not their sphere. One study found that only 28 percent of married women in Bangladesh participated in decisions about household finances.[47] White has reported that in many Bangladeshi households, the men have more scope to determine how money is used, and women are expected to rely entirely on the money the men give them.[48] There is little social pressure on wives to supplement the household income, perhaps because of the *purdah* system and because religious values encourage women's seclusion from society. Of course, low-income women do work, because their husbands do not earn enough to feed the family. Women have to assume the breadwinner role if their husbands are unemployed or if they become divorced, separated, or widowed. However, even these women work in "culturally acceptable ways."[49] International migration is definitely not "culturally acceptable," even at the lowest rung of Bangladeshi society.

The Trapping Mechanism and Circular Migration

Most migrant women plan to work abroad for a few years, but once they set foot on foreign soil, their plans and feelings tend to change. Some return home sooner than they planned and never try to emigrate again, but the large majority of migrant women either stay longer or migrate to a different country. This tendency is stronger among Filipinas: in my sample, 64 percent of those working in Hong Kong had been away from home for more than five years, and 28.5 percent for more than ten years. One of them had been working abroad for nineteen years, another for seventeen years, and three others for eleven years. The average length of stay was eight years. Those whom I interviewed in the United Arab Emirates had been there for a shorter time—sixteen months on average. However, this was mainly a result of sample bias: the respondents in the UAE were "runaway migrants" who had taken refuge in the Philippine Embassy. Since Arab employers normally do not allow days off to domestic workers and most of them work sixteen to eighteen hours a day, it was impossible for me to interview these women unless they had taken refuge in shelters. When problems arose for these women (non-payment of wages, sexual harassment, and so on), it was usually during the first three to twelve months of the contract. Therefore, the average of sixteen months is not a representative figure for Filipina domestic workers in the UAE. In fact, if I include the previous migration experience of these runaway migrants, their total time overseas averaged over three years. The average time spent working abroad by all returned migrants in the Philippines was 4.8 years.

Sri Lankan women also stay abroad for quite long periods of time. In my sample, their average length of stay overseas was 6.2 years for those inter-viewed in Hong Kong and 3.8 years for returned migrants in Sri Lanka. One-third of the Sri Lankan women in Hong Kong had been away from home for more than ten years—a higher proportion than for Filipina long-stayers. Bangladeshi migrant women tended to stay overseas the shortest time: 2.7 years on average, and none of them stayed longer than five years.

Circular migration—the phenomenon in which migrants return home and go overseas again—was also commonly observed in my study. Some mi-grant women return to the same employer in the same country. Others re-apply for a different employer in the same country, and still others try an en-tirely new country. Whatever the case, many women emigrate more than once. In my sample, the proportion of migrant women who have worked in multiple countries was the highest among Sri Lankans: 56 percent of them had worked in more than one country, and of these and 39.3 percent had worked in three or more countries. Yapa found that 61 percent of migrant women had previously worked in a different country—most often in the Middle East.[50] Filipinas also repeated migration but were more likely to re-turn to the same country: 61.8 percent had worked in only one country and 38.2 percent in more than one country. The national data for the Philippines suggest that the percentage of Filipino "repeaters" could be as high as that of Sri Lankans. In 1993, the number of Filipino workers who emigrated for at least the second time exceeded the number of new migrants, and this trend has continued since. In 2000, 60.6 percent of all legal migrant work-ers were "repeaters."[51] As for Bangladeshi women, only one respondent had worked in more than one country; one other respondent had worked twice in the same country.

TRAPPING MECHANISM

Why do so many women repeatedly emigrate to a foreign country or stay for unexpectedly long periods of time? It is because labor migration entails a "trapping mechanism" that drives migrant women to prolong their stay, to repeat migration, or both. This mechanism operates at three levels: recruit-ment process, household, and individual migrants.

The most crucial factor is the recruitment process—in particular, the placement fees that women must pay in order to emigrate. As discussed ear-lier, many migrant women must pay exorbitant fees to the recruitment agency to obtain a job overseas. Less cash is required up front these days, but many women still pay some cash deposit and commit themselves to pay the total amount from their future salaries. Even those who find jobs through their own personal connections are not necessarily exempted from high fees: because of the limited supply of jobs and the relatively high overseas salaries, even friends and relatives feel entitled to charge some money—albeit often below market rates. Only 13 percent of the women in my sample paid no fees. Besides placement fees, migrant women must also pay numerous other fees—medical exam, visa, passport, government registration, insurance, departure tax, and so on—which quickly add up.

Women from low-income households find these fees extremely high. For instance, the average household income for Sri Lankan migrant women in my sample was US$50 a month, and one-third of these women lived on less than US$15 a month. Even the relatively low fees for the Middle East were equivalent to eight to ten months of a Sri Lankan factory worker's salary. Because of the low savings rates among poor households, many women had to borrow money to cover migration costs: 69 percent of Sri Lankan women received loans from friends, relatives, or moneylenders. To my surprise, almost all these friends and relatives charged 10 percent interest, which admittedly was lower than the market rate of 20 percent.

These high fees affect migrant women in several ways. First, women normally have to work for at least the first few months without a salary simply to pay off their fees and interest; only then can they start saving money. Savings are further delayed in some countries, such as Taiwan where a six-month salary deduction is common. In addition, most salary deduction schemes are combined with an initial cash payment up front, and many women borrow money at high interest in order to cover those fees as well as other costs, such as domestic transportation and board and lodging for a few days in the capital before departure. Since most contracts are for two years, the period in which these women can actually save money is limited, and the total amount they can save is not significant because of their low wages.

EMPLOYMENT MALPRACTICE

Even after paying off the fees and other migration-related debts, migrant women often find that their plans to save money do not work out as they hoped. Employers can fire them abruptly and whenever they feel like it. Some Chinese employers in Hong Kong are especially fussy about *feng shui*, which involves superstitious beliefs about women's physical features; these employers have been known to fire migrant women at the airport as soon as they see a mole in the "wrong" spot or any other physical features that might bring bad luck to the family. An NGO worker in Manila refers to this as "A-to-A," meaning "from the airport to the airport": that is, the migrant worker flies from the Manila airport to the destination airport, where she is fired and immediately returns to Manila. Crying is also seen as inviting bad luck; thus, predeparture orientations in the Philippines often instruct prospective migrants to Hong Kong and Singapore not to cry in front of their employers.

Even when a migrant woman is not fired, saving money can be difficult when the employer does not pay her salary regularly or decides not to pay her at all. In fact, non-payment and underpayment are common problems. In 1994, there were 14,314 reported problem cases involving Filipino migrant workers, and 25 percent of these were related to contract and payment problems.[52] In my sample of "runaway" Filipina migrants in the United Arab Emirates, 23 percent had not received any salary since arriving in the country, even after the salary deduction period was over. The situation was similar for Sri Lankans: 28.4 percent of complaints lodged by migrant Sri Lankan women in 2002 were related to non-payment of wages.[53] Although only 6 percent of the interviewees received no wages, 46 percent were paid less than had been promised. Somawathi, a fifty-year-old Sri Lankan woman, worked in Kuwait for two years without receiving any salary until just before she returned to Sri Lanka. The employer gave her only 20,000 rupees (US$280) as a lump sum salary for two years' work. With this money, she paid off the recruitment fees she owed and bought a bicycle for herself. That was all she got for two years' work in Kuwait.

In cases of non-payment and underpayment, migrant women have very limited choices: they can stay until the end of the contract, hoping they will be paid in full when they leave, or they can simply flee the employer. However, leaving the present employer does not necessarily lead to a new employer. Most destination countries in Asia do not allow unskilled migrants to change employers while in the country, and require them to return home before applying for a new job. This means that migrants will have to start the emigration process all over again, which necessarily involves paying another set of fees and taking on more debt.

In Hong Kong, where migrant workers are allowed to sue an employer for non-payment or underpayment, some migrant women do run away and file suit for their back wages. However, the rate of success is marginal since court cases take a very long time and many employers do not even appear in court. Furthermore, the "two-week rule" in immigration regulations stipulates that migrant women must return to their home country within two weeks from the date of contract termination. Migrants are allowed to stay longer if they have filed suit in a court but are not allowed to work while the case is being heard. Since most migrants cannot afford to wait for the entire legal process to unwind without earning any income, they either give up on suing the employer and go home, or illegally engage in temporary work. If they follow the latter course, they earn even lower wages and also risk deportation. Most migrants in this position give up and go home, planning to apply for an overseas job again to recuperate the loss.

Some migrant women return home early because of abuse and sexual harassment by the employer. According to the Philippine Department of Labor, 31 percent of problem cases have been related to abuse, rape, sexual harassment, and other maltreatment.[54] The Sri Lankan government reports that 21.6 percent of complaints by migrant women in 2002 involved harassment.[55] Just as with cases of non-payment and underpayment, migrant women who cannot tolerate abuse and harassment return home only to find that the debts they owe have grown considerably because of the high interest rates. It is difficult for them to pay back these huge debts while remaining in their own country, because employment opportunities are limited for unskilled women and the wages paid by the jobs they can find are very low. In this situation, they must borrow money again, pay more fees, and give working overseas another try, hoping that this will be the last time they have to migrate.

FINANCIAL MISMANAGEMENT
AND INCREASING CONSUMERISM

Migrant women tend to make substantial financial contributions to their families back home. Most of the migrant women I interviewed were sending 80 to 100 percent of their earnings back home. Another study has reported that single female migrants send their families an average of 6.7 months' salary per year, whereas single male migrants send only 2.8 months' salary.[56]

However, the filial piety and altruism shown by migrant women is not always rewarded. Other family members are sometimes the source of the financial problems that lead to circular migration. Migrant women's parents, husbands, or other relatives often mismanage the remittances so that by the time the women return home, the situation that compelled them to migrate has not improved. Indeed, sometimes it is worse. One of the problems is that low-income people, especially agricultural workers and day laborers in rural areas, have never seen such large sums of cash before and find it difficult to manage these windfalls. During my fieldwork, I heard many stories about husbands who spent all the remittances on "monkey business," by which was meant alcohol, gambling, and women.

Fiona, a thirty-four-year-old Filipina migrant now in Hong Kong, had worked in Qatar for seven years and kept sending money to her husband. Then she came home and found that nothing had changed for the better in all that time. "All the money disappeared because of my husband," she said, "and I had to start all over again." A year after returning from Qatar, she migrated to Hong Kong as a domestic worker. She no longer sends her husband money; instead, she saves most of her salary in her bank account in Hong Kong and only sends some money to her parents to take care of her children. "I will stay here until I save enough money for my kids' college and my own reintegration," she said.[57] Upula, a forty-nine-year-old Sri Lankan, worked in Lebanon for four-and-a-half years, only to find that her husband had spent all her money on alcohol. "He was a drinker before but started drinking more after I left," she said. Upula had to emigrate again, this time to Saudi Arabia. She decided to send her husband only 50 percent of her salary; she saved the rest in her own bank account. In the end, she had to emigrate three more times for a total of twelve years before she could save a sufficient amount of money.

Single migrant women are not exempt from similar risks. Myra, a twenty-eight-year-old Filipina migrant in the United Arab Emirates, had been sending her money to her older sister for many years. Her parents were old and the sister was making the financial decisions for the entire family. Myra had a joint bank account with her sister in the Philippines, and that was where she had been sending the money. However, the sister took Myra's money and electronic appliances with her when she got married and moved elsewhere. Myra has lost everything and must keep working in the UAE to support herself and her parents. Lalani, a forty-two-year-old Sri Lankan divorcée who worked in Kuwait for seven years, had a similar experience. She had sent her entire salary to her sister; on her return, she found that her sister had spent all the money on her husband and children without saving any for Lalani. She had to leave again for Kuwait at the end of 1999 in order to save money for herself.

Remittances certainly change the consumption patterns of migrants' families. Family members and relatives often spend the money without any long-term goals. In particular, almost all of them purchase electrical appliances immediately, such as a television, a VCR, and a stereo; these are the status symbols of the middle-class, to which most low-income people aspire. Migrant women usually tolerate this behavior. In fact, they believe these appliances are good for their children and their family. A television is especially valued because it unites the family and encourages the children to stay home and away from drugs. Rosa, a returned migrant in the Philippines, said: "In a village like ours, we don't have much entertainment. No movie or concert. So young kids often hang around and do drugs. But if you have a TV, you sit together with your family and watch it after dinner. You talk together while watching it. Kids don't have to go outside to do drugs at night."

The entertainment these gadgets provide is very much appreciated by migrant mothers. Furthermore, these appliances signify the success of the migrant women themselves. In most households I visited in the Philippines, Sri Lanka, and Bangladesh, a television and VCR were placed in the most visible corner of the house so that visitors would notice them as soon as they stepped inside. These shiny electrical appliances often seem out of place in the shabby residence. They are sparklingly clean and are sometimes decorated with a nice cloth cover or some ornaments so that they almost resemble household shrines. Whenever I took a photograph inside a house, the woman always asked me to include her TV and VCR in it. Even after all the remittances have been spent and no money is left, these appliances are not sold; they are still the centerpieces of the home.

Many migrant women, when they come home and find that the family has saved little, emigrate again. However, many of them have a clearer strategy for this second time. Some tell their family members outright how to spend the remittances and how much to save in a bank account. Lucila, a thirty-five-year-old Filipina migrant in Hong Kong, now sends her husband only half her monthly salary, with detailed instructions how to budget it. Yet things do not necessarily go smoothly. "He still lends money to his friends and drinks more," she said. Other women send less money home and save a large part of their wages in a personal bank account. Often this is not easy, because they receive letters asking for more money. Some yield to the pressure, but most of them who learned from the past are determined to set aside some money for themselves.

Some migrant women encounter their own problems managing money. Having grown up in low-income households in developing countries, they find themselves intoxicated with city life with its shopping malls and entertainment centers. The experience of migration permanently changes their expectations as consumers. Some young Filipinas admitted to me that they were excited at the beginning and spent too much money on clothes, cosmetics, perfume, jewelry, and so on. Paz, a Filipina secretary in the UAE, remembers that she could not save very much money for the first few years after her arrival. "When I was single, I was worldly," she recalls, "I went to discos and parties with my friends. I liked to spend money."

Other migrant women—especially those who were domestic workers in the Middle East and who had no holidays and had little chance to spend money while abroad—spend more after they return home. In Sri Lanka, returned migrant women find it hard to readjust to rural life, having grown used to the lifestyle in wealthy countries. There is even a derogatory term for this—"Dubai Syndrome," referring to the tendency of women to wear excessive make-up, flashy clothes, and accessories after they return from overseas. A local woman was critical of returned migrants: "They prefer to take three-wheelers [a taxi-like motorcycle] to travel short distances instead of walking. They want more and more." Comments like these are tinged with jealousy, but even so, it is clear that migration alters many women's expectations as consumers. The longer they work abroad and the more money they make, the wealthier the lifestyle they desire for themselves. Some of them feel driven to achieve it and thus emigrate repeatedly.

Migrant women's overspending also has a complex social dimension. In part, it reflects the difficulties migrant women have with reintegration. Some migrant women in Sri Lanka engage in conspicuous consumption in response to the envy, stigmatization, and other negative reactions they sense from their neighbors and other community members. They try to compensate for their reduced social status by displaying their heightened economic status. Even in the Philippines, where there is little bias against female migration, some women still overspend, treating their family, friends, and relatives and sometimes lending money to them. Migrants feel social pressure to help the people around them. The community perceives them as "nouveaux riches" regardless of their actual financial situation, and expects them to act like benevolent providers.

The lack of savings, overspending, and rising expectations all drive many women toward circular migration. Yet working overseas for many years does not guarantee a better life. Rosita, a forty-three-year-old Filipina, said she had saved very little money even after working in Hong Kong for ten years. All the money she sent home had been spent by family members—for their daily needs at first, and later for medical treatment for her husband and parents, and after that for their funerals. Generally, most migrant women find that it takes at least five years to save sufficient money. Among those who worked abroad for five or more years, 54 percent of Filipinas and 67 percent of Sri Lankans said they had saved enough money. Among the short-timers who worked four years or less, only 23 percent of Filipinas and 18 percent of Sri Lankans had been able to save money. Given that the potential to save increases with the length of overseas stay, many migrant women tend to stay abroad longer or engage in circular migration.

DISRUPTED FAMILY RELATIONSHIPS

Family problems also significantly affect migrant women's decisions to prolong their stay abroad or engage in circular migration. Once they leave home, their family situation will never be the same again. The problem is more serious for married than for single women, since the husband and children have a hard time adjusting to the absence of the wife and mother. The most common family problems that migrant women face are the husband's extramarital affairs and neglect of the children. Stella, a forty-five-year-old Filipina who worked in Hong Kong, found out from a friend's letter that her husband was having an affair with someone in the same village. "I came back home immediately," she said. When she did, she also found that family unity no longer existed: "As for meals, everyone was eating whenever and whatever he or she liked to eat. There was no sense of family. I was sad." She made strenuous efforts to bring the family back together, and her family life has been restored. Not everyone is as lucky as Stella. Apsara, a forty-one-year-old Sri Lankan woman working in Hong Kong, divorced her husband, who had left her for another woman. In the aftermath, he took the house and land she had purchased with her earnings from her long-time work abroad. A similar thing happened to Malani, a thirty-seven-year-old Sri Lankan woman. While she was working in Kuwait, her husband abandoned their children for his lover, who eventually killed him.

Many women emigrate in order to secure a happy future for their family, only to encounter problems that endanger the family. The worst cases end in separation and divorce, as Apsara and Malani experienced. Once women become separated or divorced, they become "true" breadwinners and their financial responsibilities increase—all the more reason for them to stay abroad as long as they can keep their job, or to emigrate repeatedly for higher-paying work overseas.

It often happens that problems arise which do not lead to separation or divorce but which are serious enough to keep migrant women away from home. In Fiona's case (mentioned earlier), her husband placed their children with relatives without telling her. Fiona was upset when she learned this, especially because her husband was unemployed and had plenty of time to take care of the children. She also learned that her in-laws were maltreating her youngest son and that her husband was spending all the money she was sending from Hong Kong. After all this, she now feels very differently about her husband: "I don't see him as my husband any more. I feel that he is just like a friend." Having lost her desire to be reunited in a family, she has placed her children in her own parents' care and decided to stay longer in Hong Kong.

Even when there is no serious conflict, long absence can weaken family ties to the extent that migrant women are discouraged from returning home. Imelda, a fifty-nine-year-old Filipina, came to Hong Kong in 1982 and has been working there ever since. Her husband had left her long before, and that was the original reason why she migrated. During her absence, her mother took care of her three children. All three are now adults: the oldest son is thirty-two, the youngest twenty-four. Imelda feels proud that she has been able to support them all and pay for their education. Yet when I asked her why she did not return home now that they have all become independent, she said she feels a distance from them that she is unable to bridge. She and her children can no longer communicate as mother and children. "I don't want to go home any more," Imelda said sadly. No matter how much money migrant women provide, it may not be enough to compensate for the lost emotional ties between mother and children, or to repair rifts within the family. Rosita, another Filipina, provided her thirteen-year-old boy with all she could afford: a television, a VCR, a CD player, games, toys, and many other things. However, one day her son said to her: "Mom, you don't need to come back to the Philippines as long as you send me money." "I got really hurt and felt sad," she sighed. Cecile, a thirty-five-year-old Filipina in Hong Kong, also regrets staying away from home too long: "I missed the chance to see my children growing up. I couldn't take care of them. Working abroad is good. You get money. But it's bad for children." Many migrant women come to realize what they are losing in their life, but by the time they do, it is often too late to regain it.

It seems that almost all migrant women experience family problems while they are away. I asked Fiona whether she would encourage her friends to work overseas. "No," she said. "I don't want them to experience what I have experienced. Many migrant women here have broken homes. So many of them! They might not tell you, but they actually do." These family problems, which vary in seriousness, can trap migrant women in extended stays or circular migration, further discouraging them from returning home.

LIFE CYCLES

Migrant women do not extend their overseas stays forever, nor do they engage in circular migration forever. Almost all of them return home eventually, since most receiving countries in Asia have very strict policies that forbid them to settle. It is impossible for unskilled migrant workers to obtain permanent resident status, let alone citizenship. Some countries even prohibit migrant women from marrying their citizens. This means that even if they wish to, many unskilled migrant women do not have the option of retiring in their country of destination.

Furthermore, the work that most migrant women do—domestic and entertainment work—is physically demanding and becomes even more so with age. These women's working hours are also long: the domestic workers in my sample averaged sixteen hours a day, and those in the Middle East almost never received days off. Moreover, there is a demand-side factor: one recruitment agency in Hong Kong noted that employers prefer to hire young women as domestic workers because they have more energy and can work more efficiently. All of this explains why few migrant women are over forty.

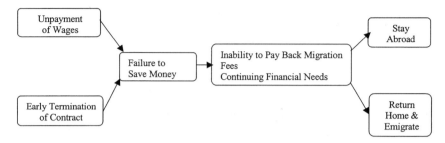

FIGURE 5.1. Trapping Mechanism for Migrant Women I: A Failure Model

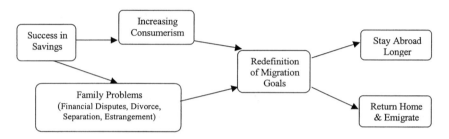

FIGURE 5.2. Trapping Mechanism for Migrant Women II: A Success Model

TRAPPING PATTERNS

The possibility that migrant women will become trapped in circular migration always exists for the reasons outlined above. The patterns for trapping can be summarized as shown in Figures 5.1 and 5.2.

I am not suggesting that circular migration and the prolonging of overseas stays occur in every single case. Some migrant women who have had traumatic experience such as rape, sexual harassment, or physical abuse do not migrate again or extend their stay. But others with similar experience still do. When such problems do not arise, the likelihood that they will prolong an overseas stay goes up even higher after the first migration, especially in cases where they have incurred greater debt because of high fees and nonpayment of wages. Another factor that contributes indirectly to circular migration is an increase in women's self-confidence. Most of my respondents said they became more independent and confident about themselves after surviving a difficult experience of living abroad and dealing with foreign employers. This self-confidence empowered them to emigrate again despite their difficult experiences in the past.[58]

STEP-UP MIGRATION

Some migrant women engage in circular migration not because of the "trapping mechanism" but because of their long-term goal—settling in North America. Most destination countries in Asia have very strict immigration policies that prevent unskilled workers from settling; by contrast, permanent residence and citizenship are more easily available in North America, especially Canada. American immigration policies allow Third World women to enter the country legally as nurses, but not as temporary domestic workers; Canada, on the other hand, accepts migrant women as caregivers. Caregivers in Canada can apply for landed immigrant status after several years. This makes the country a "dream destination" for many migrant women in Asia. Some of them hoped to meet a Canadian husband and get Canadian citizenship so that they could forever escape their poverty back home. The reality, however, is that most women find it extremely difficult to apply for a job in North America because of the high fees and because of the work experience required before they can apply.

Given such a circumstance, some women adopt a long-term strategy that I call "step-up migration." They start out working in Asian countries; having accumulated money and experience, later on they apply for a job in Canada. Many of them start out in Middle Eastern countries, which require the lowest migration fees, then move to Hong Kong or Singapore and eventually to Canada. McKay's data indicate that 43 percent of caregivers in Canada were migrant women with experience in Asian countries such as Hong Kong and Singapore.[59] In these cases, women end their circular migration once they obtain Canadian citizenship and settle there.

Conclusion

This chapter has cast light on the faces of migrant women and highlighted the similarities and differences among them. Various microlevel factors such as poverty and social networks push many women to emigrate from the Philippines and Sri Lanka (much less so from Bangladesh). The effects of "migration culture" are especially noteworthy in the Philippines and Sri Lanka where the socialization processes of migrant women's daughters have fostered intergenerational female migration.

This chapter has also elucidated the importance of women's autonomy in decisions to migrate. Contrary to the conventional assumption that views households as primary decision-making units, my study found that women's decisions to migrate were mainly in their own hands. Women's power to make decisions was a function of their role and degree of autonomy within the household. Women's financial responsibility within the household was crucial: the more responsible they were in this regard, the more keenly they were aware of the short- and long-term financial needs of all the family members, and the more motivated they were to work abroad to meet those needs. At the same time, migrant women were not entirely selfless. Many emigrated to meet their own goals and purposes, not just those of family members. Overall, in the Philippines and Sri Lanka, migrant women have much greater autonomy and decision-making power than they have been given credit for in much of the literature on migration.

Bangladeshi women were not quite motivated to migrate, perhaps due to their household positions. Compared with women in the Philippines and Sri Lanka, these women have much less decision-making power within households. This was reflected in women's decision-making for migration: many Bangladeshi migrant women had been persuaded by their husband or family members to work overseas instead of taking the initiative themselves. Overall, low-income Bangladeshi women still do not assume a sufficient financial responsibility that compels them to emigrate. The lack of mentality for setting long-term financial plans, partly as a result of little education, is another reason. These examples clearly indicate that women's individual autonomy and gender roles within households are just as important as state policies and other macrostructural factors.

This chapter has also examined the "trapping mechanism" faced by migrant women. Whether they fail or succeed in making money, the possibility of getting trapped in extended migration or circular migration always exists as a consequence of wage non-payment or underpayment, financial mismanagement by themselves or other family members, heightened consumerism, and family problems. Furthermore, some women perceive temporary migration in Asia as a stepping stone to permanent migration to North America.

Individual factors have a tremendous impact on the processes and patterns of female migration. However, they do not operate in isolation from the social environment that surrounds women. The next chapter will focus more on the mesolevel factors in society, explaining how individual actions are affected by a particular social environment, and vice versa.

CHAPTER 6

Social Legitimacy: The Nexus of Globalization and Women's Migration

WOMEN'S INTERNATIONAL MIGRATION entails different meanings for different countries. In the Philippines, it signifies courageous sacrifice for the family and the nation, and every president proclaims migrant women as national heroines. It carries a more negative image in Bangladesh, where migrant women are stigmatized and sometimes blamed—despite a lack of any solid evidence—for carrying venereal diseases. Why are there such discrepancies in the social environment that surrounds international female migration? Which factors yield positive or negative perceptions of migrant women?

In this chapter, I present the concept of *social legitimacy* as a useful heuristic tool for linking microlevel with macrolevel factors. Social legitimacy—which is often manifested in various discourses in society as well as the state—can be defined as an endorsement that a society or community attaches to individuals' particular behavioral patterns. I contend that social legitimacy is an important determinant of large-scale international female migration because it directly shapes and influences women's decisions whether to migrate. Social legitimacy for international female migration arises from (1) historical legacies of women's gainful employment; (2) feminization of the labor force caused by globalization; (3) the resulting rural–urban mobility of women; and (4) overall gender equality, especially in education. My research suggests that social legitimacy for international female migration exists in the major sending countries of migrant women such as the Philippines, Sri Lanka, and Indonesia but not in non-sending countries such as Bangladesh, India, and Pakistan.

Social legitimacy is never static; it is subject to steady change over time. Economic globalization and the export-oriented industrialization that has resulted from it have had an especially strong impact on this change. Multinational corporations' preferential hiring practices for women have triggered rural–urban female migration, which in turn has feminized the industrial workforce in urban areas, including export processing zones (EPZs). However, the EPZs and export-led industrialization do not have a direct impact on international female migration. Whatever the existing literature on migration suggests,[1] my research did not find that women's rural–urban migration has created a labor reserve for international migration. The impact of EPZs on women's internal and international migration is much smaller than has been suggested in the existing literature. Industrialization across countries has become an important driver of women's rural–urban migration but has not directly resulted in their international migration.

Rather, export-oriented industrialization has helped create a social environment and social legitimacy conducive to international female migration. How has this happened? In this chapter, I examine how social legitimacy for international female migration emerged in some countries (such as the Philippines and Sri Lanka) but not in others (such as Bangladesh). In particular, I will consider and try to disentangle the complex linkages among globalization, export-oriented industrialization, rural–urban migration, and women's international migration.

Globalization and Women's Work

Globalization during its various stages has always had a strong impact on Third World women. From the nineteenth to the mid-twentieth century, the imperial powers incorporated local women in their colonies into the large agricultural estates as day laborers. Cheap female labor was vital to colonial economies. The World Bank distinguishes three waves of globalization: the first between 1870 and 1914, the second between 1945 and 1980, and the third from 1980 to the present.[2] However, globalization in its more recent phase has had an even stronger impact on women in developing countries. This phase opened with the shift from import substitution industrialization to export-oriented industrialization in the developing world. The strategy of import substitution was an outgrowth of dependency theory which attributed underdevelopment to inequalities in the international trade system. Its goals were to develop domestic industrial capacity and to reduce outflows of foreign exchange. Under this policy framework, states significantly reduced their imports of manufactured goods from industrialized countries and substituted locally made products. However, this nationalistic, closed-economy policy met with limited success because in order to develop local industries, these states still had to import expensive capital goods and raw materials. Moreover, their markets were not large enough for the industries to grow. As a result of these factors—as well as oil price hikes and falling prices for agricultural products—many developing countries faced deterioration in their balance of payments.[3]

By the early 1960s, Taiwan, Korea, and Singapore had shifted from import substitution to export-oriented industrialization. The success of these newly industrialized countries slowly convinced other Asian countries to follow suit. The Philippines liberalized its economy in the late 1960s, which was earlier than many other developing countries in Asia. Sri Lanka only did so in 1977, and Bangladesh took even longer—it did not liberalize its economy until the mid-1980s. The shift to export-oriented industrialization was a major component of the structural-adjustment programs imposed on troubled developing economies by international financial institutions such as the International Monetary Fund (IMF) and the World Bank. These countries had to accept such programs in order to receive loans. Based on neoclassical economic models and free-market principles, structural adjustment entailed a series of reforms which these states were required to undertake. Since they were implemented in 1979, structural adjustment reforms have included trade/financial liberalization, privatization of industrial sectors, currency devaluation, and promotion of foreign investment.[4]

The economic retrenchment that structural adjustment imposed had a significant impact on women's employment in many developing countries. In order to balance their budgets, developing countries were forced to take austerity measures. This meant cutting subsidies to many industrial sectors. The poor were most severely affected: in most countries where structural adjustment programs were implemented, unemployment rose among low-income populations, and so did poverty. Yet at the same time, new industrial policies, especially the establishment of EPZs, began to create jobs for women in urban areas, and this encouraged internal female migration. The percentage of women in the urban manufacturing labor force increased in many developing countries.

The EPZs were established to attract foreign investment by providing various tax incentives and financial benefits while forbidding workers to unionize.[5] Most of the MNCs that were setting up factories in EPZs actively recruited female workers because they accepted low wages, were obedient, and (so it was presumed) had "nimble fingers" for the work. The traditional gender ideology categorizes women as supplementary wage earners, and this also gave the MNCs a competitive edge—"the comparative advantage of women's disadvantage."[6] The EPZs absorbed the unemployed female labor force in both rural and urban areas. Hordes of young single women migrated from the former to the latter. Most production workers in the EPZs were—

and still are—women. The following sections examine more closely each country case and the actual impact of economic globalization on women's employment and their rural–urban mobility.

In the Philippines, the shift in economic strategy took place rather early. In the late 1940s and more extensively in the late 1950s under President Carlos Garcia, import substitution industrialization had been tried to a limited extent.[7] However, Garcia's "Filipino First Policy"—which restricted imports and gave preferential treatment to local companies—failed, partly because of American interference. In 1961, after the U.S.-backed Diosdado Macapagal became president, export-oriented industrialization gradually replaced import substitution strategy.

Economic liberalization and export-oriented industrialization were further accelerated under the Marcos regime after 1965. For instance, the Investments Incentives Act of 1967 allowed foreign firms with less than 51 percent local shares to operate under certain conditions; it also allowed 100 percent foreign equity in pioneer industries.[8] The first EPZ was opened in Bataan in 1967, and the institutional structure was further strengthened by the Export Incentives Act of 1970 and by the Republic Act 5490 of 1969.[9] The number of the EPZs has continued to grow over the following two decades. By 1997 there were as many as thirty-five EPZs in the country.[10] Direct and indirect employment in the four main zones rose from 56,525 in 1980 to 459,272 in 1997.[11] By 1994, 74 percent of the workers in the zones were women.[12] Most of them had migrated to the zones from rural areas.

The establishment of EPZs and export-oriented industries in urban areas increased the overall demand for labor—especially female labor—and eventually led to an increase in rural–urban migration. This, coupled with poverty and unemployment in rural areas, accelerated urbanization. In 1970 the Philippines was still largely an agrarian country, with 68.2 percent of the population in rural areas. However, by the end of the 1990s, the urban population exceeded 50 percent.[13]

Women have comprised a large segment of internal migration flows since the 1960s. They accounted for 61 percent of rural–urban streams in 1973, whereas men still outnumbered women in rural–rural streams.[14] However, by the late 1980s, women outnumbered men in almost all interprovincial flows in the Philippines.[15] Of course, not all of these migratory flows were associated with export-oriented industrialization; migration for education—especially for higher education—was common. Furthermore, expansion in the service sectors was generating a large demand for female labor in urban areas. Even so, various data suggest that the growing export-oriented sectors are closely related to the increase in rural–urban migration of women who were heading to the large cities to find high-paying jobs. The MNCs preferred hiring women, and this contributed to the feminization of migratory flows. The vast majority of women who migrated from rural to urban areas were young and single. Total employment in manufacturing increased from 0.6 million in 1973 to 1.1 million in 1993, and women comprised over 40 percent of these workers.[16] In the garment and apparel sectors in 1993, about 70 percent of the workers were women. The number of production workers in the informal sectors also soared. By 1978 there were around 2,000 manufacturing contractors employing 214,000 factory workers and 500,000 "homeworkers" who were employed out of their homes on a piece-rate basis. Most of these workers were also women.[17]

SRI LANKA

In Sri Lanka, structural adjustment and the resultant influx of cheap imports severely undermined small, rural-based industries such as the pottery and handloom industries. These had long been a source of employment and income for women. Hardest hit was the handloom industry, which had been supported by the state and which employed 600,000 workers, most of whom were women.[18] After structural adjustment programs were implemented, power looms were introduced in private corporations, and small, cooperative handloom centers were closed down. As a result, 400,000 workers lost their jobs between 1977 and 1980.[19] Jayaweera contends that it was around this time that Sri Lankan women began emigrating to the Middle East as domestic workers.[20]

However, economic liberalization did not simply result in the job loss for women. Soon after the reforms started, foreign direct investment (FDI) in Sri Lanka grew rapidly, which led to an increase in the demand for female labor in urban sectors. Although net FDI was negative (−US$2 million) in 1978, within a year, it drastically increased to US$47 million.[21] The manufacturing industries, especially the garment industry, were the main beneficiaries of this growth. Garment exports rose from 481 million to 95 billion rupees between 1978 and 1995; during the same period, their share of the total national economy also soared from 4 to 48.6 percent.[22]

Growth in the garment industry meant more employment opportunities for women, since the industry employed mainly female workers. According to a study on Sri Lanka's four EPZs, 80 percent of the workers in those zones were female.[23] The percentage of women was even higher (90 to 97 percent) in some factories outside the EPZs. Within the EPZs, men were employed mainly in administrative and supervisory positions, and presumably the same was true outside them.[24] These women accounted for most of the internal female migration from rural to urban areas. In her study of rural–urban migration of women, Abeywardene reported that 65 percent of the women from villages became factory workers. Most of them were young, single, and relatively well educated—over 32 percent had postsecondary education.[25] These women worked for about ten hours a day under harsh working conditions. Entry-level workers earned only about 2,700 rupees (US$50) a month—the minimal subsistence level. Yet many of these women wanted to keep their jobs because of the poverty back home and the lack of alternative means of survival.[26] Between 1981 and 1985 the percentage of women in the manufacturing sector increased from 30 to 49 percent.[27]

BANGLADESH

Women's labor force participation in formal sectors is a more recent phenomenon in Bangladesh. Because of the Islamic legacy of female seclusion, women's productive contributions remained hidden within households or within courtyard compounds called *bari*.[28] Some women were working as wage workers, but they comprised only a small minority. In 1974, women's labor force participation rate was estimated at only 4 percent.[29]

Moreover, the shift from import substitution took place rather late in Bangladesh. Economic liberalization began only in 1982, after import substitution strategy had failed. After the state instituted export-oriented industrialization policies, the number of factories grew rapidly—from a handful in 1976 to around seven hundred in 1985. Most of these factories were in large cities such as Chittagong and Dhaka.[30]

In response to the World Bank's recommendations, Bangladesh began following the path taken by other developing countries: attracting foreign direct investment by establishing EPZs. The government enacted laws to create the Bangladesh Export Processing Zones Authority in 1980, and established the country's first EPZ in Chittagong in 1983. Levels of investment and production have been increasing dramatically since then. Investment in the Chittagong EPZ was only US$0.9 million in 1983; by 1999 it had risen to US$243.7 million.[31] Over the same years the number of investing companies also grew, from 4 to 120. Following this success, another EPZ was established in Dhaka in 1993.[32] To meet the increasing demand from both local and foreign investors, three more EPZs—in Comilla, Khulna, and Ishurdi—are under construction.[33]

The rapid expansion of EPZs generated employment across the country. In 1984 only 624 workers were employed in the Chittagong EPZ; by 1998 the number was 47,000.[34] The private EPZ, which began operating in 1998, is expected to create direct employment for 150,000 people.[35] As elsewhere in Asia, the majority of EPZ workers in Bangladesh are female. In the Chittagong EPZ, women comprised 66.2 percent of workers in 1998.[36] Women are especially concentrated in low-skilled jobs at the production level: they constituted 98 percent of those workers but only 15 percent of administrative and supervisory workers.[37] Most of the female workers in the EPZs and in other manufacturing sectors in Bangladesh are young and single.

When Bangladesh's garment industry is taken as a whole, both within and outside the EPZs, women's employment levels have grown phenomenally over the past decade. In 1984–85, 2,699,000 workers were in manufacturing industries and only 24.3 percent of them were women. By the beginning of 1998, 2,600 garment factories had been established and employed 1.3 million people, 90 percent of whom were young women. In Bangladesh, the garment sector accounts for over 70 percent of female formal-sector employment.[38]

Kibria studied female workers in garment factories and suggests that many of these women are single rural migrants.[39] Paul-Majumder and Begum report that 73 percent of female workers in the ready-made garment industry migrated from the suburbs of Dhaka and more distant rural areas.[40] The percentage of female migrants among workers in non-export industries is only 35 percent; clearly, the role the export-led garment industry is playing in the rural–urban migration of women is significant.

Nevertheless, although export-oriented industries have certainly triggered women's rural–urban migration, most of these rural migrant women cannot actually land factory jobs because of the limited opportunities. Huq-Hussain found that only 5.5 percent of long-term migrant Bangladeshi women from rural areas and 1.8 percent of recent arrivals were working in the garment industry in Dhaka.[41] In fact, these women were more likely to be engaged in low-paid domestic work and other informal work: 40.5 percent of long-term migrants and 37.3 percent of recent migrants were doing domestic work; and 36.3 percent of long-term migrants and 43.6 percent of recent migrants were in other informal sectors.[42] Many are in home work in which they were engaged in piece-rate work subcontracted by local factories. These facts suggest that a large number of Bangladeshi women are still concentrated in the "invisible" informal sectors. Women's lack of visibility in the public workspace further reinforces society's view that men and women have "separate spheres."

Rural women have been drawn to the cities by the possibility of finding work in export-oriented industries. Yet even these large, growing industries have failed to provide enough opportunities for all female migrants from rural areas. In addition, rural–urban migration in Bangladesh is still dominated by men. The sex ratios (the number of males per 100 females) in the major metropolitan areas are heavily skewed: Chittagong had the highest sex ratio (133), followed by Dhaka (127), Khulna (119), and Rajshani (110).[43] Furthermore, one study has found that although many women have begun working in garment industry, many local factories in other urban sectors still hire more men than women.[44] At the national level, in the sphere of paid employment, Bangladeshi women are neither as mobile nor as visible as Filipina and Sri Lankan women.

Rethinking the Role of Export-Oriented Industrialization in Migration

As seen in the above case studies, export-oriented industrialization has helped increase the demand for female labor in urban areas and triggered the rural–urban migration of women. However, when it comes to the *international* migration of women, the direct role played by export-oriented industrialization strategies is unclear. The existing literature has generally assumed that EPZs create large pools of potential international migrants.[45] However, the empirical data gathered so far do not suggest that EPZs have any significant impact on women's international mobility. On the contrary, many studies have found that most migrant women from Sri Lanka were housewives who had never engaged in wage employment prior to migration.[46] Even in the Philippines, only a small percentage of emigrants once worked in EPZs.

In fact, the impact of EPZs on the overall female workforce and on migration is very limited. While EPZs tend to attract much attention, they actually employ a relatively small proportion of the female workforce in most developing countries. In Bangladesh, women working in EPZs comprised only 0.4 percent of the total female workforce in 2002.[47] Sri Lanka has twice as many EPZs as Bangladesh, but their impact on employment is still limited: in 2002, female workers in EPZs constituted only 3.9 percent of the total female labor force. Even in the Philippines, where the presence of EPZs is the strongest in Asia, EPZs still accounted for only 5.0 percent of the total female labor force in 2002.

The actual size of EPZs is generally small. Furthermore, the differences between EPZs and non-EPZ sectors have narrowed. When first introduced, EPZs were the only areas where companies could enjoy tax holidays, exemption from labor laws, better exchange rates, and other benefits. However, soon after the manufacturing industries began growing, the same benefits became available outside EPZs. In Sri Lanka in 1992, President Ranasinghe Premadasa declared the entire country a free trade zone; this offered foreign corporations an incentive to invest in rural areas as well.[48] The situation is similar in the Philippines: the incentives to foreign investment have been extended beyond the EPZs. The Foreign Investment Act of 1991, the 1993 Investment Priorities Plan, and the Philippine Export Development Plan have

TABLE 6.1
Differential Integration into the Global Economy

	Trade in Goods as % GDP	Export as % of GDP	FDI as % of GDP
Senders of Migrant Women			
Philippines	22.1	12.3	0.7
Sri Lanka	17.9	9.3	0.4
Indonesia	15.2	7.9	0.9
Non-Senders			
Bangladesh	7.0	2.7	0.2
India	3.9	2.0	0.1
Pakistan	8.2	3.0	0.3

SOURCES: World Bank (2000); UNDP (2000).

provided various benefits to investors regardless of where they locate.[49] As a consequence, many MNCs have been investing outside EPZs, and this has blurred the distinctions between EPZs and non-EPZs. The EPZs have lost their uniqueness and become mere symbols of foreign direct investment. Therefore, in assessing the impact on women's employment, export-oriented industrialization policies must be considered as a whole rather than focusing on EPZs alone.

Export-oriented industrialization directly induces women's rural–urban migration, but not necessarily international migration. Even so, export-oriented industrialization seems related somehow to high levels of international female migration. Moreover, as seen in Table 6.1, the major sending countries of migrant women (such as the Philippines, Sri Lanka, and Indonesia) have larger export sectors and are better integrated into the global economy than "non-senders" (such as Bangladesh, India, and Pakistan). In addition, the "senders" of female migrants tend to have high levels of women's rural–urban migration whereas the "non-senders" do not (see Table 6.2).

The Macro–Micro Link: Social Legitimacy

How, then, can we interpret the relationships between export-oriented industrialization and international female migration? I contend that export-oriented industrialization makes significant contributions to the development of "social legitimacy" for women's employment and geographical mobility, initially at the local level. This eventually legitimizes international female migration. In this section I examine how export-oriented industrialization has transformed community norms and values by inducing women's internal (rural–urban) migration, and how this has led to social legitimacy for international female migration.

TABLE 6.2
The Sex Ratio in Urban Populations

		SEX RATIO: MALES PER 100 FEMALES	
		National	Urban Areas
Senders of Migrant Women			
Philippines	1970	98.8	93.3
	1980	100.7	95.5
	1990	101.1	97.7
	1998	n.a.	94.4
Indonesia	1961	97.3	100.1
	1971	96.8	100.0
	1980	98.8	100.2
	1990	99.5	99.9
Sri Lanka	1963	108.2	117.9
	1971	106.1	113.3
	1981	104.0	109.6
	1996	97.4	n.a.
	2001	97.9	102.2
Non-Senders			
Bangladesh	1961	107.6	142.2
	1974	107.7	129.4
	1981	106.4	125.8
	1991	106.1	118.1
India	1961	106.3	118.4
	1971	107.5	116.6
	1991	107.9	111.9
	2001	107.2	111.0
Pakistan	1961	111.1	130.1
	1968	113.8	122.7
	1981	110.5	115.3
	1998	108.3	111.9

NOTE: n.a. = not available.

SOURCES: Gugler (1997); Population Reference Bureau (2001); and national statistics.

In many developing countries, women's internal migration is not necessarily a new phenomenon. However, before export-oriented industrialization accelerated, most of them migrated with their husbands or other male family members. Only after many multinational factories began operating in the cities and the demand for female labor grew did women begin migrating to cities by themselves.

The increase in women's rural–urban migration reflected the needs of the poor who were suffering from the effects of structural adjustment programs. Because of rising poverty levels and the increasing demand for female labor both in cities and in foreign countries, societies began changing their perceptions of women's work. Many low-income families became more willing to send their daughters to a city for employment—a phenomenon that will be examined more closely in later sections. Neighbors also accepted this, seeing it as a way for households to improve their financial security. Eventually, societies became more tolerant and accepting of the idea that women leave home and work in factories. The following section discusses how social legitimacy for female migration has emerged in the Philippines and Sri Lanka but not in Bangladesh.

PHILIPPINES

In the Philippines, society has long been open to the idea of women playing independent economic roles. Even before Spanish colonial rule, women not only participated in agricultural work but also handled most of the trade.[50] The Spanish historian Wenceslao Retana has described the Filipina women during Spanish colonial rule as "capable and eager to earn a living, with a talent for business."[51] This tradition remains: many women today own small businesses such as *sari-sari* stores. According to Lauby and Stark,[52] a woman's migration from home in search of work in cities is thus perfectly consistent with the acceptance in the traditional Philippine culture of such economic roles for women. Their geographical mobility and wage employment have been widely accepted by the society because of this historical legacy.

Women's migration beyond cities—to foreign countries—has encountered little social resistance in the Philippines. The legitimacy provided by the state has certainly played some role: migration was initiated and legitimated by the state under the Marcos regime, when the country was desperately in need of foreign currency. Overall societal acceptance of and dependence on women's international migration has also been strong. As discussed earlier, when the Aquino administration banned the migration of unskilled women in 1988, the public resisted this ban, as did migrant women themselves, who accused the state of taking away their employment opportunities. Public pressure forced the state to moderate its restrictive policy. Furthermore, the ban on migration of domestic workers to Kuwait, which remained intact for many years, proved ineffective; the pressure among women to emigrate was so high that they circumvented the ban and kept emigrating there. In the mass media, the public often accused the state of not doing enough to protect migrant women. Yet my review of local newspapers over the past three decades found that public criticism has never been directed against the women themselves for working overseas.

The Philippines now treats migrant workers better than any other migrant-sending country. This is true of both the state and society. Migrants are hailed as national heroes and heroines, and December 18 is celebrated as

International Migrants' Day as a tribute to the hard work of migrants overseas. Every year before Christmas, the president personally welcomes migrant workers on a red carpet at the Ninoy Aquino International Airport. Migrant workers are treated with great dignity and respect for their contributions to their families and to the national economy. The international migration of both men and women has been widely accepted and even praised by society.

This high level of social legitimacy for migrant women is related to the high mobility of women within the country. Interregional and rural–urban migration was initially male-dominated; for the past three decades, however, Filipino women have constituted the majority in these migratory flows. Between 1948 and 1960, owing to industrial growth, especially in the manufacturing sectors, the sex ratio of the population in Manila dropped from 101.6 to 88.8 males per 100 females.[53] Rural–urban migratory flows had been feminized as early as 1965, when 60.6 percent of migrants were women.[54] In 1998, the urban population was female-dominated, with 94.4 males per 100 females; whereas the rural population was male-dominated, with 103.3 men per 100 females.[55]

The feminization of rural–urban migration is partly an indication of the high educational attainment of women in the Philippines. One of the most consistent findings of internal migration studies is that a positive correlation exists between educational attainment and migration. This is because workers with better education have greater chances of finding work.[56] Hart attributes the rapid feminization of internal migration to the number of new job opportunities that have become available for women in factories, hospitals, corporations, and public schools.[57] Filipinas have not only achieved parity with men in literacy rates but quite early on also surpassed them at the postsecondary level. By 1958, women already comprised 48 percent of the total college enrollment; even in the United States that year, the figure was only 38 percent. By 1970, female college students exceeded males by 5.3 percent in the Philippines.[58] The gap has continued to widen since then: 56.9 percent of college students were female in 1994.[59]

However, women's high educational attainment is not the only explanatory factor for the feminization of internal migration. Social legitimacy for female migration seems to exist even in earlier stages of women's lives. According to the data from the National Statistics Office, girls dominate even more heavily in the rural–urban migration of children. The national survey on children between five and seventeen found that across the country in 1995, 190,953 of them were living away from home, and that 64.7 percent of these were girls.[60] The fact that parents allow (or force) more girls than boys to leave home for wage employment at this early stage of life indicates that there is a great deal of social legitimacy for women's mobility. This is in stark contrast to what is found in Bangladesh and Pakistan where girls are kept home and strictly protected by male guardians until marriage.

Lauby and Stark[61] suggest two possible reasons why Filipino families are more likely to send daughters than sons to urban areas. First, the work of sons on farms and in craft manufacturing may be more valued than that of daughters, given the strenuous physical labor involved. Other research confirms this hypothesis. In Heinonen's study on rural households in southern Luzon, the respondents contended that women were physically weak and thus could not do certain agricultural tasks requiring physical strength.[62] Another study suggests that a clear gender division of labor exists in rural Philippine society, with the "[agricultural] field" designated as men's place.[63]

Lauby and Stark offer the second reason why parents prefer to send daughters to urban areas.[64] The low-wage jobs that are easily available to women in cities—such as factory work and domestic service—are more stable than the ones available to males. Typical male jobs such as construction work and dock work are seasonal, and the earnings are subject to factors such as weather and the size of the crop. Risk-averse families that are seeking to minimize income variations prefer the stability of "female jobs." It should be noted that Lauby and Stark's study only infers the role of the family and does not provide empirical evidence that family members actually influence their daughters in their migration decisions. Furthermore, they assume that women's rural–urban migration was not their own decision but rather their parents,' which has been contested by many scholars as already discussed. However, the data on the feminization of children's migration at least indicate that parents do send their daughters to cities to earn extra income for the family because of the stability of "female jobs." Daughters' loyalty to the family is another important factor. Families prefer to send daughters out of the home because they are likely to send more remittances back home. In fact, many studies have shown that women actually do send more money back home than men do.[65]

The overall stance of religious authorities toward women's employment also partly determines the level of social legitimacy for international female migration. The Catholic Church, which is the religious and moral authority in the Philippines, has never been against women entering the labor force. Unlike the Muslim organizations in Bangladesh, which have come out strongly against women's work in factories, the Catholic Church has been fairly open to women's employment. In 1974, Fr. Leonardo Legaspi, the rector of the University of Santo Tomas, declared in a speech that "women's

destiny should not be limited solely to keeping house and looking after husband and children." [66] The newspaper reported on his speech as follows:

> [If women's place were limited to home], he said, "the opening of universities to
> women is a waste of time and money and a travesty on the concept that women
> are the equals of men, not just in dignity but also in intelligence, capability and
> potential. Why should a girl study to be a doctor, if after such an expensive edu-
> cation all the medicine she will practice will be to apply a band-aid on a child's
> bruised knee?" [67]

The same article quoted a speech by Pope Paul XII:

> [Women's] entry into public life came suddenly as a result of social upheavals
> which we see around us. It does not matter.
>   You are called to take part. . . . [in] this powerful motive which impels a
> Catholic woman to enter upon a way that is now opened to her activity, there is
> added . . . dignity as woman. . . . Each of the two sexes must take part [*sic*] that
> belongs to it according to its nature, special qualities and physical, intellectual and
> moral aptitudes. Both have the right to cooperate towards the good of society and
> of their country. [68]

The Catholic Church has also been supportive of international migration,
be it of men or women. It has affirmed many times in various official documents that the right to emigrate is one of the basic human rights, and it has
not discriminated against women, whom it sees as having the same right as
men. [69] Pope John XXIII, for instance, in his Encyclical "Pacem in Terris"
of 11 April 1963, wrote the following:

> Again, every human being has the right to freedom of movement and of resi-
> dence within the confines of his own State. When there are just reasons in favor
> of it, he must be permitted to emigrate to other countries and take up residence
> there. The fact that he is a citizen of a particular State does not deprive him of
> membership in the human family, nor of citizenship in that universal society, the
> common, world-wide fellowship of men. [70]

Another Vatican document on regulating migration within the Church, the
"De Pastorali Migratorum Cura," states:

> But where a state which suffers from poverty combined with great population
> cannot supply such use of goods to its inhabitants, or where the state places con-
> ditions which offend human dignity, people possess a right to emigrate, to select
> a new home in foreign lands, and to seek conditions of life worthy of man. This
> right pertains not only to individual persons, but to whole families as well. There-
> fore "in decisions affecting migrants their right to live together as a family [is to
> be] safeguarded," with consideration of the needs of family housing, the educa-
> tion of children, working conditions, social insurance, and taxes. Public author-
> ities unjustly deny the rights of human persons if they block or impede emigra-

tion or immigration except where grave requirement of the common good, considered objectively, demand it.[71]

In recent years the Archbishop of the Catholic Church in the Philippines has begun reminding people of the social costs of migration, including family disintegration, but the church still endorses migration officially, declaring that "a person, because of an intolerable political or economic situation in one's country has a right to emigrate, to select a new home in foreign lands, and to seek conditions of life worthy of human being."[72]

The high proportion of highly educated women among Filipino migrants is another indicator of the high level of social legitimacy for international female migration in the Philippines. As discussed earlier, Filipina migrant women are the most highly educated migrant group in the world. Even about one-third of Filipina domestic workers have some college education. This testifies clearly that working overseas as an unskilled worker does not carry much social stigma for women in Philippine society.

SRI LANKA

Sri Lankan society has also been relatively open to international female migration. One reason may be that the country's economy has long relied heavily on female wage labor. Women began to turn into a steady labor force in the nineteenth century, when the British began recruiting them for the tea plantations as leaf pickers.[73] Women's wage employment has been socially acceptable since then. According to the Ceylon Census Report, by 1911 women were already 46.6 percent of the plantation labor force.[74] In 1971 in the Nuwara Eliya district it was as high as 53.1 percent.[75]

Nor was the internal migration of women uncommon in Sri Lanka. Such migration flows were generally male-dominated; however, the 1971 Census showed that female in-migrants outnumbered male in-migrants in the districts of Kandy, Matara, and Galle. Kearney and Miller[76] assume that this was due to employment opportunities in the coir (coconut) industry which produces coconut fiber rope and matting. Many Sri Lankan women were engaged in such work.

In 1979, after economic liberalization, Sri Lankan women's high literacy levels helped attract foreign investors, who set up factories. Since the 1960s the literacy rate among Sri Lankan women has been one of the highest among developing countries. Under the socialist government, the enrollment of girls in primary schools had increased from 36.0 to 48.1 percent by the 1970s.[77] The women's literacy rate had already reached 80 percent in the 1970s; by 2000 it was almost 90 percent, which was much higher than the Third World average for women of 66 percent.[78]

In the early 1980s, women's geographical mobility and their high education levels made it more acceptable for them to migrate to cities to take the new jobs in the EPZs and other export sectors. Women's employment in the EPZs did not face too much opposition from society because working for foreign companies and dealing with new technology and equipment brought them some social status. Perera cites one worker who boasted: "The employees could tell the world that they worked in the EPZs."[79]

Although there was a supportive environment for women's rural–urban migration and employment in cities, it took a while before Sri Lankan society came to accept their international migration. When women began migrating to the Middle East in the early 1980s, they enjoyed very little social acceptance. When these migrant women returned, they encountered many difficulties in their communities. Despite the lack of any solid evidence, young unmarried women were accused of having lost their virginity and ostracized for it, and married women were stigmatized for their alleged sexual misconduct.[80] The negative impact of female migration was a focus of public debate in the mid-1980s.[81] And because the social stigma could have affected marriage prospects, few young single women emigrated overseas. The most typical Sri Lankan migrant was an older married woman with limited education and a compelling need to support her family. Rural women with little education got only low-status jobs at home, although these sometimes exposed them to the same risks of abuse and exploitation that they would experience in the Middle East anyway.[82]

However, Sri Lankan society's reactions to the international migration of women have been changing over the past two decades. Perera contends that the experience of overseas travel, familiarity with modern appliances, improvements in housing, and other material advantages have brought status and acceptance to returned migrant women and their families.[83] Many of my respondents reported that their family's status within the community had somewhat improved as a result of the money they brought.

This does not mean that the international migration of women has shed its negative image entirely. During my fieldwork, I found that the reality was not as simple as Perera's respondent suggested when she said: "When we bring back money, society will accept us."[84] For example, some migrants and their families have chosen to donate large sums of money to local temples to compensate for their tarnished image and to improve their social standing in the community. The middle- and upper-middle-classes still look down on migrant women. During an interview, one senior female professor at the University of Colombo made this comment:

> Social stigma against premarital sex is still strong [in Sri Lankan society]. So, the prejudice against migrant women, especially unmarried women, still exists. How

do you know? She [a migrant woman] could have slept with someone else [over-seas]. People don't say it outright, but they think in their heart, "This girl may not be pure."

The prejudice against migrant women is particularly strong among the up-per social strata. Those in the upper middle-class are especially critical of women who show off, flash their money, and act proud after they return from abroad. They are not happy with these women wearing jewelry and nice dresses, or even taking a trishaw for short distances they used to walk. "They became lazy," a senior villager said. Actually, what makes the village leaders most uncomfortable is not these trivial changes, but the fact that some returned women have more money than *they* do—at least temporarily—and partly as a result they treat the community leaders differently. This could threaten the community's hierarchical structure. In their view, migrant women should "know their place" and act accordingly.

Pushpa Chandrasekera, an educated woman who runs a local women's NGO, was frustrated with the migrant women in her community for this very reason: they no longer treated her with enough respect and courtesy. When she was trying to organize an association for these female returnees to help them set up small businesses, some returnees told her she was not the right person to chair the association since she had never migrated abroad. This came as a shock to her because she is from a prestigious family that had rarely been challenged by people in the lower social strata. While she was describing this incident to me, she seemed furious:

> They [migrant women] are very uneducated and very poor. They don't know how to behave. . . . We have to train them how to behave. I don't allow them to come to the association [meeting of migrant women] wearing like "Dubai women" [wearing flashy clothes and earrings, etc.]. I don't allow them because they are Sri Lankan women. There are so many problems. . . . In Sri Lanka, NGOs don't want to work with these women. They come back to the country with big money [and act like a different person]. We have to change their mind.

Clearly, some prejudice against female migration still exists in Sri Lankan so-ciety. Overall, however, the strong stigma against migrant women has been fading, at least among the lower and middle classes, if not among older gen-erations and the upper social strata. Migration is no longer a serious obstacle to the marriage prospects of young middle-class women. Gamburd found that in 1997, more unmarried women were traveling abroad than in 1994.[85] During my fieldwork, I was surprised to meet many young, single Sri Lan-kan migrant women with a good education. One of my respondents, Fa-tima, came from a respectable family and had an "A level" (thirteen years) education, yet she had gone to the Maldives to work in a garment factory and later to Kuwait as a domestic worker. Her family was against her working abroad, but she had insisted. Her parents' misgivings were apparently unfounded: she married a successful businessman when she returned. Fatima does not believe that her migration experience hindered her search for a husband; in fact, it helped her, because of the money she had accumulated overseas and the skills she learned there. Women who have worked as garment workers are especially valued, because they have demonstrated their potential for earning extra income for the family.

It is possible that domestic work carries less social stigma if it is done for foreigners. I asked Fatima if she had considered working as a domestic worker in Sri Lanka. She said she would never do such work for a local family, not only because of the low wages but also because it would be a disgrace to "wash other people's pots and pans" in her own society. The question actually upset her:

> I am an educated girl. I can't do such work. My parents won't let me work in someone's house like that. Our society thinks that working abroad [as a domestic worker] is good, but working [as a domestic worker] here for a Singhalese family is not.

Dayani, who had worked in Kuwait and who had begun working for a Japanese expatriate in Colombo at the time of the interview, also told me she would never do domestic work for a local family. Housekeeping for foreigners brings recognition and some status whereas doing the same work for local residents is viewed as shameful.

Social legitimacy for women's migration overseas has slowly established itself in Sri Lanka. There is no way to measure precisely the degree of social legitimacy; however, the behavior of educated women perhaps indicates how well certain jobs are perceived. When a job carries a strong social stigma, it is unlikely that many educated women will take it. The proportion of educated women among migrants has been increasing, and this suggests that social legitimacy for international female migration is beginning to emerge. Since there is no consistent longitudinal study on the education level of migrant women, it is hard to measure the changes in a precise manner. The only way to estimate those changes is by reviewing studies carried out over the past two decades (see Table 6.3). These studies are not strictly comparable because of differences in sampling methods. Even so, they indicate that the educational qualifications of migrant women have been rising significantly. Brochmann found that in 1985–86, only 3 percent of migrant women had nine or more years of education.[86] Eight years later, the proportion was much higher: the Marga Institute found that 29.3 percent of migrant women had more than nine years of education, and Yapa observed that 40 percent had nine to twelve years of education.[87] My own research, conducted in

TABLE 6.3
Increasing Educational Levels of Sri Lankan Migrant Women

Years of Education	Brochmann (1985–86) (%)	Marga (1994) (%)		Yapa (1995) (%)		Oishi (1999) (%)
9 years or more	3	More than 9 years	29.3	9–12 years	40	College — 6.3
8 years	31	6–9 years	45.6	6–8 years	44	12 years (A level) — 10.4
5–7 years	31	1–5 years	22.4	1–5 years	15	10 years (O level) — 52.0
Less than 5 years	35	No schooling	2.6	No schooling	1	9 years and less — 31.3
N	100	N	2,000	N	100	N — 50*

NOTE: *Including two missing variables.

1999, indicated a rapid increase—about 70 percent of migrant women had more than nine years of education.

Emerging social legitimacy also implies broader acceptance of more liberal gender roles, especially those relating to female virginity and marriageability.[88] With more and more women working abroad, the social stigma attached to this choice has weakened. More parents are now allowing their daughters to follow the paths of their relatives and neighbors working abroad. While some lingering prejudice continues among small segments of the population, more and more Sri Lankans are coming to see migration as an acceptable employment option for women.

BANGLADESH

In Bangladesh, the colonial authorities did not integrate women into wage labor as they did in Sri Lanka and the Philippines. As a consequence, Bangladesh has maintained the Muslim tradition of *purdah* and female seclusion easily until recent years. This has contributed to women's limited geographical mobility and labor force participation. While not strictly practiced widely, it was considered ideal for women to be confined within four walls and protected by male guardians. Seclusion is especially important for young single women whose marriage prospects could be at stake. The father's presence and protection are especially crucial. Single women find it difficult to attract a marriage partner when the father is absent. Even when the family has considerable money, if the father has been working overseas, his daughters are less preferred for marriage because the father's lack of supervision implies a lack of chastity.

Moral restrictions on women's mobility do not end after marriage. Married women are discouraged from traveling long distances without a male guardian.[89] This social environment has strongly affected Bangladeshi women's overall mentality concerning their mobility. Even in slums where female seclusion is not strictly practiced, women usually live in a very confined world. They feel vulnerable and helpless to go "out there" where they do not know anyone. One woman in a slum told me: "I even feel scared of going outside this area. How could I go abroad?"

Whether a Banglasdeshi woman is married or not, her freedom of movement is fairly restricted. This is not necessarily because of Islamic law. In fact, Islamic law guarantees the right to freedom of movement.[90] It is rather that cultural practices do not extend the right to women. This tendency is stronger in rural areas, where the social institution of *shamaj* governs people's lives more strictly than in cities. *Shamaj* is a community organization that brings households together at times of birth, death, and marriage and that also plays a powerful moral role.[91] According to Kabeer, *shamaj* acts as "the guardian of the social and moral order, representing the interests of the rich and powerful, through its dominance of the *shalish*."[92] The *shalish*, an informal village court for local disputes, lays down the codes of "proper" behavior and sanctions those who do not comply.[93] The *shamaj* exerts its own values through the *shalish*, which is supported by local religious leaders, *mullahs* and *moulanas*, who make "vociferous allegations about women's improper activities which often go well beyond what is laid down in the sacred scriptures."[94] These social institutions have been quite powerful in enforcing the practice of *purdah* and in placing constraints on the types of work that women can do. In rural areas, only women from poor, landless households could devote a significant amount of time to wage employment outside the home until recent years.[95]

Given such an environment, women's entry into wage employment in the 1980s was perceived as a radical change in Bangladesh. The strong presence of young "unaccompanied women" on the streets was almost a scandal. Kabeer records that the media caricatured women who were employed by urban factories:

> A group of girls . . . with faces in cheap makeup, gaudy ribbons adorning their oily braids and draped in psychedelic colored sarees with tiffin carriers in their hands are a common sight [these] days during the morning and evening hours. These are the garment workers, [a] new class of employees.[96]

The religious community also denounced women's wage employment, contending that it would contribute to the breakdown of the "natural" principle of sexually segregated spheres.[97] For their part, Islamic economists contended that women's employment would bring many "disasters" to the society, one of which was "moral degradation":

> Men and women sit in the same working place face to face. Whatever liberal arguments are put forward in favour of this arrangement, in reality the close proximity of opposite sexes arouses lust and love for each other which on many occasions lead to immoral and scandalous affairs between them. What are [*sic*] happening to their children left at home? Are they getting enough love and proper rearing? The answer is 'No.'[98]

The public's response to "factory women" was sharply negative, and at first these women had to endure antagonistic campaigns mounted by the religious community near their workplaces. However, as the demand for female labor increased and a large number of women entered wage employment, the situation gradually changed. Women's wage employment has now become more socially acceptable.

Another significant change was that not only urban women but also rural women began taking wage employment in urban areas. The autonomous migration of rural women to cities was once extremely rare in Bangladesh; today it is becoming more common. Kibria notes that among low-income families there was almost no opposition to women's migration to cities for factory work.[99] For low-income households in Bangladesh—the poorest of the poor—survival mattered more than social prestige. Lower middle-class families, whose daily survival is more or less secured, still offer some resistance, although for economic reasons some of them have started allowing their daughters to work in factories in cities.[100]

Despite these positive changes, however, the impact of export-oriented industrialization on women is much smaller in Bangladesh than in the Philippines and Sri Lanka. As Table 6.2 shows, rural–urban migration in Bangladesh is still heavily male-dominated. In addition, women in the export-manufacturing sector are still a minority, comprising only 10 percent of the total female labor force in Bangladesh in 2002;[101] the vast majority—80 percent—of Bangladeshi women are still working in agriculture.

MIGRATION AS "IMPURITY"

For women, going overseas alone carries far more negative connotations than working in a city. In Bangladesh, the international migration of women as domestic workers or entertainers—the most readily available jobs for low-income women—is often associated with sexual impurity and promiscuity. During my fieldwork in the Dhaka slums, many low-income women—including those who wanted to work overseas—often used the word *khati* (purity) when talking about the indecency of domestic workers. According to them, domestic work was not *shal kaaj* (pure work) because the employer could take sexual advantage of the woman. Asha, a forty-five-year-old slum dweller, was critical of women working abroad as domestic workers, saying:

> When girls work [abroad] as a domestic worker, it's not good. It's not pure. No guardian [to protect them], no say [to employers], so she gets [sexually] abused.

The prejudice against female migration is also based on the widespread belief that women pretend to be migrating as domestic workers while actually working as full-time or part-time prostitutes. Another common belief is that Bangladeshi domestic workers are often forced to have a sexual relationship with the male employer. There is no way to tell what percentage of migrant women actually engaged in sex work or sexual relationship with employers, because no one would have revealed as much even if they had encountered such an experience. At the same time, it is impossible for women to prove that they did *not* work as prostitutes. No matter what they say, people are still suspicious about what work they actually did. A forty-two-year-old woman in a slum told me: "I don't know what they [migrant women] actually do overseas." When I heard this, I understood why Bangladeshi women often told me they wanted to go abroad as factory workers, or that they would do any work as long as they got paid, but none of them told me specifically that they wanted to go abroad as domestic workers. The local interpreter even told me not to ask the respondents directly whether they would like to find domestic work overseas: the question would have offended them.

The reactions from local women being so negative, one can easily imagine how harsh men are likely to be toward international female migration. In a male-dominated society there is no difference between domestic work and factory work in terms of moral values. Women who work overseas, however, are to be censured no matter what work they do because of their alleged sexual promiscuity and misbehavior. They are even perceived as the source of HIV/AIDS in Bangladesh. One newspaper article put it this way:

> Ask a male Bangladeshi villager how AIDS has been spreading in his country and nine out of 10 will reply, "Bangladeshi 'nongra' (dirty) women bring it from outside." Female Bangladeshi migrants who return home are often seen by their male contemporaries as "loose" or "bad charactered" women. Whether they were in garment factories or domestic work in the Middle East or Southeast Asia, the overwhelming male perception is that they almost always become part-time sex workers.[102]

Of course, this sort of stigma does not stop all Bangladeshi women from emigrating abroad. Despite the social stigma and official bans, destitution has driven some unskilled women to venture abroad through unofficial channels, mostly as domestic workers. According to one estimate, 32,000 undocumented Bangladeshi migrant women were working in the Middle East in 2000.[103] Even though this is a rather high-side estimate made by the NGO, it is only 0.1 percent of the total female workforce in the country. Sri Lanka's population is less than one-sixth that of Bangladesh, yet about 680,000 Sri Lankan women were working overseas around the same time,[104] constituting roughly one-fifth of Sri Lanka's total female labor force.[105] The Philippines has an even larger female workforce overseas: in 2002, the overseas stock of migrant women comprised almost one-fourth of the total female labor force.[106] Compared with these countries, Bangladesh is emphatically a non-sending country with regard to migrant women. Bangladesh's ban on women's migration was lifted in 2003, but social illegitimacy continues to discourage unskilled low-income women from migrating.

Conclusion

Globalization has undoubtedly exerted significant influence on women's employment in developing countries. New global production processes have opened up new opportunities for women because of their low wages, perceived dexterity, and docility. Despite poor working conditions, more and more women have been entering the export-oriented manufacturing and service sectors. These job opportunities have been bringing about massive social change in traditional societies in terms of women's increasing visibility in the formal employment sector and, more importantly, their autonomous migration. Many of these women are migrants from rural areas. It has long been assumed that these internal migrants form potential pools of international migrants.

However, my data do not confirm a direct link between internal and international migration. Internal migrants do not necessarily become international migrants; many international migrants are housewives with no work experience who come from rural areas. Furthermore, the impact of EPZs is not as significant as often believed, in terms of job creation and productive output.

The link between globalization and international migration is more subtle and yet powerful. Globalization processes and the resultant export-oriented industrialization do not produce international migrants directly. They do, however, help bring about important changes in social perceptions of women's employment and of their independent mobility. The sudden increase in the demand for female labor is gradually transforming traditional norms that long restricted women's geographical mobility in small communities. Moreover, women's rising education levels are helping boost their levels of internal migration. With women's rural–urban migration gaining more social legitimacy, societies are finding it easier to accept their international migration.

The most significant challenge to traditional social norms is that women are leaving home and exposing themselves to the "outside world" before getting married. The actual distance of migration—whether it is to a city or to another country—is less important. The point of controversy within communities centers on the fact that young single women are leaving home without being accompanied by a male guardian. A woman's independent move, when it first happens, generates moral resistance among conservatives in the community. However, this resistance fades once a large number of women begin to take factory work; at some point, female migration to cities becomes more "normal" and migration over longer distances and even to foreign countries gradually becomes acceptable. For this reason, in countries where the internal migration of women has been legitimized, international female migration also tends to gain social legitimacy.

Furthermore, social legitimacy influences policy makers' perceptions, since it gives them more confidence to support international female migration. The average education level of prospective migrant women is a key factor affecting policy decisions. The state officials I interviewed in the Philippines and Sri Lanka emphasized the high levels of educational attainment among their migrant women overseas, arguing that education made these women more alert and helped them solve problems overseas and counteract abuse and exploitation.

The lack of social legitimacy and the existence of a strong stigma against female migrants—as in the case of Bangladesh—tend to discourage women from leaving the country. Women fear being ostracized, being labeled as promiscuous, risking their marriageability, and tarnishing their family's reputation. In such cases, women emigrate only when they are desperate to survive and cannot afford to care about social perceptions. Most of them have very little education. Such profiles of women do not persuade policy makers to support female migration, since they believe that these uneducated, unskilled women would be not only vulnerable to abuse and exploitation by foreign employers but also entirely helpless when encountering problems. The policy makers I interviewed in Bangladesh, when they discussed the reasons why they had banned the migration of unskilled women, often mentioned the illiteracy and vulnerability of these women.

Social legitimacy for international female migration is difficult to measure because it is subject to changes that constantly affect and are affected by individuals, communities, and policy makers. However, the data on rural–urban migration and on the increasing education levels among migrant women at least suggest that social legitimacy for women's domestic mobility is a crucial prerequisite for international female migration.

Together with historical legacies of women's employment and gender equality in education, economic globalization, particularly growing export sectors, is a powerful factor developing social legitimacy for women's international migration. As it attracts more rural women to the urban area, communities grow accustomed to the phenomenon and eventually accept women's mobility, even beyond national borders. In other words, social legitimacy is the key to understanding the nexus between globalization, economic development, and the international migration of women.

CHAPTER 7

Conclusion: Toward Global Governance of Migration

THIS STUDY HAS examined the cross-national variations and causal mechanisms of international female migration in Asia. It has adopted an integrative approach in order to analyze receiving, sending, and non-sending countries at four levels (see Table 7.1). With regard to receiving countries, globalization has affected the patterns of international female migration in different countries in different ways. Often, the demand for foreign domestic workers and caregivers grew in industrialized and semi-industrialized countries when local women began to engage in wage employment. The erosion of welfare-state policies and the resultant gap between state care provisions and the needs of working families have stimulated a strong demand for migrant women. In other countries, rapid accumulations of wealth have boosted the demand for foreign domestic workers who are perceived as symbols of conspicuous consumption. The oil-rich GCC countries in the Middle East are an example of this. In Japan, on the other hand, the presence of female migrant "entertainers" (or quasi-sex workers) has been more significant; the demand for these workers has been growing and met through global networks of crime syndicates. This book has not focused on irregular migration or human trafficking *per se*; however, it has shown that even legal migration of "entertainers" raises many serious issues.

Immigration policies establish an overall framework for international female migration in all of these countries. They do so by restricting occupational categories and sometimes even the nationalities of migrant women through "political selectivity" based on state interests and diplomatic partnerships. At the same time, employers and recruitment agencies exert "social selectivity" based on certain national stereotypes and biases. These ste-

TABLE 7.1

Integrative Approach to International Female Migration

Levels of Analysis	Major Analytical Dimensions of Women's Migration Inflows	Major Analytical Dimensions of Women's Migration Outflows
Macro (Suprastate)	• Globalization of production and services	• Globalization of production and services
Macro (State)	• Immigration policies • Development policies • Welfare policies • Political selectivity	• Emigration policies • Development policies • Social policies
Meso (Society)	• Social selectivity • Social networks	• Social legitimacy for international female migration • Social networks
Micro (Individual)	• Employers' selectivity	• Women's autonomy and decision-making power • Trapping mechanism

reotypes and biases, which are shaped and reinforced by the media and by recruitment agencies, create general preferences for migrant women from particular countries and also determine their market wage rates.

THE DETERMINANTS IN DEVELOPING COUNTRIES

International migration is a demand-driven phenomenon, and immigration policies determine the general levels of international female migration. However, demand-side factors cannot on their own explain the cross-national patterns of migration. In particular, they cannot entirely explain why women in some countries are not willing to respond to the overseas job demand. This book has pointed to three social factors in developing countries—emigration policies, women's autonomy, and social legitimacy—that affect the levels of international female migration in Asia.

Emigration policies tend to exert more control over women than men. Some countries limit women's emigration by placing restrictions on certain feminized sectors such as domestic work and entertainment. The severity of these restrictions varies significantly among states. Socialist states tend to place the strongest controls over emigration because of their closed economic policies. However, even some capitalist states have adopted restrictive emigration policies for women. There are several factors in play here, but the most important is national identity. A nation's self-understanding affects migration policies in fundamental ways.

In Bangladesh, where emigration policies for women have been restrictive, policy makers and elites emphasize the Muslim nature of their state.[1] Referring to the Quranic teaching that men should be the "protectors" of women, they believe that the state has to assume this role at the macro level. Restricting women's mobility is, in this sense, justified in order to protect them from abuse in the hands of foreign employers. Nevertheless, Islam does not always result in restrictive policies for female migration. In Indonesia, the Muslim identity was overridden—at least initially—by the country's identity as a "developmental state." In the 1980s and early 1990s, its state initiatives for economic development included an aggressive labor export policy. Both men and women were encouraged to work abroad because the foreign currencies they remitted would strengthen the national economy. Sri Lanka took a similar stance, but on the basis of its democratic philosophy. State officials often emphasized that their country was a "democratic state" that respected the human rights of its citizens, including their right to free movement. In the Philippines, female migration has been banned several times in the past on a temporary basis; however, most policy makers identify strongly with democracy and have generally adopted open emigration policies for both men and women over the past three decades.

National identity is never static; it is always subject to "symbolic politics of gender" through which a country's migrant women become the symbolic focus of public debates. The public—whose opinions are often male-dominated—is extremely sensitive to any abuses of "its women" by foreign employers. Abuses against migrant women abroad tend to generate much more public outrage than similar abuses of women at home. This is because women are symbols of national dignity and pride once they leave their country. It follows that the public often considers their abuse and rape by foreigners as atrocities against the nation. Faced with this reality, states often try to adopt more restrictive emigration policies for women. Female migration brings to the fore a whole separate set of policy issues that are not important for male migration.

Finally, civil society plays some role when migration policies for women are being formulated. In the Philippines, pressure from migration NGOs helped repeal the ban on the emigration of domestic workers. By contrast, in Bangladesh, where only a handful of NGOs focus on migration issues, there was only a limited protest when the emigration of unskilled women was banned. Bangladesh is well known for its strong civil society, yet the vast majority of its NGOs do not work on migration issues because those issues do not appear on the radar of Western donors. Many NGOs in Bangladesh rely for their funding on donations from North America and Europe, and those donors' interests cannot help but influence their activities. This is why local NGOs find it difficult to expand their activities to cover migration issues. Overall, then, a strong presence of migration NGOs in a given country results in more open emigration policies for women, especially when those NGOs have political clout.

WOMEN'S AUTONOMY

For large-scale female migration to take place, there must be strong conducive factors at the micro level—in other words, individual women must be motivated to work abroad. This study found that high levels of women's autonomy and financial responsibility within households are closely associated with the motivation to migrate and with the actual migration process.

In countries where women have decision-making power over household finances, rates of female migration tend to be high; this is because these women are acutely aware of the need for additional income. For these women, migration is an obvious option. Among single women—especially younger single women—the level of autonomy is important, because parents or elder siblings could exert control over their emigration decisions.

In countries where women have little autonomy and little control over household finances, fewer women are willing to migrate abroad because their families tend to restrict their mobility, or because it is not their responsibility to support financially the family. In these countries, female migration is found only among low-income households where women are allowed to migrate and are sometimes encouraged to do so.

SOCIAL LEGITIMACY

This study has presented a new concept—"social legitimacy"—as a key to understanding the nexus between macro-policies and micro-individual factors. The degree to which a society accepts and legitimizes international female migration significantly influences the decisions women make. Social legitimacy flows out of several conditions. Colonial legacies provided a foundation for societal acceptance of women's employment. In some countries (for example, the Philippines and Sri Lanka), women were an integral part of the colonial economy; after these countries achieved independence, less stigma was attached to women's wage employment. Societies that lack this legacy (such as Bangladesh) tend to view women's employment as a threat to traditional values at least initially.

More recently, globalization has affected social legitimacy for international female migration. Export-oriented industrialization has increased women's labor force participation and rural–urban mobility. In the Philippines and Sri Lanka, this has helped transform the traditional social norms that declared women's place to be the home and that prohibited young single women from leaving home until after marriage. Women's employment and their independent migration to cities at first generated community resistance. However, as their earnings actually improved the living conditions of the families, more women began to work in cities, during which process the stigma gradually faded. In other words, globalization has helped make societies more accepting of women's employment and geographical mobility. Social legitimacy for women's rural–urban migration eventually led to greater acceptance of their international migration, because communities had already softened their resistance to young single women leaving the village for any reason. It became acceptable for women to leave home for cities, and this legitimated their migration to foreign countries.

In countries such as Bangladesh, where globalization and export-oriented industrialization have proceeded rather slowly, social legitimacy for women's international migration has not been well developed. The vast majority of women still remain in the agricultural sector and are less mobile than men in rural–urban migration. Women's limited geographical mobility is related to the underdevelopment of social legitimacy for international female migration.

Albeit indirectly, women's educational attainment has helped foster social legitimacy for international female migration. Policy makers often find it acceptable for educated women to work abroad;[2] the assumption is that these women will know what to do if they encounter trouble and will be able to protect themselves from foreign employers who would otherwise abuse them. This assumption is not necessarily valid, since abuse can occur in any workplace, whatever the worker's education level. Conversely, policy makers believe that uneducated women lack the capacity to protect themselves; thus the state must protect them by restricting their mobility. This mentality is endemic among policy makers and elites in those countries where women's education levels are relatively low. In countries where women have achieved parity in education, there are fewer restrictions on female migration, because both policy makers and social elites trust women's overall ability to deal with problems in foreign workplaces. The better educated a country's women are, the more social legitimacy they are extended when it comes to international migration.

The degree of social legitimacy also depends on state policies. In the Philippines, President Ferdinand Marcos aggressively promoted overseas employment, and every government since has largely supported the migration of both men and women. In the Philippines, migrants are lauded as national heroes and heroines for helping their loved ones and the national economy. In Sri Lanka, the state has never aggressively promoted female migration *per se*, but it has encouraged migration in general. This laissez-faire policy has

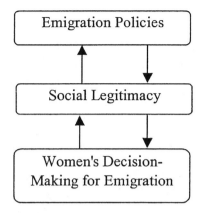

FIGURE 7.1. Interactions of Determinants in Developing Countries

extended some political legitimacy to female migration. In Bangladesh, by contrast, the lack of social legitimacy for international female migration has been accentuated by state emigration policies such as bans and restrictions.

Interactions of Factors

In developing countries, international female migration is determined by the interactions among these multilevel factors (see Figure 7.1). Export industrialization and open state policies for emigration bring about a positive social environment for women's employment and mobility; this facilitates women's decisions to go overseas. Conversely, closed emigration policies and the lack of social legitimacy for women's work and migration discourage women from migrating. However, women are not simply subjugated to the state and society. Even when traditional social norms stigmatize female migration, some women—often those who are too desperate to care about how society views them—resist community pressure and emigrate abroad. As they bring back money and improve their economic status, other women emulate them. As the numbers of migrant women increase and their wealth exerts some "demonstration effect," community norms begin to change. Migrant women's sheer numbers, and the economic contributions they make to families and the country, gradually legitimize female migration. Social legitimacy for female migration then influences the perceptions of policy makers; this in turn can result in more open emigration policies for women. Women's international migration is an outcome of constant interactions between multilevel factors.

As I made clear at the outset, this study has focused on Asia. It thus reflects regional specificities in terms of economic development and labor market dynamics. The applicability of my findings to other regions must not be assumed. However, various other studies suggest that my findings may well be applicable to other regions. In Latin America, where economic development has followed a somewhat similar course as in the Philippines, Sri Lanka, and Indonesia, migration flows have also been feminized.[3] On the other hand, in sub-Saharan Africa, where export-oriented industrialization has not expanded significantly, migration flows are still male-dominated both internally and internationally, although more women have begun to migrate in recent years. It would be interesting to systematically apply the same integrative approach to other developing regions when analyzing their patterns of female migration.

Further studies are needed to uncover the extent to which state policies, women's autonomy, and social legitimacy determine levels of female migration elsewhere in the world. For example, well worth exploring is women's migration from Eastern Europe and the former Soviet Union. These regions are quickly becoming important sources of migrant women—particularly the victims of human trafficking. How have communist/socialist legacies affected these societies' views of women's employment in general and their employment in foreign countries in particular? Has globalization increased these women's rural–urban migration and international migration? More comparative research is necessary to answer these questions.

The most significant challenge for migration scholars is to establish a theoretical framework that can integrate irregular migration—in particular, human trafficking. My study included some respondents who were irregular migrants. However, I did not address this specific issue because their numbers were too small for me to make any generalizations. Furthermore, human trafficking and irregular migration seem to have their own distinct mechanisms and for that reason require separate studies. Irregular migration is becoming a large component of international migration, and many case studies have been produced over the past few years.[4] Yet more systematic and theoretically oriented studies are needed, especially from a gender perspective. Although there are problems of data and methodology, it is imperative that migration scholars tackle these challenges. How does it differ from regular labor migration in terms of women's profiles and risk-awareness? Is irregular migration likely to occur more when women's socioeconomic status is low? What impact do state policies have on this type of migration? Once further studies address these questions and integrate them into the existing research framework, we will be closer to understanding women's international migration.

The Challenges to the State and the International Community: Policy Implications

This study has analyzed the cross-national patterns and causal mechanisms of women's migration, and its findings have a number of policy implications, both national and international. Given the intensification of global competition and the growing care gap in industrialized societies, the demand for migrant female labor will continue to grow. As globalization continues to transform the social environment and remove obstacles to female migration, more women will be joining the migrant labor force. It is thus an urgent necessity that more effective protection mechanisms be established for migrant women. This last section addresses some of the key issues and challenges for individual states and the international community regarding the protection of migrant women.

THE STATE'S RESPONSIBILITY FOR THE PROTECTION OF MIGRANT WOMEN

As seen above, states exert bans and restrictions on female migration for protection purposes. However, one of the fundamental problems of such measures is that information about these bans and restrictions is not necessarily communicated well to potential migrant women. This study found that migrant women were not always informed of emigration policies. The vast majority of Filipina migrant women knew the basic emigration regulations. Sri Lankan migrants were less well informed; many of them had never heard of the state agency, the SLBFE, and did not even know they had to register with it before their departure.

Bangladeshi migrant women were by far the least informed. Almost all the respondents, including non-migrants, had never heard that there was a ban or even that a state agency existed for registering migrants. Women who came back from abroad had also never heard of the state agency, BMET, even though they were supposed to have registered with it prior to their departure. This problem is quite complex in Bangladesh, because potential migrants have very limited access to education. Many village women I spoke to did not even know what the government was. One of them could not distinguish the government from recruiting agents: "They [the government] are bad guys. They sell us to India." Because they lacked educational opportunities and had little exposure to society outside their own community, these women had little understanding of how the social system operated. Their illiteracy prevented them from reading newspapers, and their poverty did not allow them to buy a radio or a television. These poor women were the ones most likely to apply for overseas employment and therefore should have known about the ban, yet they were the least likely to be informed. Given this information gap, the rationale for the ban on female migration is highly questionable.

Bans on female migration are not an ideal solution with regard to protection, either. They make women even more vulnerable by diverting them into irregular/undocumented migration and by reducing the likelihood that protection will be available to them. Furthermore, as long as pressures to emigrate continue to exist, it will be difficult to enforce bans, because of the growing trafficking industry operated by crime syndicates. With the numbers of undocumented migrant women increasing, a much more effective protection strategy would be to launch campaigns to warn prospective migrant women about illegal recruiters and traffickers. Women in foreign workplaces, or thinking about foreign employment, need information in order to protect themselves from these organizations. Some awareness-raising programs are presently being launched by local and international NGOs; these should be expanded. International donors should be encouraged to provide financial support for these prevention programs.

STATE CAPACITIES FOR PROTECTION

Migrant-sending states try to protect their workers, both male and female. The effectiveness of protection varies, however. The Philippines is perhaps ranked at the top in this regard. It has made predeparture orientations mandatory for migrants.[5] Moreover, it has assigned a number of labor attachés and welfare officers to its diplomatic missions specifically to attend to the problems that migrant workers encounter in destination countries. Many diplomatic missions offer temporary shelter and legal counseling for migrants who have run away from an employer after encountering serious problems. The Philippine embassies and consulates even organize social events and offer vocational training courses for migrants who are willing to learn additional skills while working abroad.

However, it is still difficult for sending states to solve problems by themselves because of their limited capacities. For instance, even in the Philippine embassies and consulates, where the protection system is most developed, there are still far from enough labor attachés (thirty-five in 1999), considering that over seven million Filipino migrants work abroad. Other states offer much less protection for migrants; they lack predeparture orientation programs, shelter facilities in embassies and consulates, and sufficient numbers of labor attachés and welfare officers. Some states even take the side of foreign employers for the sake of maintaining good relations with them; clearly, their hope is to continue sending a large number of migrants and benefiting from their remittances. I met some migrant workers who complained that their embassies and consulates not only paid little attention to their problems but also deported some workers who complained about their employers. These cases reflect the unequal political and economic power between sending and receiving states. Such an imbalance often makes it extremely difficult for sending states to protect migrants on their own.

THE ROLES OF MIGRANT-RECEIVING STATES

The key to protecting migrants is largely located in destination states. The most important measure that migrant-receiving states could take is to extend their legal protections to encompass migrant workers, especially domestic workers and entertainers. The fundamental problem is that migrant women are concentrated in occupations like these which are not protected by labor laws. It is not just migrant women who are suffering from maltreatment and unfavourable working conditions; so are the nationals in these occupations. To protect *all* workers in these occupations is extremely important, for the welfare of both national and migrant workers.

Migrant-receiving states should also work harder to educate employers and raise their awareness. In Singapore, for instance, after a number of migrant domestic workers were murdered by their employers, the state introduced a compulsory orientation for first-time employers of domestic workers. It also decided that all agencies for domestic workers must be accredited by the state.[6] Comprehensive labor inspections and interventions are almost impossible, given the limited state capacity; even so, major migrant-receiving states should assign at least some inspectors specifically to monitor the conditions of migrant workers. To better protect migrant women, labor inspectors should be allowed to randomly monitor the houses of employers' home where migrant domestic workers are employed.

And lastly, migrant-receiving states should consider providing financial resources for migrants' shelters and counseling centers, most of which have been operated by migrant-sending states' embassies or NGOs to a limited extent. The needs of maltreated migrants have always exceeded the capacities of these institutions. For the better protection of migrants, it is highly recommended that migrant-receiving states extend their assistance to the operation of shelters and legal counseling for migrants.

Challenges to the International Community: Toward Global Governance of International Migration

The crucial challenge facing the international community is to improve the existing mechanisms for protecting migrants. As discussed earlier, restrictive policies for female migration arise in part from the disadvantaged position of sending states in the international labor market and from the lack of global governance mechanisms for international migration. Many state officials told me that if suprastate institutions such as the UN could intervene effectively to protect migrant workers, they would not need to institute restrictions on women such as migration bans.

Global governance of international migration is still in its rudimentary stage, though some international legal instruments have been adopted to protect the rights of migrant workers abroad. For example, the ILO has the Migrant for Employment Convention (Revised), 1949 (No. 97); the Migrant Workers (Supplementary Provisions) Convention, 1975 (No. 143); the Migration for Employment Recommendation, 1949 (No. 86); the Migrant Workers Recommendation, 1975 (No. 151). More recently, the UN General Assembly adopted the International Convention on the Protection of the Rights of All Migrant Workers and Members of Their Families (popularly called the "UN Migrant Workers Convention") in 1990. However, the UN Migrant Workers Convention came into force only in July 2003, thirteen years after it was adopted, due to the insufficient number of ratification. Furthermore, these legal instruments have not been very effective for several reasons. First, most states in major migrant-receiving countries have not signed or ratified them. In the case of the UN Convention, all ratifications came from migrant-sending states, not from even a single major receiving state. Receiving states are not willing to ratify these conventions partly because of the lack of political pressure from the domestic electorate, but also because of the commitments that they entail; once it has ratified any convention, the state must often revise its domestic laws and report on the implementation. In addition, given the large number of migrants on its soil, the perfect implementation of these conventions would be impossible. Yet the ratification of these conventions would immediately raise the expectations of migrants and sending states. They might soon find violation cases of the conventions and criticize receiving states at international meetings. The ratifications of these conventions, in many officials' minds, do not bring enough political benefits to receiving states.

The second major reason why the "migrant conventions" are not effective is that they lack substantial enforcement mechanisms. At present, no international body can directly intervene in cases of violations of migrants' rights. The receiving state, having ratified a convention, is the only actor that could act on it by punishing local employers or unscrupulous recruitment agencies. Nevertheless, nothing happens even if no action is taken; the worst possible penalty on the state for its negligence would only be a few minutes of accusations at international meetings. Clearly, the international legal mechanisms for protecting migrant workers, at least in the current form, have only limited effectiveness.

Migration issues are politically sensitive. Almost all countries have migrant workers on their soil who are not being treated well, but no state wants to be blamed or intervened by others for this situation. Many states have long insisted that migration is a sovereignty issue. This political environment has affected global politics on migration. In fact, for these reasons, the UN has been unable to convene a Conference on International Migration and Development, although one was proposed by the UN Population Conference in Cairo as well as by a General Assembly Resolution in 1994.[7] In the same resolution, the General Assembly also proposed that a UN conference be convened to thoroughly review the problems facing refugees, returnees, displaced persons, and migrants. This conference still has not materialized because of a lack of consensus among member states.[8]

CHANGING GLOBAL LANDSCAPE IN MIGRATION

The UN has been finding it difficult to convene a conference on migration. Even so, the environment surrounding international migration has been changing gradually. "Global governance" is far from being achieved, but many multilateral initiatives have been taken at various levels. At the international level, the UN and other international organizations have been increasingly active in addressing issues relating to international migration. For more than three decades the General Assembly has been adopting resolutions on measures to improve the situation of all migrant workers and ensure their human rights and dignity; however, its interest in protecting migrants grew much more rapidly in the 1990s. The International Convention on the Protection of the Rights of All Migrant Workers and Members of Their Families, adopted in 1990, was of course an important milestone in the process.

In 1992 the General Assembly adopted a resolution on violence against migrant women workers—the first resolution ever to specifically address international female migration. This indicates that the international community has become aware of the plight of migrant women who have long been threatened by sexual abuse and various other forms of maltreatment. The General Assembly has adopted a resolution on migrant women almost every year since then. Between 1993 and 2002 the UN Human Rights Commission issued twenty-four resolutions on migrant workers as a whole. In addition, the UN Economic and Social Council has issued seven resolutions on migration-related issues since 1983.

Institutional structures have been strengthened at the international level. In 1997 the UN Human Rights Commission appointed a Working Group of Intergovernmental Experts on the Human Rights of Migrants mainly to (1) gather all relevant information on obstacles to protecting the human rights of migrants, and (2) recommend ways to promote, protect, and implement the human rights of migrants.[9] In 1999, one of this working group's recommendations resulted in the appointment of a Special Rapporteur on the Human Rights of Migrants. Among other things, the special rapporteur was instructed to take gender into account when requesting and analyzing information and to pay special attention to occurrences of discrimination and violence against migrant women.[10]

In 2000 the UN General Assembly adopted three resolutions on migration issues. One was the Resolution on Violence Against Women Migrant Workers which asked states to cooperate fully with the special rapporteur and urged them to make "further efforts to protect and promote the rights and welfare of women migrant workers."[11] The UN resolutions are political statements, not legal instruments with enforcement mechanisms. Therefore, they do not have a direct impact on improving the situation of migrants. However, they are official declarations of the UN's concern for particular issues; they foster a global normative framework and have an impact on public opinion as it relates to the countries involved in migration. They also shape the ways in which funding resources are channeled in that major donors such as development agencies, international NGOs, and other private donors often consult the UN's agenda and concerns when developing future projects.

In 1998 a group of national and international NGOs and intergovernmental organizations established the Global Campaign for the Ratification of the UN Migrant Workers Convention. Between 1998 and 2002, signatories of that convention increased from seven to twelve and ratifications from nine to twenty. This was unprecedented success, relative to the slow progress made over the preceding eight years. After Guatemala ratified the convention in March 2003, it finally came into force on July 1, 2003. As of February 1, 2005, there were twenty-two ratifying states.[12]

A global governance framework for migration has yet to be established, but progress is being made. Various states are now cooperating, and since the 1990s regional initiatives have been growing all over the world. In recent years, multilateral initiatives beyond regional boundaries have also been emerging. The Dialogue "Five-Plus-Five," which focuses on migration in the western Mediterranean, links migrant-sending countries in North Africa with receiving countries in southern Europe. Ministerial meetings have been taking place every year since 2001. At these, the issues discussed include irregular migration and the humane treatment of affected individuals, migration and development, and the integration of migrants.[13]

Another consultative process is the Berne Initiative, launched by the Swiss government in 2001. This convenes policy makers, NGOs, and scholars from all regions to discuss migration issues and to identify common interests. Its goal is to develop "a broad policy framework aimed at facilitating co-operation between states in planning and managing the movement of people in a humane and orderly way."[14] Through annual consultations, the Berne Initiative has been enhancing multilateral dialogues and cooperation on international migration.

In 2003, with the encouragement of the UN Secretary-General and the governments of Sweden and Switzerland, the Global Commission on International Migration was established to "provide the framework for the formulation of a coherent, comprehensive and global response to migration issues."[15] The commission, on which thirteen states and the Holy See (Vatican) are represented, has convened various meetings and regional hearings to analyze gaps in current policy approaches to international migration, to examine the implications of migration issues in other areas, and to place international migration on the global agenda.[16] It will submit its final report to the UN Secretary-General and other stakeholders in the summer of 2005. This is the first time that the UN Secretary-General and major industrialized countries have taken a strong initiative to provide a multilateral forum on international migration—an indication that the global environment surrounding this issue has begun to change. Its actual effect on state policies is debatable, but it is helping transform this issue from "low" to "high politics" for the global community in this new century.

These initiatives have been helping pave the way for a global framework for migration. At the ILO Conference in 2004, governments, employers, and workers agreed to adopt a new action plan which called for the development of a non-binding multilateral framework for a rights-based approach to labor migration. They also agreed to establish an ILO dialogue on migration in partnership with other international and multilateral organizations. This is a tremendous change given that migration could not be placed on the agenda until recently because of the political sensitivity.

These examples suggest that a consensus on building a global migration framework and on starting dialogues to attain this goal has been developing over the past few years.

THE CHANGING SITUATION IN ASIA

The changing global landscape is affecting Asia specifically. For many years, any discussions about international migration had also been taboo in official regional dialogues. Most migration flows in Asia take place within the region, yet until the mid-1990s there was no regional cooperation or discussion concerning the protection of migrant workers.

One reason for this lack of regional cooperation and dialogue has been the absence of political unity in the region. Asia is the only region in the world that lacks a political body equivalent to the European Union (EU), the Organization of American States (OAS), or the African Union (AU). Asia has found it difficult to organize itself as a regional political entity because of its weak regional identity, given the vast differences in language, religion, and culture and the very uneven economic levels. The long historical legacy of wars and conflicts has also deepened mistrust among Asian nations. This absence of regional political unity has contributed to the fact that Asia is the only region in the world that lacks a regional human rights commission. In Asia there is no institutional mechanism through which regional human rights issues can be addressed.

Nevertheless, in recent years many countries in the region have begun to realize the need to cooperate on migration because of the alarming increase in the trafficking of women and children. Consultations are beginning. In 1996 the first regional consultation process was launched in Manila by seventeen countries. This "Manila Process" provides a regular forum for migration authorities to exchange information on trends and policy measures concerning irregular migration and trafficking.[17] Another forum, the Asia-Pacific Consultations (APC), is cosponsored by the International Organization for Migration (IOM) and the UNHCR. It provides a forum for Asian and Pacific countries to consult on population movements in the region, including those of migrants, refugees, and internally displaced persons.[18]

The Asian financial crisis of 1997 further enhanced this trend toward cooperation. After experiencing serious problems with the repatriation of migrant workers, the states in the region felt an acute need for more effective regional approaches to migration.[19] The crisis also led to grave concerns about the extremely large volume of irregular migration which cannot be reduced simply by erecting legal walls against prospective migrants. Against this backdrop, the first regional initiative took place in the form of a ministerial-level symposium, "Towards Regional Cooperation on Irregular/Undocumented Migration," held in Bangkok in April 1999. The end result—the Bangkok Declaration—was adopted by nineteen Asian and Pacific states.

Regional cooperation on irregular migration has expanded further since then. The Bali Ministerial Conference on People Smuggling, Trafficking in Persons and Related Transnational Crime was convened in 2002. Attending were thirty-eight Asian and Pacific states as well as the IOM and UNHCR. The states in attendance acknowledged the human rights dimensions of human trafficking and agreed to cooperate on law enforcement and visa systems and to exchange information, with the goal of deterring irregular migration.[20]

Multilateral cooperation among migrant-sending states is also beginning to emerge. In 2003 the Philippines led a coalition of six countries—the other five were Indonesia, Thailand, Vietnam, Myanmar, and Sri Lanka—to pressure Hong Kong to withdraw its wage cuts for foreign workers. The coalition explored countermeasures against those cuts and investigated the working conditions of domestic workers in other destinations where unjust labor practices were rampant.[21] This initiative would have been impossible in the past, while states were focused on competing with one another for niches in the international labor market. However, through various regional meetings, they have recognized their common interests and the importance of building a coalition against receiving states. This is a positive development that will help protect migrant workers in the region.

The efforts of NGOs to address the plight of migrant workers, especially of women, have also accelerated since the late 1990s. Local migration NGOs have developed various regional networks and strengthened cooperation in the area of migration. Every year since 1998, regional NGOs have organized the Joint Campaign for Migrants' Rights in Asia; protection of migrant women is one of its key goals.[22] In 2002, regional NGOs organized the Regional Summit on Foreign Migrant Domestic Workers in Sri Lanka. This summit was attended by state officials, NGOs, and other stakeholders from twenty-four countries. At the closing session, it issued the Colombo Declaration, which acknowledged the importance of cooperation in protecting the rights of foreign domestic workers.[23]

Given these emerging regional initiatives at the official and grass-roots levels, it is high time that an official human rights body in Asia—preferably a regional human rights commission and a human rights court—be created to take up the issues in a formal manner. Asia is the only region in the world without a regional human rights body equivalent to the European Commission on Human Rights, the Inter-American Commission on Human Rights, and the African Commission on Human and People's Rights. The establishment of a regional human rights commission—preferably along with a court of human rights—would be an important step toward protecting migrants' rights in the region as well as in the world. The human rights commission could also provide a permanent forum for policy makers and NGOs to devise better mechanisms to protect migrants.

It is going to take a while longer for a broader global governance system of international migration to materialize. However, emerging regional and interregional dialogues point toward such possibilities. The global community, including the UN agencies, intergovernmental organizations, and international NGOs, should continue endorsing and encouraging this new trend in international cooperation, and advocate the protection of migrants—especially of migrant women—in these processes. Only through such long-term concerted efforts at the national, regional, interregional, and global levels will more effective protection of migrant workers—both men and women—be made possible.

Epilogue:
Migration and Women's Empowerment

DURING MY FIELDWORK, many migrant women opened my eyes to a broader dimension of migration—that is, what migration means to women and their empowerment. This dimension was not directly related to my research and will require more in-depth examination and analyses. My knowledge and expertise are limited in this area; even so, I present this dimension here in the hope of stimulating future discussions and research.

As we have seen, the international migration of women has often been associated with negative consequences such as abuse and exploitation. The mass media portray migrant women as helpless victims, or they point out the many family problems to which it leads, such as higher school dropout rates among children and alcoholism among husbands. The international migration of women certainly has these negative aspects. But does it only bring money and harm? What implications does migration have for women themselves? Does it empower them or disempower them?

Many scholars contend that migration has both empowering and disempowering effects. The latter effect, however, tends to receive more attention. Numerous studies have highlighted the disempowering effects of harsh working conditions and maltreatment that migrant women encounter overseas.[1] Furthermore, migration leads to downward social mobility, since migrant women tend to be concentrated in sectors that are not commensurate with their professional qualifications.[2] In particular, undocumented migration and trafficking disempower women because "recruiters and employers hold power over them by virtue of the fact that contact with the authorities would result in the repatriation."[3] Migration does little to improve women's social status because of the types of jobs they take—domestic worker, entertainer, factory worker—jobs that are often characterized by low wages, poor working conditions, and lack of unionization. Many studies tend to describe migrant women as victims of abuse and harassment.

It is indeed true that migrant women are often vulnerable. Cases of abuse, harassment, and wage non-payment are far too common. Migrant women are "sometimes completely powerless in facing their employers."[4] However, does it mean that migration disempowers women? This question is not easy to answer, and to do so we need to carefully examine the concept of empowerment. According to Pillai, empowerment is

> a multidimensional process which should enable individuals or a group of individuals to realize their full identity and powers in all spheres of life. It consists of greater access to knowledge and resources, greater autonomy in decision making to enable them to have greater ability to plan their lives, or have greater control over the circumstances that influence their lives and free them from shackles imposed on them by custom, belief and practice.[5]

If we take this definition at face value, migration may not be a fully empowering experience for women because while working overseas they lack legal protections, decision-making autonomy, and control over their working conditions. Hugo contends that these workers often move "from one household-based patriarchy to another in which their status is no better or even worse than at the origin."[6] Entertainers and factory workers are vulnerable to abuse and exploitation at their workplaces; domestic workers, especially in West Asia, are in an even worse situation because most of them are forbidden to leave the employer's house and are allowed very little freedom.

Reactions from the community of origin are another factor blocking migrant women's empowerment. Research on Indonesian domestic workers who had been employed in the Middle East indicated that a two-year migration experience did not have much positive effect on their status when they returned to their villages. This was partly because the traditional village-based hierarchies had an interest in maintaining the temporary nature of migration and the existing social order.[7] My fieldwork in the Philippines and Sri Lanka suggested that despite the sense of empowerment, some returned migrant women made efforts to remain as quiet and docile as they used to be; they were afraid of negative reactions from household members and neighbors.

The issue of empowerment becomes more complex when it comes to subjective empowerment after migrant women return home. My fieldwork showed that migration had some positive effects on women: 87 percent of migrant women from the Philippines and 58.3 percent of those from Sri Lanka agreed that they noticed positive changes in themselves, such as increased self-confidence and independence. Ismael and Momsen also found that Muslim women in Sri Lanka experienced greater decision-making power after they returned from overseas:

The women were now making the primary decisions with regards to expense allocation, savings, dress, social obligations, the size of the household and the size of the extended family that lived with them. Although these women did not enjoy a free hand in making these decisions, their experience overseas brought them more respect and the confidence to take an active interest in the welfare of the family and in social activities. They had ventured into the unknown to help their family and themselves lead a better life. These same women were not about to let all that hardship be forgotten once they were back home. Improved status, self esteem, confidence and a feeling of empowerment were the greatest social and psychological changes that were detected. Over 90 per cent of the women felt that their sense of self worth and status as a woman had been enhanced by their trip overseas.[8]

Women were concentrated in low-wage jobs with harsh working conditions and patriarchal working relationships; yet many of them still experienced some sense of empowerment. Brockett reports that Thai sex workers in Sydney thought their migration experiences had indeed empowered them.[9] Most of my respondents who worked as domestic workers also reported that their migration experiences had changed them substantially. They felt more confident about themselves than before, having gone through the difficult experience of living abroad and dealing with foreign employers. Following are typical comments from returned migrant women:

> [After I came back,] everything has changed. I feel more independent. I feel proud. It was a great achievement. Before, my neighbors looked at me low but not now! [smile] . . . I also became more important to my family. I get more respect from kids.

> I feel proud that I worked abroad. I can say that I have accomplishment. . . . I learned a lot, mingling with people from other cultures. I learned to adjust. My patience became longer. I learned cooking, more knowledge, and many things. Before, I didn't even know how to use a vacuum cleaner.

Positive comments like these were heard not just from women who had positive migration experiences. Even those who faced difficulties looked back on their experience positively. Loraine, who worked in Saudi Arabia, had a terrible experience of sexual abuse by her employer. Yet she saw her migration experience as follows:

> Before [I migrated], I was too behind of people. I just sit here doing nothing. I had inferiority complex. . . . But now I learned discipline, patience, and perseverance. I have more self-confidence. . . . I grew more in a new country.

Some Filipinas in the shelter of the Philippine Embassy told me they experienced spiritual growth. One of them said her faith had been strengthened by migration. Maria said that her experience was spiritually meaningful:

> I really learned a lot. I thank God for it. Now I know how to deal with different people like Arabs, Indians, Pakistanis, and so on. I know what's going on in the world. I became closer to God. I learned a blessing of God.

Overall, 63 percent of Filipinas and 69 percent of Sri Lankans said their migration experience had been a positive one. These numbers are very high, considering that about a half of my respondents from the Philippines and Sri Lanka were at legal counseling centers or in shelters accommodating women who had run away from their employers because of unpaid wages, sexual harassment, rape, or physical abuse. Their positive assessments perhaps reflected a degree of self-rationalization. However, the majority of the respondents (72 percent of Filipinas and 56 percent of Sri Lankans) were still willing either to stay where they were currently working as migrants or to migrate again elsewhere. The work, however "unliberating" or "disempowering" it may seem to outsiders, has a positive effect on migrant women in terms of helping them develop a sense of independence and self-confidence.

In a new country where support networks are minimal or absent, a migrant woman has to solve almost all her problems by herself and make her own decisions about every single aspect of her life: how to deal with hostile employers; what to do about unreasonable demands or abuse; how to discuss her salary when it is different from what the contract states; and so on. Migrant women also develop some decision-making power over financial arrangements back home. In particular, those who have caught household members wasting remittances try to exert control over what happens to that money. Whenever they send money back home, they give detailed instructions to their parents or husbands specifying how to spend it. Some of them calculate the amount to be sent home and keep the rest in a personal bank account in the destination country. The experience of working abroad requires migrant women to practice a variety of new organizational skills— skills they had not had a chance to learn before.

Other aspects of self-development, such as learning a new language and culture, also have empowering effects on migrant women. Most of my respondents told me they did not understand what their employer wanted at the beginning because of the language problem. But they tried very hard to learn the language on the job, and after three or four months most of them had acquired enough of it to hold simple conversations with their employers. Whenever they told me about the language-learning process, they seemed very proud and confident. Chandra, a twenty-six-year-old Sri Lankan migrant woman, said: "After four months, I can speak Arab [*sic*]. I now speak the language and have a lot of thinking power." Women who grew up in small villages or closed societies find a new world opening to them once they begin learning about a foreign culture and dealing with people from different backgrounds.

Civic engagement also contributes to migrant women's empowerment. In some destinations where foreign citizens have the right to organize themselves, migrant women form unions and associations to fight against abuse, exploitation, wage cuts, and policies threatening their human rights. These activities provide them with administrative and leadership skills. While most of the major receiving countries in Asia are quite repressive about migrant workers' civic organizations, Hong Kong, Japan, and Korea are relatively lenient in this regard. Therefore, migrant women in these places have established various organizations to address their concerns and interests.

Migrant women have not gained full empowerment in the sense of achieving total control over their lives, work, and decisions. But most of them perceive that their overseas experience had a positive impact on their lives overall, even when they did not receive the expected salary and even when they were maltreated or sexually abused. Many studies have suggested that migrant women resist their oppression in subtle and complex ways in their everyday lives when dealing with their employers.[10] They do not remain simply oppressed by foreign employers and institutionalized forms of power while abroad; rather, they exercise their own agency. It is true that migrant women are often in vulnerable positions abroad, and thus we should continue to address their need for protection (see Chapter 7). However, the fact that many migrant women also experience *internal empowerment* should be acknowledged. When abused women tell us that they have been internally empowered, it is not our place to deny it by imposing our own judgments on them.

Empowerment has subjective dimensions as well as structural ones. The "sense of agency" constitutes an important part of women's empowerment in that it enables them to "define their goals and act upon them" by "bargaining, negotiation, manipulation, subversion, resistance and protest as well as the more intangible cognitive processes of reflection and analysis."[11] Although Kabeer points to other dimensions such as economic, social, and human *resources* that "serve to enhance the ability to exercise choice" and *achievements* or actual realizations of individual goals,[12] her recognition of the subjective and cognitive aspects of empowerment opens a new path for studies on the empowerment of migrant women.

Recent studies on women's empowerment are an exciting starting point for advancing our understanding of the social dimensions of international female migration. More research is needed to clarify the concept of empow-

erment—for instance, the relationship between internal and external empowerment (for instance, "Does the latter always result in the former?"). We
need to recognize the importance of subjective empowerment, while striv-
ing simultaneously to bring about structural empowerment for all migrant
women in the world.

Reference Matter

Notes

1. Although there are more popular terms for describing these workers, such as "housemaids" and "domestic helpers," these are rather problematic. The former is somewhat derogatory, and the latter is not an accurate description in that migrant women take care of most of the housework—they do not simply "help" with household chores. They are "helpers" only from an employer's perspective. To highlight that they are legitimate workers, I will use the term "domestic workers" to describe individuals who are engaged in productive work within households.

2. UN 2004. This figure is based on the stock data of UN Population Division. It refers to the stocks of "migrants" who are defined as people who were living outside their country of "usual residence" at the time of the survey. In general, international migration can be classified into four major categories: (1) permanent migration; (2) temporary migration; (3) irregular migration; and (4) forced migration. Temporary migration is further divided into contract migration and professional migration. The former refers to migration of semiskilled and/or unskilled workers under seasonal or short-term (one or two year) contracts; the latter refers to highly skilled technicians or managers in multinational corporations who are transferred from one country to another (see Stalker, 1994, 4). This book deals mainly with the first type of temporary migration—migration of semiskilled and unskilled workers.

3. UN 2002.

4. UN 2004.

5. ILO 2001, 1.

6. Anker 1998, 264.

7. McKay 2005.

8. Anderson 2000.

9. Hochschild 2000.

10. Parreñas 2001.

11. Gereffi and Korzeniewicz 1994.

12. Sturgeon 2001.

13. The term "newly industrialized *countries*" (NICs) refers to Hong Kong, Korea, Taiwan, and Singapore and is popular in North America. However, "newly industrialized *economies*" (NIEs) is a more internationally recognized term that refers

to these countries because Hong Kong is not a "country" and also Mainland China still claims that Taiwan is one of its provinces.

14. Nash and Fernandez-Kelly 1983.

15. Lim 1998, 8.

16. U.S. Department of State 2004.

17. Lim 1998, 8—9.

18. This book follows the UN definition of "Asia" which includes "West Asia" (e.g., Saudi Arabia, Kuwait, and the United Arab Emirates). In 1994, 99.7 percent of Pakistani migrants, 95.9 percent of Indian migrants, and 94.9 percent of Sri Lankan migrants moved for employment to other Asian countries, most of which were in West Asia (Huguet 1995).

19. Another common alternative for legal migration involves seeking asylum—that is, applying for refugee status. This approach has been generating heated debate in many industrialized countries. This book will not be dealing with refugee issues, because they bring different causal factors to the fore.

20. The terms "semi-skilled" and "unskilled" are highly contentious. Female migrant domestic workers are categorized as "unskilled"; this is because society attaches little significance to reproductive labor, particularly household work, and does not acknowledge that it entails any skills. Yet domestic work actually requires a variety of skills, including the following: the proper use of electronic household gadgets, cooking and cleaning skills, and management skills. In the Philippines and Sri Lanka, prospective migrant women must take a training course to improve their "skills" in these areas prior to their departure. Also, these workers generally bring with them other skills that they acquired from past experience in other sectors, such as expertise in teaching, factory work, and office work. Nevertheless, I will follow the general usage of the term "unskilled" women or migrants in order to differentiate these women from those in professional categories such as medicine, the law, business, and so on.

21. POEA 2004; Commission for Filipinos Overseas 2004.

22. This estimate was made by applying various types of data. In Sri Lanka, India (Kerala only), and Indonesia, the public data on total female emigrant stocks were used. For the Philippines and Bangladesh, the data on total emigrant stocks were multiplied by women's percentage of annual emigrant outflows, on the assumption that the gender composition of stock data must be similar to flow data. To these data, I added the data from the receiving side on Vietnamese and Thai women whose emigration data were not available from the government. The total estimate of 4 million is still modest, as it only includes the seven main nationalities. Further data will have to be collected in order to arrive at a clear estimate of the number of Asian migrant women.

23. "Irregular migrants" and "undocumented migrants" refer to various populations, ranging from those who went through illegal channels to emigrate overseas to those who emigrated legally and whose status became illegal because they overstayed. Some migrants overstay unwillingly when they get stuck with unscrupulous middlemen or employers who take away their passports and force them into prostitution. Because it sounds derogatory, the term "illegal migrants" is often avoided at international meetings and conferences.

24. Lim and Oishi 1996.

25. Harris and Todaro 1970; Todaro 1976.

26. Palma-Beltran 1992; Vasquez et al. 1995; Asis 2001.

27. Piore 1979.

28. ILO 2004.

29. The situation has not improved much. For more about the statistical weaknesses in studies of female migration, see INSTRAW (1994).

30. Thadani and Todaro 1979, 26.

31. The good examples for rural–urban migration include Chant (1992) and UN (1991). Those for international migration are Heyzer et al. (1994), Palma-Beltran (1992), and UN (1995).

32. Taylor 1986; Massey and Garcia España 1987; Gurak and Caces 1992.

33. MacDonald and MacDonald 1974; Massey 1986.

34. Hagan 1998; Menjivar 2003.

35. Curran and Rivero-Fuentes 2003.

36. Kritz et al. 1992.

37. Harbison 1981; Lauby 1987; Lauby and Stark 1988.

38. Wood 1981, 1982; Radcliffe 1986.

39. Grasmuck and Pessar, 1991; Chant 1992.

40. Phillips 1989; Sen 1990; Wolf 1992; Goss and Lindquist 1995.

41. Hondagneu-Sotelo 1994.

42. Sen 1990; Wolf 1992; Grieco and Boyd 1998.

43. Palma-Beltran 1992; Eelens 1995; Gurak and Kritz 1996; Ortiz 1996.

44. Constable 1997.

45. Parreñas 2001.

46. Gamburd 2000.

47. Chin 1998.

48. Chant 1992; Fairhurst et al. 1997; Momsen 1999.

49. Parreñas 2001.

50. Lim and Oishi 1996.

51. Goss and Lindquist 1995.

52. Ibid., 326.

53. The recent consensus among migration scholars is that the long-held distinction between "migrant senders" and "migrant receivers" no longer suffices in that most countries are both, or are even "transit countries" in which migrants stay for a short time before emigrating elsewhere. I fully acknowledge this reality but even so have decided to use these terms simply to highlight a more prominent aspect of each country. In addition, terms such as "source countries of migrants" and "country of origin/destination" will be used interchangeably. The term "migrant sending/receiving states" will be used to refer to states in migrant-sending/receiving countries, treating them as actors in migration processes; but this is not at all to imply that the state is the only actor causing migration by "sending" or "receiving" workers. This study fully recognizes the importance of women as agents in international migration.

54. The original idea was taken from J.S. Mill (1967) [1843]. See also Skocpol and Somers (1980) and Wickham-Crowley (1992).

55. Sassen-Koob 1984; Sassen 1991; Parreñas 2001.

56. Nayyer 2002; WCSDG 2004.

57. Here I will be applying Stepan's definition of the "state": "all the administrative, legal, bureaucratic and coercive systems" within a certain geographical territory (Stepan 1978, xii). There are many possible definitions of the state and of government; in this study, when I use the term "government," it will be in reference to the central political and administrative apparatus only.

58. Weiner 1990, 1995; Cornelius et al. 1994; Russell 1995.

59. Brubaker, 1992.

60. Peek and Standing 1982; Chant and McIlwaine 1995.

61. Battistella and Paganoni 1992; Abella 1995; Hugo 1995; Lim and Oishi 1996; Gonzalez 1998.

62. One of the few exceptions to this is Heyzer et al. 1994.

63. Sassen 1988, 116.

64. Because I could not conduct fieldwork in Singapore and Kuwait, the information on these countries are based on the secondary sources.

65. In this book, the term "migration NGOs" refers to those non-governmental organizations whose activities are tailored specifically to the needs and interests of migrant workers and/or their families. Many "migration NGOs" are not organized or operated by former migrants; that said, as long as their specific aim is to serve migrants and their families, they fall within this category. Another term, "migrant associations," refers to those only comprised of former or current migrant workers.

CHAPTER TWO

1. Gaw 1991, 67.

2. Ibid., 73.

3. Husbands were usually arranged by the master or his family members. See Gaw (1991) for more detail.

4. Jaschok 1988, 106.

5. Ibid., 101.

6. Huff 1994: 154.

7. Ibid.

8. Ginsberg and Roberts 1958, 251.

9. Stockard 1989, 169.

10. Gaw 1991, 78.

11. Chiang 1994, 239.

12. Welsh 1997, 404.

13. Vogel 1991, 68.

14. Salaff 1990, 102.

15. Mak and Yue-ping argue that the drop in the men's labor force participation rate reflects the effect of educational expansion: impact of greater opportunities for education: more young men are staying in school longer and taking up employment later. See Mak and Yue-ping (1997,19).

16. Salaff 1974, 11; cited in Constable 1997, 24.

17. Census and Statistics Department [Hong Kong] 1991.

18. Constable 1997, 27.
19. Ibid., 29.
20. Salaff 1995, xxvii.
21. Hong Kong Government 1965, 5–6; cited in Pui-lan et al. 1997.
22. Stalker 1994, 258.
23. Sasaki 1994, 29.
24. Hong Kong Government 2004.
25. Stalker 1994, 259.
26. Sasaki 1994, 30.
27. Johnson, 1982.
28. Vogel 1991, 77.
29. In fact, Singapore had a serious unemployment problem at the time of independence. Thus, the government had to launch an intensive population control program to relieve the population pressure. For the evolution of population policy in Singapore, see Palen (1990).
30. Wong 1997, 142.
31. Then 1996, 5; cited in Wong 1997, 144.
32. Wong 1986, 209; ILO 2004.
33. ILO 2004.
34. Wong 1986, 212.
35. Wee 1987, 5–12.
36. The officially approved "non-traditional sources" also included Bangladesh, India, Indonesia, Thailand, and Myanmar for other types of occupations such as construction worker.
37. Hui 1992, 267; cited in Wong 1996, 92.
38. Ministry of Labour [Singapore] 1998, 60.
39. Wong 1996, 92.
40. Yeoh et al. 2004.
41. Yeoh and Huang 1995, 448.
42. *Straits Times*, November 7, 1997.
43. Yeoh and Huang 1995, 450.
44. Filmo Communications 2001.
45. Ofstedal et al. 1999, 26.
46. Stalker 1994, 256; Henson 2002.
47. Stalker considered that the ratio of one domestic worker in fifteen Singaporean households in 1990 was already among the highest in the world. See Stalker (1994, 256).
48. AMC and MFA 2001, 133.
49. Chia 2004.
50. Chin 1998, 123.
51. Council of Labour Affairs [Taiwan] 2004; cited in Lan, forthcoming.
52. Choi 2001, 464.
53. Lee, forthcoming.
54. De Vos 1971; Yoshino 1977; De Vos and Wetherall 1983; Weiner 1997.
55. Another distinct minority, albeit not an "ethnic" group per se, are the Bura-

kumin who are racially Japanese yet who were treated as outcasts or untouchables until the end of nineteenth century. They experience discrimination even today.

56. Stalker 1994, 248.

57. Ministry of Justice [Japan] 2004.

58. Ibid.

59. Ibid.

60. Ibid.

61. Komai 1995, 104.

62. *Asahi Shimbun*, July 22, 1995.

63. De Dios 1989, 139–40. Those who enter Japan as tourists are allowed to stay only three months. Yet sex tourism still exists, despite the protests by women's groups.

64. In the mid-1990s, to address this problem, the Philippine government introduced an audition system. Before he or she can emigrate overseas as an entertainer, the applicant must pass a singing and/or dancing test. Having passed, that person becomes a "qualified" entertainer and receives a qualification pass from the POEA office.

65. De Dios 1989, 139–40.

66. Ministry of Justice [Japan] 2004.

67. CFO 1999.

68. Associated Press, December 7, 2004.

69. U.S. State Department 2004.

70. The newspaper reports that nursing homes in some regions are heightening their dependence on Japanese Brazilian care assistants (*Asahi Shimbun*, January 14, 2000).

71. Ozawa 1995, 62–65.

72. Ibid.

73. Cabinet Office [Japan] 2004.

74. Nakamatsu 2005.

75. Choshi 2004.

76. Cabinet Office [Japan] 2004.

77. UNDP 2002, 162.

78. UN 2000a, 50.

79. IMF 2004, 12, 18.

80. *Asian Migration News*, March 1–15, 2000.

81. *Daily Yomiuri*, April 26, 2000.

82. Ministry of Justice [Japan] 2000.

83. Ministry of Foreign Affairs 2004.

84. *Yomiuri Shimbun*, November 17, 2004.

85. *Asian Labour News*, January 15, 2004.

86. *Yomiuri Shimbun*, July 1, 2004.

87. *Japan Times*, January 19, 2000.

88. JISEA 2004.

89. I will sometimes use the term "Gulf States" to refer to destination countries in West Asia.

90. UN 2004.

91. Stalker 1994, 239.
92. Birks and Sinclair 1980, 131.
93. ILO 1973.
94. Ogawa 1987, 285.
95. Birks and Sinclair 1980, 160.
96. Ibid., 14–15.
97. Ibid., 4.
98. Choi 2001, 464.
99. Evans and Papps 1999.
100. ESCWA 1993.
101. Russell 1995, 258.
102. Ibid., 260.
103. UN 2004.
104. Shah et al. 2002.
105. Humphrey 1990, 8.
106. Shah 1995, 1012.
107. Ibid., 1009.
108. Stalker 1994, 245.
109. Scalabrini Migration Center 2004a; POEA 2004.
110. ESCWA 1997b, 102.
111. Bakan and Stasiulis 1995, 323–24.
112. Chin 1998, 108.
113. Whether this policy was abolished or the economic cooperation was simply extended to other countries is unknown, but the data show that Malaysia started accepting domestic workers from Thailand in 1997 and from Sri Lanka in 1998.
114. *Manila Times*, September 27, 1998.
115. The ethnic composition of Malaysia is Malays and other indigenous 58 percent, Chinese 24 percent, Indian 8 percent, and others 10 percent. See *CIA World Fact Book* (2000).
116. *Hong Kong Standard*, April 14, 1999.
117. Lan, forthcoming.
118. Humphrey 1990, 11.
119. Constable 1997; Lan, forthcoming.
120. Pei Chia Lan reports a similar situation in Taiwan where Indonesians already outnumber Filipinas in migrant domestic workers. This is partly due to the growing perception that Filipinas are too outspoken; another reason is that recruitment agencies encourage their clients to hire Indonesians who pay higher fees to the agencies. See Lan (forthcoming).

CHAPTER THREE

1. Especially since the 9/11 terrorist attacks, national security has become an important pillar of immigration policies in many countries.
2. Abella 1995; Lim and Oishi 1996.
3. During the initial period of labor export promotion, technological transfer and the formation of human capital were added to the list of economic benefits from la-

bor emigration (see Stahl, 1982). Many governments expected that their workers would acquire new skills for free while working overseas and help economic development on their return. However, it turned out that the jobs open to migrant workers were generally unskilled and offered little opportunity for advancement or skill acquisition. Recent studies have shown that the economic record regarding human capital formation is actually dismal, because most migrant workers (even trainees) are engaged in manual labor or unskilled work. See Kuptsch and Oishi (1995).

4. IMF 2003.

5. At least 25 percent of Indonesian migrant workers are undocumented, compared with 4 percent of Filipinos and 10 percent of Sri Lankans. It is estimated that about half a million Indonesians are working abroad without documentation. Asian Migrant Centre (AMC) and Migrant Forum in Asia (MFA) 1999.

6. *Migration News* 2(5), May 1995.

7. It was reported that the Indian Minister of State for External Affairs commented that the ban on domestic workers to Kuwait would be lifted before the end of 2001 (NRIOL, July 10, 2000).

8. The initial requirement of forty-five years has gradually been lowered to thirty-five over the past ten years.

9. Although there have been no official announcements, the governments of Indonesia and Nepal are increasingly restricting female migration. The first secretary in the Indonesian Embassy in Abu Dhabi told me in 1999 that the immigration of domestic workers to the Arab region has been temporarily suspended. In the same year, the gender expert in the ILO office in Delhi mentioned to me that the Nepali government is now trying to strictly control the departure of women at the airport, presumably because of trafficking concerns.

10. Raj-Hashim 1994, 123.

11. Calculated on the basis of unpublished government data which was cited in Hugo 1998, 14.

12. Teodoro 1981, 3; Kitano and Daniels 1988, 80.

13. Tyner 1999, 679.

14. Presidential Speech, July 20, 1982; cited in Tigno 1990, 76.

15. Abella 1979, 3.

16. This institutionalization of labor migration was largely due to severe economic difficulties at the time. President Marcos was trying to alleviate high domestic unemployment and increase the volume of remittances to help the balance of payments (the Labor Code required migrant workers to send their overseas earnings back home). However, these efforts failed in the end; the overseas demand for labor increased drastically until it exceeded the government's capacity to manage it. By 1978 the government had been forced to give up the idea of controlling labor migration; as an alternative, it began to rely on the private sector for the recruitment and placement of Filipino workers. See Asis (1992, 71–72).

17. Abella 1979, 8; POEA 2004.

18. Migration data in the Philippines are classified into two categories: land-based and sea-based. However, the latter category, which refers to "seafarers" (ship workers and crews), is not included in some migration statistics which show destinations. Although seafarers are hired by foreign ships, they actually travel to and work in var-

ious other countries which are most often unrelated to ship ownership. Thus it is difficult to specify "destination countries."

19. POEA 2004.

20. Asis 1992, 74.

21. Abella 1995, 247.

22. DOLE 1995, 36.

23. Imson 1992, 17.

24. DOLE 1995, 36–37.

25. In the United States, Canada, and Europe, for instance, the working hours for domestic workers tend to be shorter than in Asian and Middle Eastern countries where working more than fifteen hours a day is the norm. In North America and Europe, most domestic workers are allowed to take at least one day off each week; this is not the case in the Middle East.

26. Enloe 1990, 188.

27. Constable 1997, 207–8.

28. Ministry of Justice [Japan] 1992.

29. Simon and Thomas 1995.

30. Gonzalez 1998, 127.

31. U.S. Department of State 1996, 10.

32. This information is based on my interview with a former cabinet member on July 22, 1999.

33. Manalansan 2003.

34. Alcuitas 2002.

35. Korale 1984, 1.

36. Gunatilleke 1986, 167.

37. Rodrigo 1997, 52.

38. Korale 1984, 5.

39. SLBFE 2003.

40. ILO–ARTEP 1985; cited in Eelens and Speckman, 1990.

41. SLBFE 2003.

42. Ibid.

43. This information is based on my interview with David Soysa, September 1999.

44. Interview by Abha Dayal and Puneet Tandon in September 1999, videotaped for the UNDP.

45. SLBFE 2003.

46. Interview with Director-General of the SLBFE by Abha Dayal and Puneet Tandon, September 1999, videotaped by the interviewers.

47. Soysa 1999, 20; Weerakoon 1998, 106.

48. *Sunday Times Plus*, August 22, 1999.

49. *Asian Migration News*, April 30, 2000.

50. Abdullah 2003.

51. Gamburd 2000.

52. *Sunday Times Plus*, August 22, 1999.

53. Ibid.

54. Here I use the term "Bengalis" literally to refer to "those who speak Bengali"

204 Notes to Pages 74–80

and/or "those who are from Bengal," since Bangladesh did not exist as an independent state until 1971. I use the term "Bangladeshis" when I refer to citizens of the People's Republic of Bangladesh after independence.

55. Mahmud 1989, 59.

56. The cause of the Independence War was not Bangladesh's negation of its Muslim identity but rather its expression of ethnic identity. Bangladeshis (which literally means "people who speak Bengali") rebelled against the Pakistani government's policy of imposing Urdu as the official language. The conflict then took on a broader ethno-cultural context.

57. ASK 1999, 31.

58. This promotion was directed largely toward semiskilled or unskilled workers. The emigration of professionals was discouraged. The Third Five-Year Plan stated that "the country must adopt a clear policy of identifying the specific skills required within the home economy and the professionals needed in the country should be restricted from going abroad" (REPELITA III 1979, 431).

59. Government of Bangladesh 1983, 382; cited in ASK 1999, 23.

60. AMC and MFA 2001.

61. During the First Gulf War in 1991, only 3 percent of returnee migrants were women. See INSTRAW and IOM (2000, 8).

62. INSTRAW and IOM 2000, 15.

63. *Inter Press Service*, December 18, 2000.

64. AMC 2001.

65. Such a policy was based on the assumption that fellow citizens would not abuse them. However, I heard about many cases where the abuse took place in a household in which the employer had the same nationality or ethnicity as the domestic worker.

66. There are mixed reports about this policy development. One NGO reports that the government banned the migration of unskilled women in 1981; however, the source of this report is unknown (ASK 1999). Sobhan (1989) contends that the ban came later. When I contacted the former Director-General of BMET again to ask about this, he told me he remembered clearly that the Cabinet decided on the ban in 1976. I also turned to the Ministry of Labour and Manpower and BMET, but no information was available to support any of these arguments.

67. ASK n.d., 29.

68. Jahan 1993, 35.

69. Ibid.

70. Ahmed 1998, 382.

71. RMMRU 1998.

72. *Asian Migration News*, September 1–15, 1999.

73. Hasan 2003.

74. Scalabrini Migration Center 2004a.

75. *Dawn*, April 30, 1999.

76. The government of India does not record the number of professionals who emigrate. If we included the statistics on these highly skilled migrants, the figure would be much higher.

77. This is to ensure that they are over thirty-five, as the Emigration Regulation

stipulates. According to Khan, he personally interviews these women to see if they are over thirty-five. He explained that this checking system was established since sometimes precise birth records do not exist and some people do not know their age. It also prevents the use of fraudulent documents. He said he had acquired the ability to determine a person's age. In fact, he was the first person I have ever met who could tell my age.

78. Lan, forthcoming.

CHAPTER FOUR

1. Evans 1997.
2. Skocpol 1985; Pierson 1994.
3. Brubaker 1992, 1.
4. Johnson, 1982.
5. Asis 1992, 74.
6. NCRFW and ADB 1995, 46.
7. POEA 1992, 9. It is reported that the Indonesian government later established institutions to train nurses to the standard that they would be accepted by industrial countries. See also Ball 1990; cited in Hugo 1995, 295.
8. Zachariah et al. 2002, 22.
9. Skocpol 1985, 19.
10. Katzenstein 1985, 235.
11. Although recruitment agencies are not government organizations, they are not "non-governmental organizations" which usually refer only to grass-roots, non-profit associations.
12. ANGOC 1995, 121.
13. POEA 2004.
14. Scalabrini Migration Center 2004b.
15. This was due to the financial crisis in the Philippines in the early 1980s, during which the balance-of-payments situation deteriorated rapidly and the country was about to run out of foreign currency reserves.
16. CIIR 1987.
17. ANGOC 1995.
18. Ibid., 131.
19. Gamburd 2005, 21.
20. Dias and Jayasundere 2002, 22–23.
21. These figures included NGOs that were not officially registered with the NGO Affairs Bureau of the Bangladesh Government. In 1994, there were 1,370 officially registered NGOs; of these, 1,223 were managed locally, 147 internationally. See Government of Bangladesh (1998).
22. ANGOC 1995, 80.
23. Dasgupta 2003.
24. The *thana* is a Bangladeshi administrative unit, ranked between the village and district levels.
25. Brubaker 1992.
26. Ibid.

27. Joppke 1999.

28. *Asian Migration News*, September 15–30, 1997.

29. UNDP 2004.

30. Khair 1998, 9.

31. At the time of my interview in 1999, the Ministry of Labour was in charge of emigration policies. An attached office called the Bureau of Manpower, Employment and Training (BMET) actually dealt with administrative work concerning the promotion and protection of migrant workers abroad. Since then, there has been a restructuring, and BMET has become an independent ministry, now called the Ministry of Expatriates' Welfare and Overseas Employment.

32. According to the *Oxford Encyclopedic English Dictionary* (1991), *purdah* is defined as "a system in certain Muslim and Hindu societies of screening women from strangers by means of a veil or curtain." In practice, people in these societies refer to keeping women from public view (as in this official's comment) and even more commonly to women's use of the veil in public spaces.

33. Crore is a South Asian term for ten million. According to the *Asian Migrant Yearbook* (2003), the remittance figure was actually US$1.8 billion in 1999.

34. RMMRU 1998.

35. Interestingly, this ban was not placed through official legislation but only through a verbal instruction from the top official of the government agency in charge of overseas employment.

36. McClintock 1997, 90.

37. Nixon 1997, 78.

38. Tohidi 1998, 279.

39. Nixon 1997, 78.

40. Ibid.

41. Kabeer 1991, 122.

42. Siddiqi 1998.

43. Later, the U.S. government agreed to conduct the third-party autopsy. Their findings supported the results provided by the Singaporean government, which indicated that Flor Contemplacion was indeed guilty of two homicides. Public anger declined after this announcement.

44. Gonzales 1998, 7.

45. *Inter Press Service*, December 18, 2000.

CHAPTER FIVE

1. All the former migrant women I interviewed in Bangladesh in 1999 had left the country before the government banned the emigration of unskilled women in 1998.

2. SLBFE 2003, 38.

3. Bangladesh Bureau of Statistics 1993; cited by UNDP 1994. In the early 1980s the figure was less than seventeen years—among the lowest in the world. See UNDP (1994, 4).

4. UNDP 1999, 33.

5. UNDP 2002, 151.

6. Palma-Beltran and De Dios 1992; NCRFW and ADB 1995.

7. Brochmann 1990; Yapa 1995.

8. Palma-Beltran 1992, 10; Vasquez et al. 1995, 26.

9. Alailima 1997; UNDP 2002.

10. World Bank 2000, 284.

11. UNDP 2004.

12. Lewis 1968.

13. Sassen 1988, 116–18.

14. Brochmann 1990; Yapa 1995; Jayaweera et al. 2002.

15. Again, I reiterate that I am referring to temporary migrants. I exclude permanent immigrants and refugees.

16. Tacoli 1996, 27.

17. Wolf 1992; Salaff 1995; Tacoli 1996.

18. UNDP 1994, 5.

19. Tsuda 1987.

20. UNDP 1994, 2.

21. Massey 1986; Massey et al. 1993.

22. Massey et al. 1993, 452–53.

23. Hondagneu-Sotello 1994.

24. Parreñas 2001, 122–23.

25. Rodriguez and Tiongson 2001, 722.

26. Gamburd 2000.

27. Wood 1981, 1982; Trager 1984; Lauby 1987; Chant and Radcliffe 1992.

28. Stark and Bloom 1985; Stark 1991.

29. Ellis 1998; Morris 1990; Selby et al. 1990; Davidson 1991; cited in Wolf 1992, 14.

30. Becker 1981; cited in Sen 1990, 131.

31. Wolf 1990, 63.

32. Yapa 1995, 84, 86.

33. Although family members outside the household also receive some money, household members tend to be the primary beneficiaries of remittances.

34. Kabeer 1999, 17.

35. Oppong and Abu 1987.

36. Geertz 1961; Jay 1969, cited in Wolf 1992, 63; Blumberg 1988; Kabeer 1999.

37. Blumberg 1988, 53.

38. Blumberg 1988, 66–69; Stichter 1990, 58.

39. Heinonen 1996, 111.

40. Yu and Liu 1980, cited in Go 1992, 263.

41. Deano 1985, cited in Go 1992, 263.

42. Eviota 1992, 35.

43. Eder 1999, 113.

44. Abeywardane 1996.

45. UN 1998; Karunaratne 1999, 22; Takakuwa 1999, 35–40.

46. Takakuwa 1999, 35–36.

47. CIRDAP 1993; cited in UNDP 1994, 6.

48. White 1992, 123.

49. Ibid.
50. Yapa 1995, 64–65.
51. Scalabrini Migration Center 2004a.
52. DOLE 1995; cited in Gonzalez 1998, 91.
53. SLBFE 2003, 26.
54. DOLE 1995; cited in Gonzalez 1998, 90.
55. SLBFE 2003, 26.
56. Tacoli 1996, 21–23.

57. The term "reintegration" is often used among Filipino migrant workers to refer to a sustainable life after their return home. Since so few migrants can improve their financial conditions, the government and NGOs have started various "reintegration programs" to help ex-migrants sustain themselves after they come back home. Reintegration often refers to starting a small business, investing in land or a home, and so on.

58. Please see the epilogue for more discussion on the impact of migration on women's empowerment.

59. McKay 2005.

CHAPTER SIX

1. Sassen 1988, 116–18.
2. World Bank 2002.
3. Nababsing 1996, 1.
4. Sparr 1994, 7; Jayaweera 1996, 108–9.

5. The EPZs are usually not covered by labor laws, and unionization is prohibited. This reflects the difficulties that developing countries face in attracting foreign investment. The governments of developing countries have to provide numerous benefits, including land, facilities, and tax relief, in order to bring foreign investment into their countries. For labor issues within the EPZs, please see ILO (1998).

6. Arizpe and Aranda 1981; cited in Kabeer 1994, 165.
7. Chant and McIlwaine 1995, 48.
8. CIIR 1987, 33; Shoesmith 1986, 17, cited in Chant and McIlwaine 1995, 49.
9. Chant and McIlwaine 1995, 60.
10. ILO 1998, 3.
11. Ibid., 20.
12. Remedio 1996, 13.
13. Chant and McIlwaine 1995, 67.
14. UN 1993, 99.
15. Jackson 1998, 122.
16. ILO 2001.
17. Eviota 1992, 112.
18. Jayaweera 1994, 105.
19. Gunatilaka 1997, 1.
20. Jayaweera 1994, 105.
21. Maex 1985, 11.
22. People's Forum for Development Alternatives [PEFDA] 1998, 27.

23. Ibid., 45.
24. Ibid., I.
25. Abeywardene 1994, cited in Vimaladharma 1997, 51.
26. PEFDA 1998, 51.
27. Jayaweera 1994, 105.
28. Feldman 1992, 116.
29. ESCAP 1981; cited in Feldman 1992, 116.
30. Kabeer 2000.
31. Bhattacharya 1998, 15; Banglapedia 2004.
32. Bhattacharya 1998, I.
33. BEPZA 2004.
34. Ibid.
35. ILO 1998, 33.
36. *The Daily Star*, July 2, 1998.
37. ILO 1998, 37–39.
38. Ibid., 7.
39. Kibria 1998, 20.
40. Paul-Majumder and Begum 1999, 21.
41. Huq-Hussain 1996, 160.
42. Informal industry work includes paper-bag making, wrapping sweets for small factories for consumption within the informal sector, stitching plastic and jute bags, making ropes and matting from coconut fiber, preparing and packing dry snacks, grinding spices for restaurants, and street vending. See Huq-Hussain (1996, 161).
43. Bangladesh Bureau of Statistics 2001.
44. Paul-Majumder and Begum 1999, 21.
45. Sassen 1988, 116.
46. Brochmann 1990; Eelens 1995; and Yapa 1995. My own survey showed similar results.
47. These figures, including those for Sri Lanka and the Philippines, were calculated by the author, using the ILO data on EPZ employment and labor statistics. See Boyenge (2003) and ILO (2004).
48. PEFDA 1998, 20.
49. Chant and McIlwaine 1995, 62.
50. Infante 1975; cited in Lauby and Stark 1988, 474.
51. Mananzan 1998, 195.
52. Lauby and Stark 1988, 474.
53. Hunt et al. 1963, 291; cited in Hart 1971, 109.
54. UN 1993, 99.
55. Population Reference Bureau 2001.
56. Barnum and Sabot 1975, cited in Todaro 1997, 29; Pathak 1997, 375, 386.
57. Hart 1971, 109.
58. *Bulletin Today*, October 18, 1974.
59. NCRFW and ADB 1995, 48.
60. National Statistics Office 1995.
61. Lauby and Stark 1988, 485.
62. Heinonen 1996, 109.

63. Ogaya 1999, 47.

64. Lauby and Stark 1988, 485.

65. See the section "Financial Mismanagement and Increasing Consumerism" in Chapter 5 and also Hart 1971, 133.

66. *Bulletin Today*, October 18, 1974.

67. Ibid.

68. Ibid.

69. The Scalabrini Migration Center in Manila compiles many church documents that touch on international migration. Except for one occasion—in 1988, when the Archbishop of the Philippines endorsed a ban on the emigration of domestic workers and suggested extending it to entertainers—the Catholic Church (including both local churches and the Vatican) has taken a positive stance toward international migration of men and women. For more details on the role of the Catholic Church in migration, visit "Migration and Religion" on the Scalabrini Migration Center website: *www.smc.org.ph/Home.htm*.

70. Pope John XXIII 1963.

71. Sacred Congregation of Bishops 1969.

72. Morelos 1995.

73. Brochmann 1990, 115.

74. Wesumperuma 1986, 90.

75. Kearney and Miller 1987, 54.

76. Kearney and Miller 1987, 52.

77. Perera 1991, 152.

78. Alailima 1997; UNDP 2002.

79. Perera 1991, 166. In the original quote, the acronym "FTZ" was used instead of EPZ. FTZ refers to free trade zone which is roughly synonymous with EPZ.

80. Perera 1991, 167; Eelens 1995, 267.

81. Eelens 1995, 267.

82. Perera 1991, 167.

83. Ibid.

84. Ibid.

85. Gamburd 2000, 242.

86. Brochmann 1990, 93.

87. Marga Institute 1995; Yapa 1995.

88. Gamburd 2000, 242.

89. Islam et al. 1987, 149.

90. Mahmood 1993, 220.

91. World Bank 1990, 7.

92. Kabeer 2000, 64.

93. A *shalish* usually consists of members of local state institutions and rural elites. Women are not represented in it. When women want *shalish* to arbitrate a conflict, they have to be represented by a male guardian. See World Bank (1990, 7).

94. Adnan 1990, 11.

95. Wallace et al. 1987, 79.

96. *New Nation*, December 22, 1986; cited in Kabeer 2000, 82.

97. Islamic Economics Research Bureau 1980; cited in Kabeer 2000, 82.

98. Hossain 1980, 270.

99. Kibria 1998, 8–10.

100. Ibid.

101. ILO 2004.

102. Dasgupta 2003.

103. *Inter Press Service*, December 18, 2000.

104. AMC and MFA 2003.

105. In calculating this percentage, for the denominator, I added the number of legal migrants to the total female labor force in Sri Lanka because the Labor Force Survey data exclude migrants.

106. This figure is based on the estimate of 7.55 million migrants overseas (AMC and MFA, 2003), on the percentage of women among migrants (POEA, 2004), and on labor force data. I used the same calculation method as I applied to Sri Lanka.

CHAPTER SEVEN

1. Politically speaking, Bangladesh is not an "Islamic state" but rather a state based on parliamentary democracy. However, policy makers and the elites often referred to Bangladesh as a "Muslim country" in which the foundations of people's faith, actions, and state policies are based on Islamic teaching.

2. The ban on the emigration of female nurses from Bangladesh was one of the very few exceptions, and even this ban was repealed after only several months.

3. Simmons and Guengant 1992, 99.

4. For example, see Kyle and Koslowski 2001; MacKlin 2003; Heckman, 2004.

5. There are two types of orientation available in the Philippines. One is pre-employment orientation for those who are still considering migration; the other is pre-departure orientation for those who have already made up their minds to work abroad and who have signed an employment contract.

6. *Asian Migration News*, August 15–31, 2002.

7. UN 1994 and 1995.

8. UN 1999.

9. UNHCHR 1997.

10. UN 2000b.

11. Ibid. 2000c.

12. UN 2005.

13. IOM 2004a.

14. IOM 2004b.

15. Global Commission on International Migration 2004.

16. Ibid.

17. Paiva 1999, 2.

18. Ibid.

19. IOM 1999, 22.

20. MFA 2002.

21. *Gulf News*, March 11, 2003.

22. AMC 2000.

23. CARAM Asia 2002.

EPILOGUE

1. Brochmann 1990, 197; Chin 1997, 387; Hugo 1998, 25.
2. Hugo 1998, 29.
3. Ibid., 24.
4. Cheng 1996, 115.
5. Pillai 1995, 60.
6. Hugo, 1998:23–24.
7. Adi 1996; cited in Hugo 1998, 22.
8. Ismael and Momsen 1997, 146.
9. Brockett 1996, 128; cited in Hugo 1998,19.
10. Constable 1997; Parreñas 2001; Hondagneu-Sotelo 2001; Lan, forthcoming.
11. Kabeer 2001, 21.
12. Ibid., 18–22.

Abdullah, Nik Imran. 2003. "Plans Afoot to Bring in 50,000 Sri Lankan Workers to Solve Labour Shortage." *New Straits Times* (Malaysian daily newspaper), August 30. Retrieved on March 2, 2005, from the Lexis-Nexis website: web.lexis-nexis.com.

Abella, Manolo I. 1979. *Export of Filipino Manpower*. Manila: Institute of Labor and Manpower Studies.

———. 1995. "Sex Selectivity of Migration Regulations Governing International Migration in Southern and South-Eastern Asia." In *International Migration Policies and the Status of Female Migrants*. New York: United Nations.

Abeywardene, Janakie. 1994. *Assessment of Gender Integration in the Poverty Alleviation Project Sri Lanka: Report on the Field Study Conducted in the North Western Province, Sri Lanka*. Prepared for the gender and poverty team of the International Development Association/World Bank. January.

Adi, Rianto. 1996. *The Impact of International Labour Migration in Indonesia*. Unpublished Ph.D. dissertation. Adelaide, Australia: University of Adelaide.

Adnan, Shapan. 1990. *"Birds in a Cage": Institutional Factors and Changes in Women's Position in Bangladesh*. Dhaka: Research and Advisory Services.

Ahmed, Shamsun Naher. 1998. "The Impact of the Asian Crisis on Migrant Workers: Bangladesh Perspectives." *Asian and Pacific Migration Journal* 7(2–3): 369–93.

Alailima, Patricia J. 1997. "Social Policy in Sri Lanka." In W. D. Lakshman, ed., *Dilemmas of Development: Fifty Years of Economic Change in Sri Lanka*. Colombo: Sri Lanka Association of Economists.

Alcuitas, Hetty C. 2002. "Seven years after Flor: Conditions of Overseas Filipino Workers Worsen." Posted in June. Retrieved on February 23, 2005, from *www.newfilipina.com/members/pngayon/02.03/HettyIBON.html*.

AMC (Asian Migrant Centre). 2000. Campaign News. "Joint Campaign for Migrants' Rights in Asia." Posted on October 5. Retrieved on October 23, 2004, from the AMC website: *www.asian-migrants.org/news/97072973070107.php*.

AMC (Asian Migrant Centre) and MFA (Migrant Forum in Asia). 1999. *Asian Migrant Yearbook 1999: Migration Facts, Analysis and Issues in 1998*. Hong Kong: Asian Migrant Centre, Ltd. & Migrant Forum in Asia.

———. 2001. *Asian Migrant Yearbook 2001: Migration Facts, Analysis and Issues in 2000*. Hong Kong: Asian Migrant Centre, Ltd. & Migrant Forum in Asia.

————. 2003. *Asian Migrant Yearbook 2002–2003: Migration Facts, Analysis and Issues in 2001–2002*. Hong Kong: Asian Migrant Centre, Ltd. & Migrant Forum in Asia

Anderson, Bridget. 2000. *Doing the Dirty Work? The Global Politics of Domestic Labour*. London: Zed Books.

ANGOC (Asian NGO Coalition for Agrarian Reform and Rural Development). 1995. *Breaking Their Silence: Report of the Fourth Asian Development Forum "Transforming Institutions for the Empowerment of Asian Grassroots Communities."* February 20–24, 1995. Quezon City, Philippines: Asian NGO Coalition for Agrarian Reform and Rural Development.

Anker, Richard. 1998. *Gender and Job: Sex Segregation of Occupations in the World*. Geneva: ILO.

Arizpe, Lourdes and Josefina Aranda. 1981. "The 'Comparative Advantages' of Women's Disadvantages: Women Workers in the Strawberry Export Agribusiness in Mexico." *Signs* 7(2): 453–73.

Asahi Shimbun (Japanese daily newspaper). 1995. "80% of Foreign Entertainers Work as a Hostess." July 22.

————. 2000. "Toward the Framework of Acceptance: Imminent Debate on Bringing Foreigners in Care Work." January 14.

Asian Labour News. 2004. "Philippines: More Nurses are Needed Abroad than Caregivers." January 15. Retrieved on February 16, 2004, from the Asian Labour News website: *www.asianlabour.org/archives/001825.php*.

Asian Migration News (bimonthly). Various issues. Retrieved from the Scalabrini Migration Center website: *www.scalabrini.org/amn*.

Asis, Maruja M. B. 1992. "The Overseas Employment Program Policy." In Battistella and Paganoni, eds., *Philippine Labor Migration: Impact and Policy*. Quezon City, Philippines: Scalabrini Migration Center.

————. 2001. "The Return Migration of Filipino Women Migrants: Home, But Not for Good?" In Christina Wille and Basia Passl, eds., *Female Labour Migration in South-East Asia: Change and Continuity*. Bangkok: Asian Research Centre for Migration.

ASK (Ain O Salish Kendra). 1999. *A Tarnished Golden Deer: The Regime for Bangladesh Migrant Workers*. Dhaka: ASK.

————. n.d. *International Migration and the Domestic Worker: Bangladesh's Undocumented Migrants*. Unpublished paper. Dhaka.

Associated Press. 2004. "Bill to Combat Human Traffickers in Japan to Reach Parliament Next Year." December 7. Retrieved on February 17, 2005, from the Lexis-Nexis Academic: *web.lexis-nexis.com*.

Bakan, Abigail B., and Daiva Stasiulis. 1995. "Making the Match: Domestic Placement Agencies and the Racialization of Women's Household Work." *Signs* 29(2): 1–33.

Ball, Rochelle E. 1990. *The Process of International Contract Labour Migration: The Case of Filipino Nurses*. Ph.D. dissertation. University of Sydney.

Bangladesh Bureau of Statistics. 1993. *Women and Men in Bangladesh: Facts and Figures, 1992*. Dhaka: Bangladesh Bureau of Statistics.

————. 2001. *Urban Area Report of Bangladesh 1991*, Vol. 1. Retrieved on October 30, 2004, from the BBS website: *www.bbsgov.org*.

Banglapedia. 2004. "Export Processing Zones." Retrieved on March 6, 2005, from the Banglapedia website: *http://banglapedia.search.com.bd/HT/E_0085.htm*.

Barnum, Henry N., and Richard H. Sabot. 1975. *Migration, Education and Urban Surplus Labour*. OECD Development Center Employment Series Monograph. Paris: OECD.

Battistella, Graziano, and Anthony Paganoni, eds. 1992. *Philippine Labor Migration: Impact and Policy*. Quezon City, Philippines: Scalabrini Migration Center.

Becker, Gary S. 1981. *A Treatise on the Family*. Cambridge, MA: Harvard University Press.

BEPZA (Bangladesh Export Processing Zones Authority). 2004. *Prologue*. Retrieved on October 24, 2004, from the BEPZA website: *www.bdmail.net/bepza/index.html*.

Bhattacharya, Debapriya. 1998. "Export Processing Zones in Bangladesh: Economic Impact and Social Issues." *Multinational Enterprises Programme Working Paper* No. 80. Geneva: ILO.

Birks, J. S., and C. A. Sinclair. 1980. *International Migration and Development in the Arab Region*. Geneva: ILO.

Blumberg, Rae Lesser. 1988. "Income under Female versus Male Control." *Journal of Family Issues* 9(1): 51–84.

Boyenge, Jean-Pierre Singa. 2003. *ILO Database on Export Processing Zones*. ILO, Sectoral Activities Department. Geneva: ILO.

Brochmann, Grete. 1990. *The Middle East Avenue: Female Migration from Sri Lanka—Causes and Consequences*. Oslo: Institute for Social Research.

Brubaker, William Rogers. 1992. *Citizenship and Nationhood in France and Germany*. Cambridge, MA, and London, UK: Harvard University Press.

Bulletin Today (Philippine daily newspaper). 1974. Special Report. "Working Woman Takes New Roles." October 18.

Cabinet Office (Japan). 2000. *Gaikokujin Rodoshani Kansuru Seronchosa 2000* (An Opinion Survey on Foreign Workers in 2000). Retrieved on October 30, 2004, from the Cabinet Office website: *www8.cao.go.jp/survey/h12/gaikoku/index.html*.

———. 2004. *Danjo Kyodo Sankaku Hakusho 2002: Danjo Kyodo Sankakuno Genjoto Shisaku* (White Paper on Gender Equality, 2002: The Current Situation and Policies Concerning Gender Equality). In Japanese. Retrieved on October 30, 2004, from the Cabinet Office website: *www.gender.go.jp/whitepaper/h16/danjyo_hp/top.html*.

CARAM Asia. 2002. "Regional Summit: Colombo Declaration." Adapted on August 28. Retrieved on October 23, 2004, from the CARAM Asia website: *http://caramasia.gn.apc.org*.

Census and Statistics Department (Hong Kong). 1991. *Hong Kong 1991 Population Census*. Hong Kong: Government Printer.

CFO (Commission on Filipino Overseas). 1999. Unpublished statistics. Manila.

———. 2004. "Statistical Profile of Registered Filipino Emigrants: Number of Registered Filipino Emigrants By Country of Destination: 1981–2001." Retrieved on September 25, 2004, from the CFO website: *www.cfo.gov.ph*.

Chant, Sylvia, ed. 1992. *Gender and Migration in Developing Countries*. London: Belhaven Press.

Chant, Sylvia, and Cathy McIlwaine. 1995. *Women of a Lesser Cost: Female Labour, Foreign Exchange and Philippine Development.* London: Pluto Press.

Chant, Sylvia, and Sarah A. Radcliffe. 1992. "Migration and Development: The Importance of Gender." In Sylvia Chant, ed., *Gender and Migration in Developing Countries.* London: Belhaven Press.

Cheng, Ada. 1996. "Migrant Women Domestic Workers in Hong Kong, Singapore, and Taiwan: A Comparative Analysis." In Graziano Battistella, ed., *Asian Women in Migration.* Quezon City, Philippines: Scalabrini Migration Center.

Chia, Sue-Ann. 2004. "Raising Junior Is Easier Now." *The Straits Times,* August 26. Retrieved on September 22, 2004, from the Straits Times website archives: *http://straitstimes.asia1.com.sg/women/story/0,4395,269297,00.html.*

Chiang, Claire. 1994. "Female Migrants in Singapore: Towards a Strategy of Pragmatism and Coping." In Maria Jaschok and Suzanne Miers, eds., *Women and Chinese Patriarchy: Submission, Servitude and Escape.* Hong Kong: Hong Kong University Press; also London: Zed Books.

Chin, Christine B. N. 1998. *In Service and Servitude: Foreign Female Domestic Workers and the Malaysian "Modernity" Project.* New York: Columbia University Press.

Choi, Jin Ho. 2001. "International Migration, Human Resource Development and Migration Policy in Korea." *Asian and Pacific Migration Journal* 10(2–3): 463–83.

Choshi, Hirohisa. 2004. "Kajiroudou—Hatashite Oikura?" (Housework—How Much Is it?) Summer 1994. Retrieved on October 15, 2004, from his personal website (in Japanese): *http://www6.ocn.ne.jp/~house/work.*

CIA World Fact Book. 2000. *Malaysia.* Retrieved on October 30, 2004, from the CIA Factbook website: *www.cia.gov/cia/publications/factbook/geos/my.html.*

CIIR (Catholic Institute for International Relations). 1987. *The Labour Trade: Filipino Migrant Workers around the World.* London: CIIR.

CIRDAP (Center on Integrated Rural Development for Asia and Pacific). 1993. *Monitoring Adjustment and Poverty.* Dhaka: CIRDAP.

Constable, Nicole. 1997. *Maid to Order in Hong Kong: Stories of Filipina Workers.* Ithaca, NY: Cornell University Press.

Cornelius, Wayne A., Philip L. Martin, and James F. Hollifield, eds. 1994. *Controlling Immigration: A Global Perspective.* Stanford, CA: Stanford University Press.

Council of Labour Affairs. 2004. *The 2003 Investigation Report on the Management and Employment of Foreign Workers in R.O.C.* Taipei: Executive Yuan, Republic of China.

Curran, Sara R., and Estella Rivero-Fuentes. 2003. "Engendering Migrant Networks: The Case of Mexican Migration." *Demography* 20(2): 289–307.

Daily Star, The (Bangladeshi daily newspaper). 1998. "Chittagong EPZ: A Success Story." July 2. Retrieved on July 2, 1998, from the Daily Star website: *www.dailystarnews.com* (no longer exists).

Daily Yomiuri (Japanese daily newspaper). 2000. "Discussion Vital over Plans to Accept Nursing-Care Workers from Overseas." April 26.

Dasgupta, Anindita. 2003. "No Warm Welcome for Returning Women Migrants." Inter Press Service, July 25. Retrieved on September 29, 2003, from the Inter Press Service website: *www.ips.org.*

Davidson, Andrew. 1991. "Rethinking Household Livelihood Strategies." In D. Clay and H. Schwarzweller, eds., *Household Survival Strategies: Research in Rural Sociology and Development*, Vol. 5. Greenwich, CT: JAI.

Dawn (Pakistani daily newspaper). 1999. "Govt Grants Right of Vote to Overseas Pakistanis." April 30.

Deano, A.M. 1985. "Socio, Cultural and Attitudinal Determinants of Female Marriage Timing." Unpublished M.A. Thesis. Quezon City: University of the Philippines.

De Dios, Aurora Javate. 1989. "Filipinas as Commodities: The Plight of the Japayukisan." In *The Trade in Domestic Helpers: Causes, Mechanisms and Consequences.* Kuala Lumpur: Asian Pacific Development Center.

De Vos, George A. 1971. *Japan's Outcastes: The Problem of the Burakumin.* London: Minority Rights Group.

————, and William O. Wetherall. 1983. *Japan's Minorities: Burakumin, Koreans, Ainu and Okinawans.* London: Minority Rights Group.

Dias, Malsiri, and Ramani Jayasundere. 2002. *Sri Lanka: Good Practices to Prevent Women Migrant Workers From Going Into Exploitative Forms of Labour.* Geneva: ILO.

DOLE (Department of Labor and Employment [Philippines]). 1995. *The Overseas Employment Program.* White Paper. April. Manila: DOLE.

Eder, James F. 1999. *Generation Later: Household Strategies and Economic Change in the Rural Philippines.* Honolulu: University of Hawaii Press.

Eelens, Frank. 1995. "Migration of Sri Lankan Women to Western Asia." In *International Migration Policies and the Status of Female Migrants: Proceedings of the United Nations Expert Group Meeting on International Migration Policies and the Status of Female Migrants.* San Miniato, Italy, March 28–31, 1990. New York: United Nations. Department for Economic and Social Information and Policy Analysis, Population Division.

————, and J. D. Speckmann. 1990. "Recruitment of Labor Migrants for the Middle East: The Sri Lankan Case." *International Migration Review* 24(2): 297–322.

Ellis, Frank. 1988. *Peasant Economics.* Cambridge and New York: Cambridge University Press.

Enloe, Cynthia H. 1990. *Bananas, Beaches and Bases: Making Feminist Sense of International Politics.* Berkeley: University of California Press.

ESCAP (UN Economic and Social Commission for Asia and the Pacific). 1981. *Population of Bangladesh.* Country Monograph Series No. 8. New York: United Nations.

ESCWA (UN Economic and Social Commission for Western Asia). 1993. *Survey on Economic and Social Developments in the ESCWA region 1990–1991.* Anman: United Nations.

————. 1997a. *Arab Women 1995: Trends, Statistics and Indicators.* New York: United Nations.

————. 1997b. *Selected Social Trends in the ESCWA Region.* New York: United Nations.

Evans, Lynne, and Ivy Papps. 1999. "Migration Dynamics in the GCC Countries." In *Emigration Dynamics in Developing Countries*, Vol.IV: *The Arab Region.* Edited by Reginald Appleyard et al. London: Ashgate Publishing Ltd.

Evans, Peter B. 1995. *Embedded Autonomy: States and Industrial Transformation.* Princeton, NJ: Princeton University Press.

————. 1997. *State-Society Synergy: Government and Social Capital in Development.* University of California International and Area Studies Digital Collection. Research Series No. 94. Retrieved on October 26, 2004, from the University of California website: *http://repositories.cdlib.org/uciaspubs/research/94.*

————, Dietrich Rueschemeyer, and Theda Skocpol, eds. 1985. *Bringing the State Back In.* Cambridge and New York: Cambridge University Press.

Eviota, Elizabeth Uy. 1992. *The Political Economy of Gender: Women and the Sexual Division of Labour in the Philippines.* London: Zed Books.

Fairhurst, U. J., I. Booysen, and P. S. Hattingh, eds. 1997. *Migration and Gender: Place, Time and People Specific.* Pretoria, South Africa: University of Pretoria.

Feldman, Shelley. 1992. "Crisis, Islam, and Gender in Bangladesh: The Social Construction of the Labor Force." In Shelly Feldman and Lourdes Beneria, eds., *Unequal Burden: Economic Crises, Persistent Poverty, and Women's Work.* Boulder, CO: Westview Press.

Filmo Communications (recruitment agency in Singapore). Retrieved on March 20, 2001, from the company website: *www.filmo.com/maids.htm.*

Gamburd, Michele Ruth. 2000. *The Kitchen Spoon's Handle: Transnationalism and Sri Lanka's Migrant Housemaids.* Ithaca, NY: Cornell University Press.

————. 2005. "'Lentils There, Lentils Here!' Sri Lankan Domestic Labor in the Middle East." In Shirlena Huang, Brenda S. A. Yeoh, and Noorashikin Abdul Rahman, eds., *Contemporary Perspectives on Asian Transnational Domestic Workers.* Singapore: Marshall Cavendish.

Gaw, Kenneth. 1991. *Superior Servants: The Legendary Cantonese Amahs of the Far East.* Singapore: Oxford University Press.

Geertz, Hildred. 1961. *The Javanese Family.* New York: Free Press of Glencoe.

Gereffi, Gary, and Miguel Korzeniewicz. 1994. *Commodity Chains and Global Capitalism.* Westport, CT: Greenwood Press.

Ginsberg, Norton, and Chester F. Roberts, Jr. 1958. *Malaya.* Seattle: University of Washington Press.

Global Commission on International Migration. 2004. "The Mandate." Retrieved on March 9, 2005, from the commission's website: *www.gcim.org/en/a_mandate.html.*

Go, Stella. 1992. "The Filipino Family in the Eighties." In *The Changing Family in Asia.* Bangkok: UNESCO.

Gonzalez, Joaquin L., III. 1998. *Philippine Labor Migration: Critical Dimensions of Public Policy.* Singapore: Institute of Southeast Asian Studies.

Goss, Jon, and Bruce Lindquist. 1995. "Conceptualizing International Labor Migration: A Structuration Perspective." *International Migration Review* 29(2): 317–51.

Government of Bangladesh. 1983. *The Second Five-Year Plan.* Dhaka: Planning Commission, Government of the People's Republic of Bangladesh.

————. 1998. *Directory of PVDOs/NGOs in Bangladesh 1996–1997: Ready Reference.* Dhaka: Association of Development Agencies in Bangladesh.

Grasmuck, Sherri, and Patricia R. Pessar. 1991. *Between Two Islands: Dominican International Migration.* Berkeley: University of California Press.

Grieco, Elizabeth M., and Monica Boyd. 1998. *Women and Migration: Incorporating*

Gender into International Migration Theory. Center for the Study of Population Working Paper. Tallahassee, FL: Florida State University.

Gugler, Josef. 1997. "Gender and Rural-Urban Migration: Regional Contrasts and the Gender Transition." In U.J. Fairhurst, I. Booysen, and P.S. Hattingh, eds., *Migration and Gender: Place, Time and People Specific.* Pretoria, South Africa: University of Pretoria.

Gulf News. 2003. "Arroyo Claims Support of Five Countries in HK Wage Protests." March 11.

Gunatilaka, Ramani. 1997. *The Problems and Prospects of Sri Lanka's Handloom Industry.* Research Studies Industrialization Series No. 6. Colombo: Institute of Policy Studies.

Gunatilleke, Godfrey, ed. 1986. *Migration of Asian Workers to the Arab World.* Tokyo: United Nations University.

Gurak, Douglas T., and Fe Caces. 1992. "Migration Networks and the Shaping of Migration Systems." In Mary Kritz, Lin Lean Lim, and Hania Zlotnik, eds., *International Migration Systems: A Global Approach.* Oxford: Clarendon Press.

Gurak, Douglas T., and Mary M. Kritz. 1996. "Social Context, Household Composition and Employment among Migrant and Nonmigrant Dominican Women." *International Migration Review* 30(2): 399–423.

Global Commission on International Migration. 2004. "The Mandate." Retrieved on October 23, 2004, from the commission's website: *www.gcim.org/a_mandate .htm.*

Hagan, Jacqueline Maria. 1998. "Social Networks, Gender, and Immigrant Incorporation: Resources and Constraints." *American Sociological Review* 63: 55–67.

Harbison, Sarah F. 1981. "Family Structure and Family Strategy in Migration Decision Making." In Gordon F. De Jong and Robert W. Gardner, eds., *Migration Decision Making: Multidisciplinary Approaches to Microlevel Studies in Developed and Developing Countries.* New York: Pergamon Press.

Harris, John R., and Michael P. Todaro. 1970. "Migration, Unemployment, and Development: A Two-Sector Analysis." *American Economic Review* 60: 126–42.

Hart, Donn V. 1971. "Philippine Rural-Urban Migration: A View from Caticugan, a Bisayan Village." *Behavior Science Notes* 6(2): 103–37.

Hasan, Rafiq. 2003. "Bangladeshi Women Eye Jobs in Saudi Arabia." *The Daily Star,* September 20. Retrieved on October 30, 2004, from the newspaper's archive: *www.thedailystar.net/2003/09/20/d3092001077.htm.*

Heckmann, Friedrich. 2004. "Illegal Migration: What Can We Know and What Can We Explain? The Case of Germany." *International Migration Review* 28(3): 1103–26.

Heinonen, Tuula. 1996. "Negotiating Ideal Womanhood in Rural Philippine Households: Work and Survival." In P. Ghaorayshi and C. Belanger, eds., *Women, Work, and Gender Relations in Developing Countries: A Global Perspective.* Westport, CT: Greenwood Press.

Henson, Bertha. 2002. "Who Will Speak up for Voiceless Maids?" *The Straits Times,* January 13.

Heyzer, Noeleen, Geertje Lycklama A Nijeholt, and Nedra Weerakoon. 1994. *The Trade in Domestic Workers: Causes, Mechanisms, and Consequences of International Migration.* London: Zed Books.

Hochschild, Arlie. 2000. "The Nanny Chain." *The American Prospect* 11(4): 32–36.

Hondagneu-Sotelo, Pierrette. 1994. *Gendered Transitions: Mexican Experiences of Immigration.* Berkeley: University of California Press.

Hong Kong Government. 1965. *Aims and Policy for Social Welfare in Hong Kong.* Hong Kong: Government Printer.

———. 2004. "Domestic Help." Retrieved on October 15, 2004, from the Invest Hong Kong website: *www.firstchoicehongkong.gov.hk/firstchoicehongkong/lifestyle/frm_domestic.htm.*

Hong Kong Immigration Department. 1999. Unpublished statistics.

Hong Kong Standard. 1999. "Maids from Indonesia 'Underpaid.'" April 14.

Hossain, Muhammad Musharraf. 1980. "The Employment for Women." In Islamic Economics Research Bureau, ed., *Thoughts on Islamic Economics.* Dhaka: Islamic Economic Research Bureau.

Huff, W. G. 1994. *The Economic Growth of Singapore: Trade and Development in the Twentieth Century.* Cambridge and New York: Cambridge University Press.

Hugo, Graeme J. 1995. "Labor Export from Indonesia: An Overview." *ASEAN Economic Bulletin* 12(2): 275–98.

———. 1998. "Migration and Female Empowerment." A paper presented for the International Union for the Scientific Study (Population's Committee) at Gender and Population's Seminar on *Female Empowerment and Demographic Processes: Moving Beyond Cairo.* Lund, Sweden, April 21–24, 1997.

Huguet, Jerrold W. 1995. "Data on International Migration in Asia: 1990–1994." *Asian and Pacific Migration Journal* 4(4): 519–29.

Hui, Weng Tat. 1992. *Foreign Workers in Singapore: Role of Government, Management and Unions in Cooperation.* Paper presented at the Conference on Present Issues of International Migration. Tokyo.

Humphrey, Michael. 1990. *Asian Women Workers in the Middle East: Domestic Servants in Jordan.* Occasional Paper No. 22. Centre for Multicultural Studies. Australia: University of Wollongong.

Hunt, Chester L., and Dani Aguila. 1963. *Sociology in the Philippine Setting.* Quezon City: Phoenix Publishing House.

Huq-Hussain, Shanaz. 1996. *Female Migrant's Adaptation in Dhaka: A Case of the Processes of Urban Socio-Economic Change.* Urban Studies Programme, Department of Geography, University of Dhaka.

ILO (International Labour Office). *Year Book of Labour Statistics.* Various issues. Geneva: ILO.

———. 1998. *Labour and Social Issues Relating to Export Processing Zones: Report for Discussion at the Tripartite Meeting of Export Processing Zones-Operating Countries.* Geneva: ILO.

———. 2001. *Family Responsibilities and Working Time: Towards an Integrated Approach to Work and Family Issues.* Paper submitted to the Conference on Gross Domestic Product vs. Quality of Life: Balancing Work and Family, Bellagio, Italy, January–February 2001. Draft. Conditions of Work Branch. Geneva: ILO.

———. 2004. LABORSTA (database of labor statistics). Retrieved on October 15, 2004, from the ILO website: *http://laborsta.ilo.org.*

ILO-ARTEP (ILO Asian Regional Team for Employment Promotion). 1985. Impact of Out and Return Migration on Domestic Employment in Sri Lanka: A Preliminary Analysis. Report for the Ministry of Labour, Government of Sri Lanka. New Delhi: ILO-ARTEP.

IMF (International Monetary Fund). 2003. *Balance of Payments Statistics*. Washington, DC.

———. 2004. *World Economic Outlook: The Global Demographic Transition*. Retrieved on September 28, 2004, from the IMF website: *www.imf.org/external/pubs/ft/weo/2004/02/index.htm*.

Imson, Manuel G. 1992. "Domestic Helper Employment: A Concern for Policy." *Overseas Employment Info Series* 5(2). December. Manila: POEA. A Contribution to the Information Network of the ILO/UNDP Asian Regional Programme on International Labour Migration.

Infante, Teresita R. 1975. *The Woman in Early Philippines and among the Cultural Minorities*. Manila: Unitas Publications.

INSTRAW (International Research and Training Institute for the Advancement of Women). 1994. *The Migration of Women: Methodological Issues in the Measurement and Analysis of Internal and International Migration*. Santo Domingo, Dominican Republic: INSTRAW.

INSTRAW and IOM. 2000. *Temporary Labour Migration of Women: Case Studies of Bangladesh and Sri Lanka*. Santo Domingo, Dominican Republic: INSTRAW/IOM.

Inter Press Service. 2000. "Women Domestics Face Tough Life Abroad." December 18. Retrieved on January 10, 2001, from the IPS website: *www.ips.org*.

IOM (International Organization for Migration). 1999. "The Beijing Platform for Action and Recent Trends in Female Migration in the Asia-Pacific Region." High-Level Intergovernmental Meeting to Review Regional Implementation of the Beijing Platform for Action, October 26–29, 1999. Bangkok: ESCAP.

———. 2004a. "5+5 Dialogue on Migration in the Western Mediterranean." Retrieved on October 23, 2004, from the IOM website: *http://www.iom.int/en/know/dialogue5–5/index.shtml*.

———. 2004b. "The Berne Initiative: A Global Consultative Process for Inter-State Cooperation on Migration Management." Retrieved on October 23, 2004, from the IOM website: *www.iom.int/en/know/berneinitiative/index.shtml*.

Islam, Muinul, Hasanuzzaman Chowdhury, M. Salehuddin, Jyoti Prakash Dutta, Muhammad Ali, and A. K. Enamul Hoque. 1987. *Overseas Migration from Rural Bangladesh: A Micro Study*. Rural Economics Programme, Department of Economics. Bangladesh: University of Chittagong.

Islamic Economics Research Bureau, ed. 1980. *Thoughts on Islamic Economics*. Dhaka: Islamic Economic Research Bureau.

Ismael, Munira, and Janet Momsen. 1997. "Migration as the Nexus of Gender and Region: The Migration of Sri Lankan Muslim Women to the Middle East." In Fairhurst et al., eds., *Migration and Gender: Place, Time and People Specific*. Pretoria, South Africa: University of Pretoria.

Jackson, Richard T. 1998. "Inter-Provincial Migration in the Philippines, 1985–1990." *Asian Migrant* 11, October–December: 120–28.

Jahan, Selim. 1993. "Impact of the Gulf Crisis on the Bangladesh Economy." In

P. Wickramasekara, ed., *The Gulf Crisis and South Asia: Studies on the Economic Impact*. UNDP. New Delhi: ILO Asian Regional Team for Employment Promotion.

Japan Times, The. Various issues.

Jaschok, Maria. 1988. *Concubines and Bond Servants: The Social History of a Chinese Custom*. London: Zed Books.

Jay, Robert. 1969. *Javanese Villagers*. Cambridge, MA: MIT Press.

Jayaweera, Swarna. 1994. "Structural Adjustment Policies, Industrial Development and Women in Sri Lanka." In Pamela Sparr, ed., *Mortgaging Women's Lives: Feminist Critiques of Structural Adjustment*. United Nations. London: Zed Books.

———. 1996. "Sri Lanka." In Uma Kothari and Vidula Nababsing, eds., *Gender and Industrialization: Mauritius, Bangladesh, Sri Lanka*. Rose-Hill, Mauritius: Editions de l'Ocean Indien.

———, Malsiri Dias, and Leelangi Wanasundera. 2002. *Returnee Migrant Women in Two Locations in Sri Lanka*. Study Series No. 26. Colombo: Centre for Women's Research.

JISEA (Japan Institute for Social and Economic Affairs). 2004. *Gaikokujin Rodoshano Ukeireni Kansuru Hokokusho* (Survey Report on the Issue of Accepting Foreign Workers). August. Retrieved on October 15, 2004, from the JISEA website: *www.kkc.or.jp*.

Johnson, Chalmers. 1982. *MITI and the Japanese Miracle: The Growth of Industrial Policy, 1925–1975*. Cambridge, MA: Harvard University Press.

Joppke, Christian. 1999. *Immigration and the Nation-State: The United States, Germany, and Great Britain*. Oxford: Oxford University Press.

Kabeer, Naila. 1991. "The Quest for National Identity: Women, Islam and the State of Bangladesh." In Deniz Kandiyoti, ed., *Women, Islam and the State*. Philadelphia, PA: Temple University Press.

———. 1994. "Women's Labour in the Bangladesh Garment Industry: Choice and Constraints." In Camillia Fawze El-Solh and Judy Mabro, eds., *Muslim Women's Choices: Religious Belief and Social Reality*. Providence, RI: Berg Publishers.

———. 1999. *The Conditions and Consequences of Choice: Reflections on the Measurement of Women's Empowerment*. UNRISD Discussion Paper No. 108. August 1999. Geneva: UN Research Institute for Social Development.

———. 2000. *The Power to Choose: Bangladeshi Women and Labour Market Decisions in London and Dhaka*. London and New York: Verso.

———. 2001. "Resources, Agency, Achievements: Reflections on the Measurement of Women's Empowerment." In Birgitta Sevefjord et al., eds., *Discussing Women's Empowerment: Theory and Practice*. SIDA Studies. Retrieved on September 20, 2004, from the Eldis Gateway to Development Information website: *www.eldis.org/static/DOC10457.htm*.

Karunaratne, Kusuma. 1999. "Women's Status in Sinhala Society and the Social Background." In Motoyoshi Omori, ed., *Sri Lanka no Josei, Kaihatsu, Minzoku Ishiki* (Women, Development, and Ethnic Consciousness in Sri Lanka). Tokyo: Social Science Research Institute, International Christian University.

Katzenstein, Peter. 1985. "Small Nations in an Open International Economy: The Converging Balance of State and Society in Switzerland and Austria." In Peter B. Evans, Dietrich Rueschemeyer, and Theda Skocpol, eds., *Bringing the State Back In*. Cambridge and New York: Cambridge University Press.

Kearney, Robert, and Barbara Diane Miller. 1987. *Internal Migration in Sri Lanka and Its Social Consequences.* Boulder, CO: Westview Press.

Khair, Sumaiya. 1998. "Women's Human Rights in Bangladesh." In Tahmina Ahmad and Md. Maimul Ahsan Khan, eds., *Gender in Law.* Dhaka: Adtam Publishing House.

Kibria, Nazli. 1998. *Becoming a Garments Worker: The Mobilization of Women into the Garments Factories of Bangladesh.* Occasional Paper No. 9. Geneva: UN Research Institute for Social Development and UNDP.

Kitano, Harry H. L., and Roger Daniels. 1988. *Asian Americans: Emerging Minorities.* Englewood Cliffs, NJ: Prentice Hall.

Komai, Hiroshi. 1995. *Migrant Workers in Japan.* Translated by Jens Wilkinson. London and New York: Kegan Paul International.

Korale, R.B.M. 1984. *Middle East Migration: The Sri Lankan Experience.* Employment and Manpower Planning Division. Colombo: Ministry of Plan Implementation.

Kritz, M., L. Lim, and Hania Zlotnik. 1992. *International Migration Systems: A Global Approach.* Oxford: Clarendon Press.

Kuptsch, Christiane, and Nana Oishi. 1995. *Training Abroad: German and Japanese Schemes for Workers from Transition Economies or Developing Countries.* International Migration Papers No. 3. Geneva: ILO.

Kyle, David, and Rey Koslowski, eds. 2001. *Global Human Smuggling: Comparative Perspectives.* Baltimore and London: Johns Hopkins University Press.

Lan, Pei-Chia. 2005. "Surrogate Family, Disposable Labour, and Stratified Others: Transnational Domestic Workers in Taiwan." In Shirlena Huang, Brenda S. A. Yeoh, and Noorashikin Abdul Rahman, eds., *Contemporary Perspectives on Asian Transnational Domestic Workers.* Singapore: Marshall Cavendish.

———. (forthcoming). *Cinderella Crossing Borders: Migrant Domestics and New-Rich Employers in Taiwan.* Chappel Hill, NC: Duke University Press.

Lauby, Jennifer. 1987. *The Migration of a Daughter as a Family Strategy: Effects on the Occupations and Marital Experience of Women in the Philippines.* Unpublished Ph.D. dissertation. Cambridge, MA: Harvard University.

———, and Oded Stark. 1988. "Individual Migration as a Family Strategy: Young Women in the Philippines." *Population Studies* 42: 473–86.

Lee, Hyekyung (forthcoming). "Migrant Domestic Workers in South Korea: An Unpopular Option?" In Shirlena Huang, Brenda S.A. Yeoh, and Noorashikin Abdul Rahman, eds., *Contemporary Perspectives on Asian Transnational Domestic Workers.* Singapore: Marshall Cavendish.

Lewis, Oscar. 1968. "The Culture of Poverty." In Daniel P. Moynihan, ed., *On Understanding Poverty: Perspectives from the Social Sciences.* New York: Basic Books.

Lim, Lin Lean, ed. 1998. *The Sex Sector: The Economic and Social Bases of Prostitution in Southeast Asia.* Geneva: ILO.

Lim, Lin Lean, and Nana Oishi. 1996. *International Labor Migration of Asian Women: Distinctive Characteristics and Policy Concerns.* Geneva: ILO.

MacDonald, J. S., and L. D. MacDonald. 1974. "Chain Migration, Ethnic Neighborhood Formation, and Social Networks." In Charles Tilly, ed., *An Urban World.* Boston, MA: Little, Brown.

MacKlin, Audrey. 2003. "Dancing Across Borders: 'Exotic Dancers,' Trafficking, and Canadian Immigration Policy." *International Migration Review* 37(2): 464–500.

Maex, Rudy. 1985. *Employment and Multinationals in Asian Export Processing Zones.* Multinational Enterprise Programme Working Paper No. 26. Geneva: ILO.

Mahmood, Tahir. 1993. *Human Rights in Islamic Law.* IOS Series: Readings in Islamic Law I. New Delhi: Institute of Objective Studies.

Mahmud, Wahiduddin. 1989. "The Impact of Overseas Labour Migration on the Bangladesh Economy: A Macro-Economic Perspective." In Rashid Amjad, ed., *To the Gulf and Back: Studies on the Economic Impact of Asian Labour Migration.* New Delhi: UNDP and ILO Asian Regional Team for Employment Promotion.

Mak, Grace C. L., and Yue-ping Chung. 1997. "Education and Labour Force Participation of Women in Hong Kong." In Fanny M. Cheung, ed., *EnGendering Hong Kong Society: A Gender Perspective of Women's Status.* Hong Kong: Chinese University Press.

Manalansan, Ely. 2003. "Who Profits from the Brain Drain? The Philippine Labor Export Policy." *Bulatlat* 2 (50), January 26–February 1. Retrieved on February 23, 2005, from the Bulatlat website: *www.bulatlat.com/news/2–50/2–50–braindrain2.html.*

Mananzan, Mary John. 1998. "The Precolonial Filipina." In Jose Y. Dalisay Jr., ed., *Kasaysayan: The Story of the Filipino People,* Vol. 2. Manila: Asia Publishing Company.

Manila Times. 1998. "OCWs Blamed for 'Bad Values.'" September 27.

Marga Institute. 1995. *Study of Female Migrant Worker.* Colombo: Marga Institute.

Massey, Douglas S. 1986. "The Social Organization of Mexican Migration to the United States." *Annals of the American Academy of Political and Social Science* 487: 102–13.

———, and Juan F. Garcia España. 1987. "The Social Organization of International Migration." *Science* 237: 733–38.

———, Joaquin Arango, Graeme Hugo, Ali Kouaouci, Adela Pellegrino, and J. Edward Taylor. 1993. "Theories of International Migration: A Review and Appraisal." *Population and Development Review* 19(3): 431–66.

McClintock, Ann. 1997. "'No Longer in a Future Heaven': Gender, Race, and Nationalism." In Anne McClintock, Aamir Mufti, and Ella Shohat, eds., *Dangerous Liaisons: Gender, Nation, and Postcolonial Perspectives.* Minneapolis: University of Minnesota Press.

McKay, Deirdre. 2005. "Success Stories? Filipina Migrant Domestic Workers in Canada." In Shirlena Huang, Brenda S. A. Yeoh, and Noorashikin Abdul Rahman, eds., *Contemporary Perspectives on Asian Transnational Domestic Workers.* Singapore: Marshall Cavendish.

Menjívar, Cecilia. 2002. "The Ties That Heal: Guatemalan Immigrant Women's Networks and Medical Treatment." *International Migration Review* 36(2): 437–67.

Migration News. 1995. "Indonesian Workers Complain of Extortion," 2(5). Retrieved on October 30, 2004, from the Migration News archives: *http://migration.ucdavis.edu/archive.*

Ministry of Foreign Affairs (Japan). 2002. "Bali Ministerial Conference on People Smuggling, Trafficking in Persons, and Related Transnational Crime." Retrieved on October 30, 2003, from the ministry's website: *www.mofa.go.jp/policy/i_crime/people/conf0202.html.*

————. 2004. *Joint Press Release: Japan-Philippines Economic Partnership Agreement.* November 29. Retrieved on February 16, 2004, from the ministry's website: *www.mofa.go.jp/mofaj/area/philippines/hapyou_0411.html.*

Ministry of Justice (Japan). 2000. *The Basic Plan for Immigration Control* (2nd edition). March 24. Ministerial Notice No. 119. Retrieved on January 10, 2001, from the ministry's website: *http://www.moj.go.jp/PRESS/000300-2/000300-2-2.html.*

————. 2004. "Immigration Statistics in 2003." Retrieved on March 11, 2005, from the ministry's website: *www.moj.go.jp/PRESS/040611-1/040611-1.html.*

Ministry of Labour (Singapore). Various years. *Report on the Labour Force Survey of Singapore.* Singapore: Ministry of Labour.

Mill, John Stuart. 1967 (1843). *A System of Logic: Ratiocinative and Inductive.* Toronto: University of Toronto Press.

Momsen, Janet Henshall, ed. 1999. *Gender, Migration and Domestic Service.* London and New York: Routledge.

Morelos, Carmelo D. F. 1995. *Comfort My People, Comfort Them: A Pastoral Letter on Filipino Migrant Workers.* Retrieved on October 30, 2004, from the Scalabrini Migration Center website: *www.smc.org.ph/religion/philippines2.htm.*

Morris, Lydia. 1990. *The Workings of the Household.* Cambridge: Polity Press.

Nababsing, Vidula. 1996. "Industrial Strategies of Less Developing Countries." In Uma Kothari and Vidula Nababsing, eds., *Gender and Industrialization: Mauritius, Bangladesh, Sri Lanka.* Rose-Hill, Mauritius: Editions de l'Ocean Indien.

Nakamatsu, Tomoko. 2005. *Unpaid Domestic Work: Gender, State Policy, and the Labour Market in Japan.* In Shirlena Huang, Brenda S.A. Yeoh, and Noorashikin Abdul Rahman, eds., *Contemporary Perspectives on Asian Transnational Domestic Workers.* Singapore: Marshall Cavendish.

Nash, June, and Maria Patricia Fernandez-Kelly. 1983. *Men, Women, and the International Division of Labor.* Albany: State University of New York Press.

National Statistics Office (Philippines). 1995. Unpublished statistics.

Nayyar, Deepak, ed. 2002. *Governing Globalization: Issues and Institutions.* Helsinki: United Nations University.

NCRFW (National Commission on the Role of Filipino Women) and ADB (Asian Development Bank). 1995. *Filipino Women: Issues and Trends.* Manila: NCRFW and ADB.

New Nation. 1986. December 22.

Nixon, Rob. 1997. "Of Balkans and Bantustans: Ethnic Cleansing and the Crisis in National Legitimation." In Anne McClintock, Aamir Mufti, and Ella Shohat, eds., *Dangerous Liaisons: Gender, Nation, and Postcolonial Perspectives.* Minneapolis: University of Minnesota Press.

NRIOL (Non Resident Indians On Line). 2000. "Kuwait: India May Lift Ban on Domestic Workers." July 10. Retrieved on March 11, 2005 from the NRIOL website: *www.nriol.com/content/snippets/archives/200/snippet171.htm.*

Ofstedal, Mary Beth, John Knodel, and Napaporn Chayovan. 1999. "Intergenerational Support and Gender: A Comparison of Four Asian Countries." *Southeast Asian Journal of Social Science* 27(2): 21–42.

Ogawa, Yuhei. 1987. "Chuto no Keizaikaihatsu to Kokusai Rodoryokuido" (Economic Development in the Middle East and International Labor Migration). In

Kiriro Morita, ed., *Kokusai Rodoryokuido* (International Labor Migration). Tokyo: Tokyo University Press.

Ogaya, Chiho. 1999. *Setainaikankeikaramiru Joseino Kokusairoudouidou: Firipinno Jireikara* (International Labor Migration of Women from the Perspective of Intra-Household Relations: The Case of the Philippines). Unpublished M.A. thesis. Japan: Hitotsubashi University.

Oishi, Nana. 1995. "Training or Employment? Japanese Immigration Policy in Dilemma." *Asian and Pacific Migration Journal* 4(2–3): 367–85.

Oppong, Christine, and Katharine Abu. 1987. *Seven Roles of Women: Impact of Education, Migration and Employment on Ghanaian Mothers.* Geneva: ILO.

Ortiz, Vilma. 1996. "Migration and Marriage among Puerto Rican Women." *International Migration Review* 30(2): 1144–67.

Oxford Universtiy Press. 1991. *The Oxford Encyclopedic English Dictionary.* New York: Oxford University Press.

Ozawa, Makiko. 1995. "Nyuyoji Seisakuto Boshikankei Shinrigaku—Tsukurareru Boseiishikino Tenkenwo Jikuni" (Psychology of Infants Personality and Mother-Child Relationship: with a focus on the examination of constructed motherhood consciousness). In Teruko Inoue et al., eds., *Bosei* (Motherhood). Tokyo: Iwanami Shoten.

Paiva, Robert. 1999. "Statement to the Commission on Population and Development." Thirty-second session of the Commission on Population and Development. Item 3: Follow-up Actions to the Recommendations of the International Conference on Population and Development. March 22, 1999. New York: United Nations.

Palen, J. John. 1990. "Population Policy: Singapore." In Godfrey Roberts, ed., *Population Policy: Contemporary Issues.* New York: Praeger.

Palma-Beltran, Mary. 1992. "Filipino Women Domestic Workers Overseas: Profile and Implications for Policy." In Mary Ruby Palma-Beltran and Aurora Javate de Dios, eds., *Filipino Women Overseas Contract Workers: At What Cost?* Manila: Goodwill Trading.

———, and Aurora Javate de Dios, eds. 1992. *Filipino Women Overseas Contract Workers: At What Cost?* Manila: Goodwill Trading.

Parreñas, Rhachel Salazar. 2001. *Servants of Globalization: Women, Migration, and Domestic Work.* Stanford, CA: Stanford University Press.

Pathak, Pushpa. 1997. "Dynamics of Single Female Migration to Cities in India." In U. J. Fairhurst, I. Booysen, and P. S. Hattingh, eds., *Migration and Gender: Place, Time and People Specific.* Pretoria, South Africa: University of Pretoria.

Paul-Majumder, Pratima, and Anwara Begum. 1999. *The Gender Imbalances in the Export Oriented Industries: A Case of the Ready Made Garment Industry in Bangladesh.* Background Paper Prepared for Policy Research Report on Gender and Development. Dhaka: Bangladesh Institute of Development Studies.

Peek, Peter, and Guy Standing. 1982. *State Policies and Migration: Studies in Latin America and the Caribbean.* London and Canberra: Croom Helm.

PEFDA (People's Forum for Development Alternatives). 1998. *Garment Factory Women Workers: A Few Selected Interviews.* Colombo: Centre for Society and Religion.

Perera, Myrtle. 1991. "The Impact of Macro-Events on Social Structure in Sri

Lanka." In Eleonora Masini and Susan Stratigos, eds., *Women, Households and Change*. Tokyo: United Nations University Press.

Phillips, L. 1989. "Gender Dynamics and Rural Household Strategies." *Canadian Review of Sociology and Anthropology* 26(2): 294–310.

Pierson, Paul. 1994. *Dismantling the Welfare State? Reagan, Thatcher, and the Politics of Retrenchment*. Cambridge and New York: Cambridge University Press.

Pillai, Jaya Kothai. 1995. *Women and Empowerment*. New Delhi: Gyan Publishing.

Piore, Michael. 1979. *Birds of Passage: Migrant Labor and Industrial Societies*. Cambridge and New York: Cambridge University Press.

POEA (Philippine Overseas Employment Administration). 1992. *Overseas Employment Info Series* 5(1), May. Manila: POEA.

————. 2004. Overseas Employment Statistics. Deployment Statistics. Retrieved on September 25, 2004, from the POEA website: *www.poea.gov.ph*.

Pope John XXIII. 1963. "Pacem in Terris: On Establishing Universal Peace in Truth, Justice, Charity, and Liberty." April 11. Excerpts from Pope John XXIII Encyclical. Retrieved on October 29, 2004, from the Scalabrini Migration Center website: *www.smc.org.ph /religion/pacem.htm*.

Population Reference Bureau. 2001. "An Urbanized World." In *Population Bulletin* 55(3). Retrieved on October 20, 2004, from the bureau's website: *www.prb.org/ pubs/population_bulletin/bu55/55_3_demographics.html*.

Pui-lan, Kwok, Grace Chow, Lee Ching-kwan, and Rose Wu. 1997. "Women and the State in Hong Kong." In Fanny M. Cheung, ed., *EnGendering Hong Kong Society: A Gender Perspective of Women's Status*. Hong Kong: Chinese University Press.

Radcliffe, Sarah. 1986. "Gender Relations, Peasant Livelihood Strategies and Migration: A Case Study from Cuzco, Peru." *Bulletin of Latin American Research* 5(2): 29–47.

Raj-Hashim, R. 1994. "A Review of Migration and Labor Policies in Asia." In Noeleen Heyzer et al., eds., *The Trade in Domestic Workers: Causes, Mechanisms and Consequences of International Migration*. Kuala Lumpur: Asian and Pacific Development Center.

Remedio, Elizabeth. 1996. *Export Processing Zones in the Philippines: A Review of Employment, Working Conditions, and Labour Relations*. Multinational Enterprises Programme Working Paper No. 77. Geneva: ILO.

REPELITA. III (Third Five-Year Plan: 1979–1983). 1979. Jakarta: Department of Information, Republic of Indonesia.

RMMRU (Refugee and Migratory Movements Research Unit). 1998. *UDBASTU: A Newsletter on Refugee and Migratory Movements*, Issue 5, July–September. Dhaka: RMMRU.

Rodrigo, Chandra. 1997. "Migration for Employment Overseas: Some Dimensions of the Sri Lankan Experience." *Shakai Kagaku Kenkyu Nenpo* 27. Japan: Ryukoku University.

Rodriguez, Edgard R., and Erwin R. Tiongson. 2001. "Temporary Migration Overseas and Household Labor Supply: Evidence from Urban Philippines." *International Migration Review* 35(3): 709–25.

Russell, Sharon Stanton. 1995. "Policy Dimensions of Female Migration to the Arab Countries of Western Asia." In *International Migration Policies and the Status of Fe-*

male Migrants: Proceedings of the United Nations Expert Group Meeting on International Migration Policies and the Status of Female Migrants. San Miniato, Italy, March 28–31, 1990. New York: United Nations. Department for Economic and Social Information and Policy Analysis, Population Division.

Sacred Congregation for Bishops. 1969. *Nemo est* (Instruction on the Pastoral Care of People Who Migrate). Vatican City. Retrieved on October 30, 2004, from the Scalabrini Migration Center website: *www.smc.org.ph/religion/DPMC.htm.*

Salaff, Janet W. 1974. *Family Formation in Hong Kong: The Tension between Family and Individual Goals.* Unpublished paper.

————. 1990. "Women, the Family, and the State: Hong Kong, Taiwan, Singapore—Newly Industrialised Countries in Asia." In S. Stichter and J. Parpart, eds., *Women, Employment and the Family in the International Division of Labour.* Philadelphia, PA: Temple University Press.

————. 1995. *Working Daughters of Hong Kong: Filial Piety or Power in the Family?* New York: Columbia University Press.

Sasaki, Shoko. 1994. "Ajiashokokuniokeru Rodoshano Kokusaiido ni Kansuru Kenkyu" (Studies on International Migration of Workers in Asian Countries). *Houmu Kenkyu* 80(2). Tokyo: Houmu Sougou Kenkyujo.

Sassen, Saskia. 1988. *The Mobility of Labor and Capital: A Study in International Investment and Labor Flow.* Cambridge and New York: Cambridge University Press.

————. 1991. *The Global City: New York, London, Tokyo.* Princeton, NJ: Princeton University Press.

Sassen-Koob, Saskia. 1984. "Notes on the Incorporation of Third World Women into Wage-Labor Through Immigration and Off-Shore Production." *International Migration Review* 18(4): 1144–67.

Scalabrini Migration Center. 2004a. *Asian Migration Atlas* (database on migration in Asia). Retrieved on October 15, 2004, from the center's website: *www.scalabrini .org/amatlas/atlas.htm.*

————. 2004b. *Directory of NGOs for Migrants in Asia.* Retrieved on October 15, 2004, from the center's website: *www.smc.org.ph/directory/ngodir.htm.*

Selby, Henry, Arthur Murphy, and Stephen Lorenzen. 1990. *The Mexican Urban Household: Organizing for Self-Defense.* Austin: University of Texas Press.

Sen, Amartya. 1990. "Gender and Cooperative Conflicts." In Irene Tinker, ed., *Persistent Inequalities: Women and World Development.* Oxford: Oxford University Press.

Shah, Nasra M. 1995. "Structural Changes in the Receiving Country and Future Labor Migration—The Case of Kuwait." *International Migration Review* 29(4): 1000–22.

————, Makhdoom A. Shah, Rafiqul Islam Chowdhury, and Indu Menon. 2002. "Foreign Domestic Workers in Kuwait: Who Employs How Many." *Asian and Pacific Migration Journal* 11(2): 247–69.

Shoesmith, Dennis. 1986. *Export Processing Zones in Five Countries: The Economic and Human Consequences.* Hong Kong: Asia Partnership for Development.

Siddiqi, Dina M. 1998. "Taslima Nasreen and Others: The Contest over Gender in Bangladesh." In Herbert L. Bodman and Nayeh Tohidi, eds., *Women in Muslim Societies: Diversity Within Unity.* Boulder, CO: Lynne Rienner Publishers.

Siddiqui, Tasneem. 2001. *Transcending Boundaries: Labour Migration of Women from Bangladesh*. Bangladesh: The University Press Limited.

Simmons, Alan B., and Jean Pierre Guengant. 1992. "Caribbean Exodus and the World System." In Mary M. Kritz, Lin Lean Lim, and Hania Zlotnik, eds., *International Migration Systems: A Global Approach*. Oxford: Clarendon Press.

Simon, Harvey, and John Thomas. 1995. "Philippine President Fidel Ramos and the Flor Contemplacion Crisis." Kennedy School of Government Case Program C18–95–1305.0. Cambridge, MA: Harvard University.

Skocpol, Theda. 1985. "Bringing the State Back In: Strategies of Analysis in Current Research." In *Bringing the State Back In*. Cambridge and New York: Cambridge University Press.

———, and Margaret Somers. 1980. "The Uses of Comparative History in Macrosocial Inquiry." *Comparative Studies in Society & History* 22(2): 174–97.

SLBFE (Sri Lanka Bureau of Foreign Employment). 1999. *Statistical Handbook on Foreign Employment 1998*. Research and Development Division. Colombo: SLBFE.

———. 2003. *Statistical Handbook on Migration. 2002*. Colombo: SLBFE.

Sobhan, Salma. 1989. "International Migration and Women: Bangladesh." In *Trade in Domestic Helpers: Causes, Mechanisms and Consequences*. Selected Papers from the Planning Meeting on International Migration and Women, Quezon City, Philippines, November 30–December 5, 1987. Kuala Lumpur: Asian and Pacific Development Centre.

Soysa, GDGP. 1999. *Overview of Migration Policies and Practices in South Asia*. Colombo: Migrant Services Centre. BATU-SAARC Secretariat.

Sparr, Pamela, ed. 1994. *Mortgaging Women's Lives: Feminist Critiques of Structural Adjustment*. United Nations. London: Zed Books.

Stahl, Charles W. 1982. "Labor Emigration and Economic Development." *International Migration Review* 16(4): 869–99.

Stalker, Peter. 1994. *The Work of Strangers: A Survey of International Labour Migration*. Geneva: ILO.

Stark, Oded. 1991. *The Migration of Labor*. Cambridge: Blackwell Publishing.

———, and David Bloom. 1985. "The New Economics of Labor Migration." *American Economics Review* 75(2): 173–79.

Stepan, Alfred. 1978. *The State and Society: Peru in Comparative Perspective*. Princeton, NJ: Princeton University Press.

Stichter, Sharon. 1990. "Women, Employment, and the Family: Current Debates." In Sharon Stichter and Jane L. Parpart, eds. *Women, Employment, and the Family in the International Division of Labour*. Basingstoke, UK: MacMillan.

Stockard, Janice E. 1989. *Daughters of the Canton Delta: Marriage Patterns and Economic Strategies in South China, 1860–1930*. Stanford, CA: Stanford University Press.

Straits Times, The (Singaporean daily newspaper). 1997. "Child-care Centres Cannot Replace Maid's Service." November 7.

Sturgeon, Timothy J. 2001. "How Do We Define Value Chains and Production Networks?" In *IDS Bulletin* 32(3). Retrieved on October 20, 2004, from the IDS website: *www.ids.ac.uk/globalvaluechains/publications/Sturgeon.pdf*.

Sunday Times Plus, The (Sri Lankan weekly paper). 1999. "When Mother Goes Away." August 22.

Tacoli, Cecilia. 1996. *Gender, Life Course and International Migration: The Case of Fil-ipino Labour Migrants in Rome.* Unpublished Ph.D. dissertation. London School of Economics and Political Science, University of London.

Takakuwa, Fumiko. 1999. "Bukkyoto Gyoson Shakai no Josei" (Women in Buddhist Fishing Village Society). In Motoyoshi Omori, ed., *Sri Lanka no Josei, Kaihatsu, Minzoku Ishiki* (Women, Development, and Ethnic Consciousness in Sri Lanka). Tokyo: Social Science Research Institute, International Christian University.

Taylor, J. Edward. 1986. "Differential Migration, Networks, Information and Risk." In Oded Stark, ed., *Research in Human Capital and Development*, Vol. 4: *Migration, Human Capital, and Development.* Greenwich, CT: JAI Press.

Teodoro, Luis V. Jr., ed. 1981. *Out of This Struggle: The Filipinos in Hawaii.* Hono-lulu: University Press of Hawaii.

Thadani, Veena, and Michael Todaro. 1979. *Female Migration in Developing Countries: A Framework for Analysis.* Center for Policy Studies Working Paper No. 47. New York: Population Council.

Then, Yee Thoong. 1996. *Labor Migration in East and Southeast Asia.* Paper presented at the UN Expert Group Meeting on Violence against Women Migrant Work-ers, May 27–31, 1996. Manila.

Tigno, Jorge V. 1990. "International Migration as State Policy: The Philippine Ex-perience as Model and Myth." *Kasarinlan* 6(1–2): 73–78.

Todaro, Michael P. 1969. "A Model of Labor Migration and Urban Unemployment in Less-Developed Countries." *American Economic Review* 59: 138–48.

———. 1997. *Urbanization, Unemployment, and Migration in Africa: Theory and Pol-icy.* Population Council Working Paper No. 104. Retrieved on October 27, 2004, from the Population Council website: *www.popcouncil.org/pdfs/wp/104.pdf.*

Tohidi, Nayereh. 1998. "The Issues at Hand." In H. Bodman and N. Tohidi, eds., *Women in Muslim Societies: Diversity within Unity.* Boulder, CO, and London: Lynne Rienner Publishers.

Trager, Lilian. 1984. "Family Strategies and the Migration of Women: Migrants to Dagupan City, Philippines." *International Migration Review* 18(4): 1264–77.

Tsuda, Mamoru. 1987. "Firipin: Tomito Hinkonno Aidano Sonzaitoshiteno Mi-dorukurasu" (The Philippines—the Middle Class in between Wealth and Pov-erty). In Junzo Kawada and Mayako Ishii, eds., *Hattentojokoku no Seijikeizaigaku* (Political Economy in Developing Countries). Tokyo: Tokyo Shoseki.

Tyner, James A. 1999. "The Global Context of Gendered Labor Migration from the Philippines to the United States." *American Behavioral Scientist* 42(4): 671–89.

UN (United Nations). 1991. *The World's Women, 1970–1990: Trends and Statistics.* New York: United Nations.

———. 1993. *Internal Migration of Women in Developing Countries.* Proceedings of the UN Expert Meeting on the Feminization of Internal Migration. Aguascalientes, Mexico, October 22–25, 1991. New York: United Nations.

———. 1994. *International Migration and Development.* General Assembly Resolution, December 19. A/RES/49/127. New York: United Nations.

———. 1995. *Population and Development: Programme of Action Adopted at the Inter-national Conference on Population and Development, Cairo, September 5–13, 1994.* New York: United Nations. Department for Economic and Social Information and Policy Analysis, Population Division.

———. 1998. *Women in Sri Lanka: A Country Profile.* Statistical Profiles No. 13. Economic and Social Commission of Asia and the Pacific. Bangkok: UNESCAP.

———. 1999. *International Migration and Development, Including the Question of the Convening of a United Nations Conference on International Migration and Development to Address Migration Issues: Report of the Secretary-General.* General Assembly Fifty-fourth Session, August 6. A/54/207. New York: United Nations.

———. 2000a. *Replacement Migration: Is It a Solution to Declining and Ageing Populations?* Department of Economic and Social Affairs, Population Division, UN Secretariat. March 21. New York: United Nations.

———. 2000b. *Resolution Adopted by the General Assembly: Protection of Migrants.* General Assembly Fifty-fourth Session, February 24. A/RES/54/166. New York: United Nations.

———. 2000c. *Resolution Adopted by the General Assembly: Violence against Women Migrant Workers.* General Assembly Fifty-fourth Session, February 10. A/RES/54/138. New York: United Nations.

———. 2002. *Strengthening of the United Nations: An Agenda for Further Change: Report of the Secretary-General.* General Assembly Fifty-seventh Session, September 9. A/57/387. New York: United Nations.

———. 2004. *Trends in Total Migrant Stock: 1960–2000.* 2003 Revision, February 1. POP/DB/MIG/Rev. 2003. New York: United Nations. Department of Economic and Social Affairs, Population Division.

———. 2005. United Nations Treaty Collection (on-line database). Retrieved on April 8, 2005, from the UN website: *http://untreaty.un.org.*

UNDP (UN Development Programme). 1994. *UNDP's 1994 Report on Human Development in Bangladesh: Empowerment of Women.* Dhaka: UNDP.

———. 1999. *National Gender Profile.* Dhaka: UNDP.

———. 2002. *Human Development Report 2002: Deepening Democracy in a Fragmented World.* Oxford: Oxford University Press.

———. 2004. *Human Development Report 2004: Cultural Liberty in Today's Diverse World.* Oxford: Oxford University Press.

UN High Commissioner for Human Rights. 1997. *Migrants and Human Rights: Commission on Human Rights Resolution 1997/15.* 37th Meeting, April 3. Geneva: UNHCHR.

U.S. Department of State. 1996. *Country Reports on Human Rights Practices for 1995: United Arab Emirates.* Retrieved on October 27, 2004, from the U.S. Department of State website: *www.usemb.se/human/1995/neareast/united_arab_emirates .html.*

———. 2004. *Trafficking in Persons Report.* June. Retrieved on September 23, 2004, from the U.S. Department of State website: *www.state.gov/g/tip/rls/tiprpt/2004.*

Vasquez, Noel D., Letty C. Tumbaga, and Minette Cruz-Soriano. 1995. *Tracer Study on Filipino Domestic Helpers Abroad: The Socio-economic Conditions of Filipino Domestic Workers from Pre-departure until the End of Their First Two-Year Contract in Hong Kong.* Geneva: IOM.

Vimaladharma, Kapila P. 1997. "Escape Route or Blind Alley? Sri Lankan Female Migrant Labour in West Asia and Impact on Gender Relations." *Changing Gender Roles and Relations: Women in Traditional, Colonial and Contemporary Times.* Colombo: Centre for Women's Research.

Vogel, Ezra F. 1991. *The Four Little Dragons: The Spread of Industrialization in East Asia.* Cambridge, MA: Harvard University Press.

Wallace, Ben J., Rosie Mujid Ahsan, Shahnaz Huq Hussain, and Ekramul Ahsan. 1987. *The Invisible Resource: Women and Work in Rural Bangladesh.* Boulder, CO: Westview Press.

WCSDG (World Commission on the Social Dimension of Globalization). 2004. *A Fair Globalization: Creating Opportunities for All.* Geneva: ILO.

Wee, Vivienne. 1987. "The Ups and Downs of Women's Status in Singapore: A Chronology of Some Landmark Events (1950–1987)." *Commentary* 7(2/3): 5–12.

Weerakoon, Needra. 1998. "International Female Labour Migration." In Center for Women's Research, ed., *Women in the Economy: Trends and Policy Issues.* Colombo: Center for Women's Research.

Weiner, Michael, ed. 1997. *Japan's Minorities: The Illusion of Homogeneity.* London and New York: Routledge.

Weiner, Myron. 1990. "Immigration: Perspectives from Receiving Countries." *Third World Quarterly* 12(1): 140–65.

———. 1995. *The Global Migration Crisis: Challenge to States and to Human Rights.* New York: HarperCollins.

Welsh, Frank. 1997. *A History of Hong Kong.* London: HarperCollins.

Wesumperuma, Dharmapriya. 1986. *Indian Immigrant Plantation Workers in Sri Lanka: A Historical Perspective 1880–1910.* Kelaniya, Sri Lanka: Vidyalankara Press.

White, Sarah C. 1992. *Arguing with the Crocodile: Gender and Class in Bangladesh.* Dhaka: The University Press Limited.

Wickham-Crowley, Timothy P. 1992. *Guerrillas and Revolution in Latin America: A Comparative Study of Insurgents and Regimes Since 1956.* Princeton, NJ: Princeton University Press.

Wolf, Diane Lauren. 1990. "Daughters, Decisions and Domination: An Empirical and Conceptual Critique of Household Strategies." *Development and Change* 21: 43–74.

———. 1992. *Factory Daughters: Gender, Household Dynamics, and Rural Industrialization in Java.* Berkeley: University of California Press.

Wong, Diana. 1996. "Foreign Domestic Workers in Singapore." In Graziano Battistella and Anthony Paganoni, eds., *Asian Women in Migration.* Quezon City, Philippines: Scalabrini Migration Center.

———. 1997. "Transience and Settlement: Singapore's Foreign Labor Policy." *Asian and Pacific Migration Journal* 6(2): 135–67.

Wong, Aline K. 1986. "Planned Development, Social Stratification, and the Sexual Division of Labor in Singapore." In Eleanor Leacock and Helen I. Safa, eds., *Women's Work: Development and the Division of Labor by Gender.* New York: Bergin and Garvey Publishers.

Wood, Charles. 1981. "Structural Changes and Household Strategies: A Conceptual Framework for the Study of Rural Migration." *Human Organisation* 40(4): 338–44.

———. 1982. "Equilibrium and Historical-Structural Perspectives on Migration." *International Migration Review* 16(2): 298–319.

World Bank. 1990. *Bangladesh: Strategies for Enhancing the Role of Women in Economic Development.* Washington, DC: World Bank.

————. 2000. *World Development Report 2000: Attacking Poverty*. Washington, DC: World Bank.

————. 2002. *Globalization, Growth and Poverty: Building an Inclusive World Economy*. A World Bank Policy Research Report. Washington, DC: World Bank.

————. 2003. World Development Indicators 2003. CD-ROM. Washington, DC: World Bank.

Yapa, Lalana Kanti. 1995. *The Decision Making Process of International Labour Migration With Special Reference to the Sri Lankan Housemaid*. Unpublished M.A. thesis in Women's Studies. University of Colombo.

Yeoh, Brenda S. A., and Shirlena Huang. 1995. "Childcare in Singapore: Negotiating Choices and Constraints in a Multicultural Society." *Women's Studies International Forum* 18(4): 445–61.

Yeoh, Brenda S. A., Shirlena Huang, and Theresa W. Devasahayam. 2004. "Diasporic Subjects in the Nation: Foreign Domestic Workers, the Reach of Law and Civil Society in Singapore." *Asian Studies Review* 28: 7–23.

Yomiuri Shimbun. 2004. "Nurses and Caregivers Are in Shortage! Many Applications for Structural Reform Special Districts to Accept Foreigners." July 1.

————. 2004. "Japan-Philippines FTA Negotiation: The Number Not Yet Decided." November 17.

Yoshino, Roger I. 1977. *The Invisible Visible Minority: Japan's Burakumin*. Osaka, Japan: Buraku Kaiho Kenkyusho.

Yu, Elena S. H., and William T. Liu. 1980. *Fertility and Kinship in the Philippines*. London: University of Notre Dame Press.

Zachariah, K. C., K. P. Kannan, and S. Irudaya Rajan. 2002. *Kerala's Gulf Connection: CDS Studies on International Labour Migration from Kerala State in India*. Kerala, India: Centre for Development Studies.

Index